Displaying the Marvelous

The MIT Press   Cambridge, Massachusetts   London, England

Lewis Kachur

Marcel *Duchamp*, Salvador *Dalí*, and Surrealist Exhibition Installations

Displaying the Marvelous

© 2001 Massachusetts Institute of Technology

This book was set in Janson by Graphic Composition, Inc. and was printed and bound in the United States of America.

Library of Congress Cataloging-in-Publication Data

Kachur, Lewis.
    Displaying the marvelous : Marcel Duchamp, Salvador Dalí, and surrealist exhibition installations / Lewis Kachur.
        p. cm.
    Includes bibliographical references and index.
    ISBN 0-262-11256-6 (HC : alk. paper)
        1. Surrealism—Exhibitions.   2. Installations (Art)—Exhibitions.
    3. Art—Exhibition techniques.   4. Art, Modern—20th century—Exhibitions.
    5. Dalí, Salvador, 1904– —Exhibitions.   6. Duchamp, Marcel, 1887–1968—
    Exhibitions.   I. Title.

N6494.S8 K33 2001
709'.04'063074—dc21
                                                                    00-048673

Errata

The following illustration credits were inadvertently omitted:

Cover image:
© Arnold Newman/Liaison Agency

Pages i, iii, and 1:
Details of Marcel Duchamp portrait © Arnold Newman, courtesy of
Arnold Newman/Liaison Agency.

Figures 3.28, 3.30, 3.33, and back cover image:
© Eric Schaal Estate, courtesy Jan Van der Donk Rare Books.

Figure 3.37:
Works by Reginald Marsh © Artists Rights Society (ARS), New York/ADAGP, Paris.

Figure 4.2:
Works by Max Ernst © Artists Rights Society (ARS), New York /ADAGP, Paris.

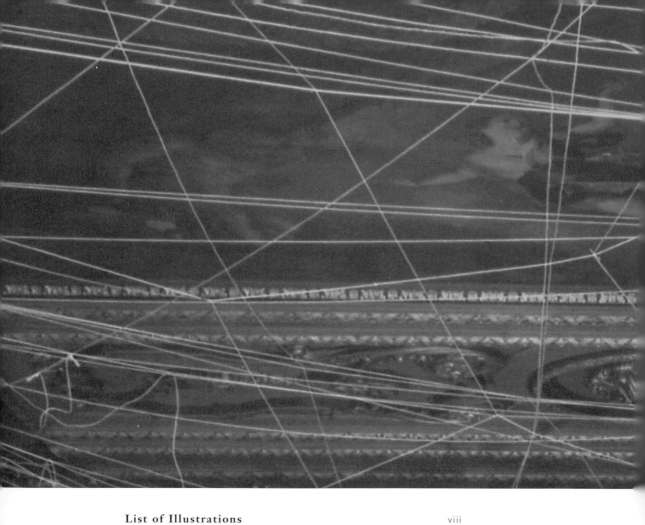

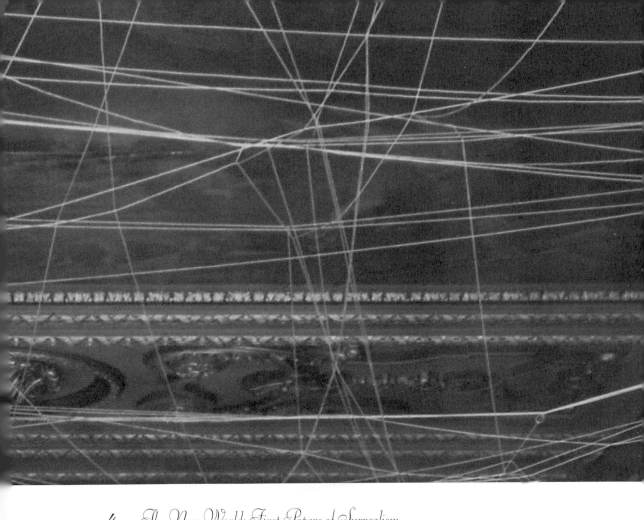

List of Illustrations

Works by Josef Breitenbach © Breitenbach Estate.
Works by Salvador Dalí: © Kingdom of Spain, universal heir of Salvador Dalí / ARS, New York, 2001. © Gala-Salvador Dalí Foundation, by appointment of the Kingdom of Spain / ARS, New York, 2001.
Works by Marcel Duchamp © Duchamp Estate.
Works by Man Ray and by Raoul Ubac © ARS, New York, 2001.

Preface

One of the main new developments in late Surrealism was its unique exhibition spaces. This was concurrent with the spread of Surrealism throughout Europe, as demonstrated in encyclopedic international group exhibitions. This book reconstructs in detail three elaborate Surrealist exhibition installations created between 1938 and 1942. They took place at, and were conditioned by, diverse sites: a traditional Old Master gallery, the amusement zone of the 1939 New York World's Fair, and a private mansion that had been converted to a war relief agency. In each setting the participants abandoned any attempt at neutrality of presentation in favor of a subjective environment that itself embodied a statement. Indeed, these exhibitions offered startled viewers an early version of installation art, before there was such a phrase for this form. Notable reporters such as Eric Sevareid and writers such as Simone de Beauvoir are among the eyewitnesses who viewed these exhibition installations as artworks in themselves, even as they searched for words to describe them. Clicking cameras, too, produced images ranging the mass-media-to-fine-art spectrum. The exhibitions were recorded by press agency and fashion cameramen as well as amateurs like Carl Van Vechten, and interpreted by artist-photographers from

Man Ray to Arnold Newman. Their photographs are the only visual documents of these displays and, taken together, enable one today to imagine proceeding through these sometimes complex and disorienting installations.

Two of the installations, for the *Exposition Internationale du Surréalisme* (1938) and the *First Papers of Surrealism* (1942), were created largely by Marcel Duchamp and significantly bracket the years of his relocation from Paris to New York at the beginning of World War II. The first exhibition, in Paris, was widely commented upon and highly influential. It directly inspired the other show discussed here, which began as Julien Levy's plan to popularize Surrealism in a pavilion at the New York World's Fair. And it would be echoed in the design of the notorious Surrealist room of Peggy Guggenheim's Art of This Century gallery. The later exhibition, *First Papers*, in New York, had less immediate impact in the press but was noticed by young local artists. Unlike the *Exposition* environment of 1938, which had in several ways fetishized the (female) body, here the installation primarily activated the total space of the room. This defiguration of Surrealist exhibition space, like the practice of automatism, contributed to the rise of abstraction in American painting of the 1940s. Duchamp's displays have continued to have an impact on subsequent installation art, even up to our day.

Each exhibition had its own art world drama, both among the changing cast of participants as well as vis-à-vis sponsors, critics, and other interested parties. I reconstruct each organizing process as much as possible from correspondence, oral histories, and reviews. I explore Duchamp's and André Breton's motives for their unlikely yet long-lasting collaboration as exhibition organizers. I also focus on Salvador Dalí, whose role in 1930s Surrealism has not been fully appreciated. A key participant in the Paris *Exposition*, Dalí immediately tried to export its highlights to the United States, notably his own *Rainy Taxi*. In 1939 his Dream of Venus pavilion at the World's Fair offered to a wider American public its first taste of Surrealist environments. Although compromised and commercialized, this was a beachhead for a broader art world presence of the Surrealists who immigrated to the United States at the outbreak of World War II. Dalí also looked west, introducing Surrealist installation to Hollywood with his "Night in a Surrealist Forest," thereby enacting the connection between Surrealism and popular culture posited by Alfred Barr. I consider Barr's landmark exhibition *Fantastic Art,*

Dada, Surrealism as a crucial forerunner—but, considered as a display, a foil—to the Surrealists' practice.

Duchamp and/or Dalí are the main players in each of these exhibitions, and their efforts largely define the character of Surrealist installation space. The former specializes in various forms of frustration or annoyance of the spectator, a problematizing of viewing which calls into question the definition of the work of art, and a certain ironic wit. Dalí adds the *dérèglement* of the senses, the establishment and then undermining of veristic space and image, as well as a focus on the actual third dimension, in the Surrealist object and architecture.

Previous histories have treated these Surrealist exhibitions only in passing, and usually with factual inaccuracies. Here I attempt a full visual and verbal reconstruction, tracing the sequence that a contemporary viewer would have encountered. The arrangement is particularly important in the first two installations. In both cases there is an unfolding in time, with an implicit narrative to the sequence. In the third exhibition, there is the contrary effect of all-at-onceness, marking a critical change in how art was perceived.

The means by which this avant-garde group proclaimed itself in the public sphere involved close collaboration between artists and writers who shared a Surrealist vision. The writers helped plan the shows and prepared the accompanying publications, which tended to be as much literary as documentary art catalogues. Yet while writers dominated the early years of Surrealism, as witnessed by the first manifesto of 1924, by the mid-thirties the tables had been turned. The momentum of these international exhibitions clearly afforded an opportunity for the artists to gain public attention, and the writers tried to join in. With the "deskilling" accompanying the adaptation of the Duchampian readymade, men and a few women of letters increasingly dabbled in object-making.

This book participates in a growing body of art historical investigation that has turned away from the more traditional monographic focus to examine the dynamics of art world systems. Exhibition space is an important maker of meaning for modern art, and is beginning to be studied as a cultural artifact. In recent years historians have delved extensively into world's fairs and international expositions; art historians and critics have analyzed contemporary and ethnographic museum practices. Like some of these, my focus is more on the case study than on theory. As such it reconstructs the forces contributing to an innovative moment in relatively neglected late Surrealism. It is thus the opposite of a heroic narrative of the founding of the movement, as it struggled to establish itself in the early 1920s. By the mid-1930s Surrealism had reached a different phase, one that involved the mixed blessings of spectacularization and commercialization. It is difficult to tell whether these are symptoms of Surrealism's extended influence or contributors to its dissolution. Probably a bit of both.

This study also seeks to counterbalance the literature on Marcel Duchamp, which has overinterpreted his readymades and *Large Glass* while minimizing his late productions as well as his substantial involvement with the Surrealists. The recent exceptions are Amelia Jones's more theoretical *Postmodernism and the En-gendering of Marcel Duchamp* (Cambridge, 1994), and Ecke Bonk's exemplary microcosm as macrocosm, *The Box-in-a-Valise* (Rizzoli, 1989). Building on these foundations, I posit that Duchamp expanded the definition of "artist" to include involvement in the art world as well as the role of the exhibition designer. However familiar this expanded definition has since become, it was quite novel in its day. Thus this book contributes to the literature of both Duchamp and Surrealism.

In the first Surrealist manifesto of 1924, André Breton famously wrote: "The marvelous is always beautiful, anything marvelous is beautiful, in fact only the marvelous is beautiful." At that point Surrealism was primarily organized as a literary movement. It took some time for this poetic concept of "the marvelous" to become widespread in painting, then later in the object. To evoke "the marvelous" in the physical and practical realm of exhibition design was one of the paradoxes that those who shaped these installations wrestled with, as we will see.

Acknowledgments

 This study has its roots in the archives of the museum. In the mid-1980s I was commissioned by then Director Thomas Messer to write a documentary book on the fifty most important exhibitions in the Solomon R. Guggenheim Museum's history. I undertook archival research and oral history interviews with the various curators in completing a lengthy manuscript. The archives and the conversations were an absorbing trove of unutilized information and unrecorded histories. I had backed into a new area of study not mentioned in graduate school: the documentation of exhibition-making.

At the prescient suggestion of Richard Martin, I next looked beyond the Guggenheim in developing a broader approach to the exhibitions influential in the defining and dissemination of modern art. These landmarks, such as the Armory Show, became the subject of a seminar I taught twice in Martin's master's program at the Fashion Institute of Technology (1989–1990). At that point I became familiar with the (then scant) literature in the field, notably Brian O'Doherty's provocative *Inside the White Cube*. For the first time I learned of the Surrealist exhibitions of 1938–1942 that are my focus here. Intrigued, I began the preliminary research that culminates in the

Acknowledgments

present book project. At the same time, art history itself became increasingly interested in how exhibitions and institutions have shaped our understanding of modern art.

Crucial support was provided by a NEH Fellowship in 1995–1996 to undertake archival research in Paris and New York, as well as to begin writing. The first draft was completed during a teaching sabbatical from Kean University in 1997–1998. Without these institutional supports, this book simply wouldn't have been possible. Kean University also provided released time for research, and my colleagues there have been very supportive.

Surrealism was a departure for me as a field of study, and its proponents are often remarkable. I was assisted by many new contacts and would like to thank them all. Early on, Francis Naumann and Martica Sawin were invaluable in helping get the study off the ground. Francis provided orientation to the research protocol at the Doucet Library and addresses in Paris, while Martica generously gave access to the clipping file compiled by Kurt Seligmann. This contained copies of many obscure newspaper and journal reviews which I have drawn on, and which could not have all been located individually.

In the commercial realm I was greatly assisted by the staff of Ubu Gallery, particularly Adam Boxer. Their exhibition on the 1938 Surrealism show early on introduced me to Raoul Ubac, Gaston Paris, and other Surrealist photographers, and Adam went out of his way to put me in touch with their sources. Later he showed me an unpublished documentation of Julien Levy's Surrealist pavilion at the New York World's Fair, one of the original bound proposals to Fair officials. Adam has remained a font of information on what's new in the field, and a valued source of encouragement.

At the outset I wanted to gather as much oral history as possible from eyewitnesses to or participants in the shows, thus I am especially indebted to those who submitted to interviews: the late Ann Alpert, Susanna Coggeshall, the late Teeny Duchamp, Charles Henri Ford, Alexander Hammid, the late Meyer Schapiro, Hedda Sterne. They racked their brains as best they could, and, although details were usually forgotten, they did evoke a sense of the spirit and tenor of the times in these circles.

Inevitably a number of fellow scholars and enthusiasts were called upon in various capacities. John Klein kindly read a chapter; Norman Bryson and Kirsten Powell tackled the whole manuscript and made eye-opening comments, as did the anonymous reviewers. I would like to acknowledge the co-operation of Timothy Baum, Dieter Bogner, Ecke Bonk, Fèlix Fanés, Lisa Jacobs, Peter Jones, Pam Meecham, Stephen Robeson-Miller, Lowery Sims, Ethaleen Staley, Mary Anne Staniszewski, Amy Winter, and Judith Young-Mallin.

In Paris I was most kindly assisted by Liza Daum of the Bibliothèque Historique de la Ville de Paris, who led me to unpublished press photos. More of the same were produced by Daniel Wildenstein, who kindly shared his memories of the Galerie Beaux-Arts show and pointed out the spaces in which it had taken place. Marcel and David Fleiss of Galerie 1900–2000 showed me a large cache of Ubac photos early on, and continued to field my inquiries. I am also indebted to Daniel Abadie, who discussed his research with me and provided more leads than I could track down. Myrtille Hugnet kindly made available the clippings compiled by her late husband Georges.

Thanks are also due to Yves Peyré and the staff of the Bibliothèque Littéraire Jacques Doucet, Dominique Bornhauser and Christine Sorin of the Centre Pompidou's Documentation, Emmanuel de l'Ecotais of their Archives, and Germaine Viatte. Thomas Michael Gunther of the Denise Bellon archives was very helpful from the earliest stages. Gregory Browner and Lucien Treillard fielded a number of Man Ray questions, as did Robert Descharnes for Dalí, Aube Elléouët for Breton, and Jackie Matisse-Monnier for Duchamp. In Great Britian Sharon Michi Kusonoki advised me and provided photos from the Edward James Foundation, West Dean. Ann Simpson, archivist of the Penrose papers, Scottish Gallery of Modern Art, patiently responded to ongoing questions. In Vienna I am indebted to Dieter Schrage. In Figueras I was kindly helped by Montse Aguer and the staff of the Dalí Theater Museum.

In New York I was regularly assisted by Janis Ekdahl and the staff of the Museum of Modern Art Library, as well as Mikki Carpenter, the Registrar's office, the Photography department, and Rona Roob of the Archives. Stephen Polcari and the staff of the Archives of American Art were unfailingly helpful, not only with their significant collection of oral histories, but also notably during the exhibition on Julien Levy. The staff of the Museum of the City of New York assisted me in their archives, and Peter Jones patiently initiated me in the options of scanning negatives. The staff of the New York Public Library, the Watson Library at the Metropolitan

Museum, and Columbia University's interlibrary loan office are also to be thanked for their help. Jan van der Donk enlightened me about Eric Schaal's photos. I am grateful to Ann Temkin, Marge Klein, Carl Strehlke, and the staff of the Philadelphia Museum for access to their Duchamp archives, and a peek at their Schiaparelli collection. Hearty thanks to Beth Guynn, Mark Henderson, and the staff of the Getty Research Institute, and David Shayt and the staff of the Smithsonian's Museum of American History, for pitching in with research questions. Thanks also to Leslie Calmes of the Center for Creative Photography, Tucson, Cathy Henderson of the Harry Ransom Humanities Research Center, Austin, Ann Shumard of the National Portrait Gallery, Washington, D.C., and to the staffs of the Ryerson Library, Art Institute of Chicago, Newberry Library, Chicago, and Beinecke Library, Yale University, for their assistance.

At the MIT Press I have benefited from the guidance and support of Roger Conover. His encouragement has been unwavering. His assistant, Margaret Tedeschi, has patiently fielded many queries. Matthew Abbate gave the manuscript his close attention, and his numerous suggestions have improved it considerably. Jean Wilcox has been open to a dialogue on how to display Surrealism in design terms, and prompted me to consider Surrealist typography. We decided to incorporate aspects of the publications related to the exhibitions under consideration, notably the initial letters used in the *Dictionnaire abrégé du surréalisme*.

A hearty thanks also to friends and family for ongoing advice and encouragement, including among the former Marlin Brenner, Stephen Brown, Michael FitzGerald, and George Singley. Miriam Kachur and Gertrude Krajic assisted with translations, Shawn Kee, Esq. with contractual advice. My wife Elizabeth has kept me on track by both word and example, and has been behind this project in innumerable ways. For their faith from the first, this book is dedicated to my parents.

Acknowledgments

Displaying the Marvelous

Ideological Exhibition Spaces and Surrealist Exhibitions

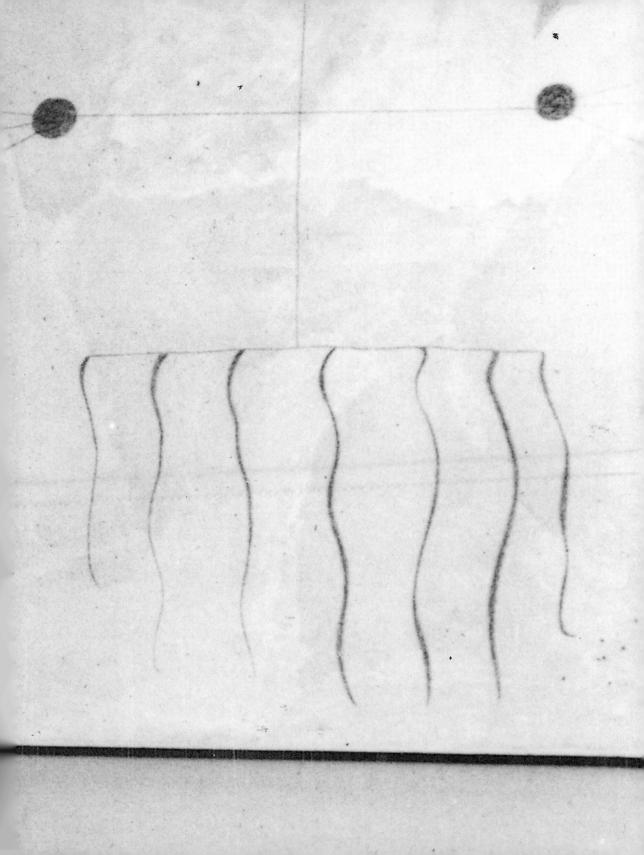

Modern Artists and the Ideological Exhibition

The Surrealist exhibitions discussed in this book are instances of what can be termed ideological spaces. They present a polemic in the format of the display itself. Before turning to the Surrealist exhibitions, it is worth considering the context and historical forces behind the subjective treatment of display, a treatment that seems especially rampant from the 1920s to the 1940s and again in recent art.

Curiously, the ideological exhibition space was a delayed development in the history of modernism. The earlier innovation was the act of exhibition itself, of bringing one's work before the public, from Courbet's pavilion of 1855 onward. (Even earlier, in London, the galleries of Benjamin West and J. M. W. Turner had presented more permanent displays of the owner-artists.) Soon the individual was supplanted by the group exhibition, as a company of like-minded avant-gardists linked together for the greater safety of numbers. The most famous example is that of the Impressionists, originally an anonymous society, who began in 1874 what became a series of eight exhibitions.[1] Their history is an almost continuous jockeying of factions and shifting allegiances up to the last show of 1886, with only one member, Pissarro, participating in all eight exhibitions. There is no photographic record of their hangings, an absence that is suggestive.

1.1   First International Dada Trade Fair, Otto Burchard Gallery, Berlin,
June 30–August 25, 1920.

With Whistler and the rise of aestheticism, there started to be more concern with the overall environs of the showcase. Thus the "greeney-yallery Grosvenor Gallery" made a mark in the 1880s. By the 1910s, the Futurists were willing to present pictures in a multimedia environment of poetic declamation and noise music. This practice was continued during the First World War by the Zurich Dadaists at a non-art space, the Cabaret Voltaire. In these manifestations, the artwork was more or less a backdrop or prelude to an aural event.

The full blossoming of ideological exhibition space comes only in the aftermath of that war. Of course every exhibition is on some level ideological, projected as it is in a particular public sphere. I have in mind, however, the abandonment of a seemingly straightforward or avowedly neutral presentation in favor of a relatively subjective format. From about 1920 such manifestations sprout up across Europe, making exhibition design one of the major new rhetorical devices of art between the wars. The earliest, appropriately, are Dadaist displays, with exhibition space echoing the tenor of political protest artworks. Thus the Cologne Dada show of April 1920, which was only accessible by passing through a men's bathroom, presented certain works that the spectator was enjoined to destroy. Across Germany at the same moment was the equally infamous Berlin Dada "trade fair" (*Messe*), its name at least an ironic enactment of commercial aegis. In this first word-environment, placards and wall posters had equal footing with collage and painting, both proclaiming Dada paradoxes and/or political slogans.[2] Every inch of the small space was packed, even overhead, where a military-uniformed, pig-faced mannequin hovered. The use of a mannequin, and the activation of the ceiling, are a foretaste of Surrealist practice at their 1938 *Exposition*. The Paris Dada group carried out related, if tamer, high jinks, such as the lights out and mockery of the spectators at Max Ernst's opening at the bookstore, Au Sans Pareil. Similarly, the Salon Dada of June 1921 had a suspended violin, a male mannequin poised on a ledge, and a row of men's ties in the installation. These activities, however, were not developed once the Dadaist group evolved into a Surrealist one, until later.

With Malevich's *Black Square* and Tatlin's counterreliefs spanning their respective corners of the *0.10* exhibition at the end of 1915 came the first inkling that abstract art would reach beyond the frame to mold its surroundings.[3] In Lissitzky's *Proun Room* (1923), the architectonics of the pictorial seemed to "naturally" extend into the architectonics of the interior or even become intermingled with it. At the same moment, De Stijl artists were experimenting with rooms and exhibition space in a coloristically dynamic way.[4] By the mid-1920s this trend was brilliantly refined in Lissitzky's exhibition projects, notably the "abstract cabinet" of Alexander Doerner's Hannover Museum, not to mention Frederick Kiesler's great soaring project at the Exposition des Arts Décoratifs. While Dadaist exhibition space proved ephemeral, these examples of what might be called Constructivist installation spread widely, its influence shaping new interiors and exhibition spaces all the way to Manhattan, in the new Museum of Modern Art, opened in 1929.[5] And at certain moments and places, the ideological quotient in exhibition space could rise to a higher or more pitched level.

The Surrealists early on manifested themselves in the almost venerable tradition of the avant-garde group exhibition, beginning at the Galerie Pierre in November 1925. Yet even with a number of group shows, as well as galleries devoted to Surrealism, they still did not attempt to inscribe their style in terms of display until 1938. Again, this seems to me a curiously delayed development, all the more so for a group that was not shy about its political posturing in the 1930s. Perhaps it was only the collapse of Surrealism's entente with the Communists that shifted energies to curating subjective installations, a major innovation and characteristic of late Surrealism. This might also be thought of as the *Minotaure* phase, in which a lavishly illustrated and designed magazine created a different kind of publication space, allowing for much more play of the image than in the early Surrealist publications. Engaged exhibition space also relates to both the internationalization and the simultaneous commercialization of Surrealism in the mid-1930s, intertwined developments that will be traced in this study.

The ideological exhibition space coincides historically with the rise of the marketing of brand name goods, as well as the spread of the site consecrated to such display, the department store. Not surprisingly, the display as spectacle has its overlapping histories in the commercial and fine art realms. Exhibition space is often where the two most obviously mingle and compete. This is notably true of the Surrealists, as witness their mannequins, borrowed from the fashion houses and dressed by the artists along a gauntletlike entry corridor for the 1938 show. There were also significant interactions with the clothing designer Elsa Schiaparelli, who launched her first theme collections at the same time as the Surrealists were packaging their own image in the form of large international shows. Fashion designers in their turn tracked the Surrealists closely, attended their vernissages, reported on the shows in the top couture magazines, and adapted aspects to their own use.[6] By the mid-1930s, in Paris or New York, a large Surrealist exhibition would set a theme for the season and be immediately reflected in the vitrines of department stores and in the press. The promotion of innovative style and stylishness thus transcended place, and became a significant part of the cultural baggage the émigré Surrealists unpacked in the new world. Their goods had a mixed reception in the already highly developed commercial and art institutional worlds of Manhattan. The collision of those worlds sparked unanticipated progeny in the New York School and beyond.

It is difficult to think of Marcel Duchamp, always pegged as a Dadaist, as having had much to do with Surrealism. Yet he collaborated closely with the group at this time, was the only artist on the editorial board of their publication *Minotaure*, and had a similarly overarching role in their exhibitions. In fact, more than any other individual, Duchamp may be said to be the "inventor" of the disorienting, obstructionist mise-en-scène that is late Surrealist exhibition display. In this way and others Duchamp was useful to the Surrealists. His tact in collaborating with Breton, and thus buffering the latter's temperamental tendency to control the artists, forged a curatorial duo that was sporadically active to the end of their lives in the 1960s. Likewise the Surrealists were useful to Duchamp in facilitating his return to the center of the thirties art world, as well as in beginning the consecration of his readymades and *Large Glass*. The later prestige of these icons was mentally backdated, as it were, and they are always discussed by critics and historians as examples of the Dada era. This obscures Surrealism's role in Duchamp's critical apotheosis, which has been going strong since the late 1950s. The intensive focus on these works ironically has been counter to the spirit of Duchamp's pioneering of roles for the artist beyond traditional object-maker. These include artist-publisher, art consultant, and, as we will see, installation artist before there was such a category. The wonder is that

Duchamp's "retirement" from art persisted for so long as a myth (albeit one that he sometimes perpetuated). By focusing on this later period of his activity and influence in the art world, we may perceive a more grounded image of Duchamp, as well as of that art world.

In recent years modern art exhibitions have increasingly been the object of study. They are often fascinating as a snapshot of art world politics at a particular moment. They also provide an obvious platform to study critical reception, as well as market and collector patronage. While there is more data about critical reception than about the market, I will consider all these areas with respect to the Surrealists. The current boom in installations also prompts one to look back at outstanding earlier examples with renewed appreciation. This is especially apropos for the Surrealist era, when critics and other participants struggled for a vocabulary and framework to explicate these new environments. To suggest the continuum and dialogue between present and past, I turn in chapter 5 to selected recent installations that hark back, in materials or themes, to the Surrealists' example.

The International Surrealist Exhibition (1936) and Fantastic Art, Dada, Surrealism (1936–1937)

At the outset of the movement, Surrealist exhibitions were generally small one-man or group shows at various locales in Paris. This began to change from the early 1930s as Surrealism took on a pan-European character. Larger shows were held in several capitals, often under the aegis of Eluard and Breton, whose conferences on Surrealist writing accompanied the exhibitions. From 1933 on, Copenhagen, Brussels, and Prague were such sites, as well as Tenerife in the Canary Islands. In Prague, for the exhibition of spring 1935, Breton told an interviewer, "we propose, in the coming period, to concentrate more on the objectification and internationalization of surrealist ideas."[7] The group exhibition became a prime vehicle of this "internationalization." Local artists also participated, lending the shows a cooperative character, or a colonizing one, depending on one's perspective, as Paris Surrealism radiated its influence.

It was in the English-speaking world, however, that the first comprehensive overviews of Surrealism's history were displayed. In the summer of 1936, the London Surrealists staged a very large *International Surrealist Exhibition* in cooperation with the Paris group, comprising some 390 works by 68 artists. These figures were nearly doubled the following winter at the

1.2   *International Surrealist Exhibition,* New Burlington Gallery, London, June 11–July 4, 1936. Collection Getty Research Institute.

1.3   *International Surrealist Exhibition,* New Burlington Gallery, London, June 11–July 4, 1936. Collection Getty Research Institute.

Museum of Modern Art in New York, site of Alfred Barr's build-ing-filling blockbuster *Fantastic Art, Dada, Surrealism.* This was not solely devoted to the latter but included historical forerunners and popular art parallels, a broad focus bitterly disputed by the Paris group, especially as spearheaded by Breton.

The 1938 Paris *Exposition* would open at Georges Wilden-stein's Galerie Beaux-Arts only a year after the Museum of Modern Art's show closed. Several French critics at the time observed that it followed in the wake of these large Surrealist surveys of London and New York; so it is useful to examine these forerunners to re-construct the context that the Parisian Surrealists were addressing. London and New York were foreshadowings in scope; indeed the same core group of artists and even some of the same pictures were found in all three shows.[8] Yet the Paris exhibition strove mightily to distinguish itself, notably in the site-specific mannequins outfitted for the show by artists and writers. Even more significantly, it deliberately sought to embody Surrealist prin-ciples in the installation. In contrast, the installations in London and New York were relatively straightforward and did not in themselves have a Sur-realist character. In fact, considering the interactions of those involved, it seems likely that the exhibition design in Paris was a competitive reaction *against* the character of the earlier installations.

For the *International Surrealist Exhibition* at the New Burlington Gal-leries, Breton, Eluard, Georges Hugnet, and Man Ray—three writers and one sole artist—selected the works for artists of French and other European countries, while the host English, headed by Roland Penrose, selected their

1.4 London Surrealist group with Breton added, 1936, from *Dictionnaire abrégé du surréalisme,* 1938, p. 54.

A l'Exposition surréaliste de Londres, en 1936. *De gauche à droite :*
A. B., Eileen Agar, S. D., P. E., R. Penrose, H. Read, E. M., G. Reavey, H. Sykes Davies.

own.[9] Penrose recalled frequent visits to Paris for deliberations with Breton and his colleagues there. Non-Western works and works by children and the mentally ill were also incorporated, an aspect that would be repeated by Barr.

In London for a little over three weeks, from June 11 to July 4, 1936, the show drew some 20,000 visitors and widespread commentary. Penrose remembered that it stirred a lot of publicity and "succeeded even finan-cially," with "large sums" from the paid admissions being carried to the bank each day.[10] The recently published installation views indicate a salon-style hanging, in closely spaced double or triple rows (fig. 1.3). The installation is jumbled, with works mixed by artist, size, and media. Polynesian shields or African masks appear periodically amidst the Western works. In the end the only guiding principle arrived at was to keep as great a contrast as pos-sible between adjacent works.[11]

Some group photos of the participants were taken in late June, includ-ing Eluard and Dalí though not Breton. The English Surrealist Eileen Agar recounted how Eluard phoned to advise her to be at the gallery for a hastily arranged shoot. She is the only woman to appear in the doctored version of this photo reprinted in the 1938 *Dictionnaire abrégé du Surréalisme* (fig. 1.4), the others consigned to oblivion by the cropping of the seated row of women. Even more astonishing than this gender cut is the appearance of André Breton at her side, montaged from another photo altogether, and tak-ing the place originally occupied by Rupert Lee and Ruthven Todd. Breton has also gained a bit in stature, in this dubious retouching of history that re-calls similar doctoring in the Stalinist-era Soviet Union. It implies more unity in the ranks than actually existed. By design, Breton was avoiding Eluard in London when the original group photo was shot.

Although now regarded as a seminal event, *Fantastic Art, Dada, Surrealism* as organized by Alfred Barr was the consequence of an-other plan falling through. Before the London show opened, in March 1936, Alfred Barr inquired about its dates and whether it would be available for his Museum of Modern Art in November and December.[12] This initial possibility apparently foundered when it became clear that Barr planned a more art historical exhi-bition, including Dada and other forerunners. A Museum press re-lease written just before his departure for Europe announced his

The *International Surrealist Exhibition* and *Fantastic Art, Dada, Surrealism*

show with the tentative title "Art of the Marvelous and Anti-Rational,"[13] thus dispensing with even the designation of a group that had existed for over ten years. By contrast, Breton and Eluard insisted on an exclusively Surrealist manifestation, and at first withheld their cooperation from Barr. According to a participant in the London show, "Breton envisaged England as the stepping stone for World Surrealism."[14] Once the London exhibition proved a success, Breton no doubt increasingly imagined that he would preside over Surrealism's expansion, even to America.

Meanwhile Barr sailed to Europe in May 1936 on the new ocean liner the *Normandie*, the very vessel that Marcel Duchamp was awaiting for his return to New York.[15] They met briefly upon Barr's arrival; no doubt Barr enlisted his support in the project. (Barr would later bemoan Duchamp's absence from Paris that summer.) Meanwhile Barr's wife Marga came from a family visit in Italy to act as translator in this "campaign." She emphasized that the recent change of government in France invigorated the populace: "One senses the liberal presence of Léon Blum. The Front Populaire creates an atmosphere of youth, liberty, and cheerfulness."[16] Buoyed by this sense of optimism, the couple made the rounds of a number of artists' studios (Ernst, Miró, Man Ray, Valentine Hugo, Arp, Tanguy, Oelze) as well as collectors and dealers (Roché, Simone Kahn, René Gaffe, Kahnweiler, Léonce Rosenberg) and poets (Tzara, Hugnet).[17] Barr also made extensive notes on the collections of Breton and Eluard, with prices meticulously elicited and noted next to each work.[18] Of necessity Breton was the first person Barr visited; he proved demanding and his attitude "severe."[19] While the poets Breton and Eluard strove to pressure Barr to limit his focus to Surrealism, they also were well aware that he wielded considerable clout on behalf of the Museum, notably acquisition funds and the commissioning of catalogue essays. The previous summer he had purchased Tanguys from Breton, Ernsts from Eluard, and documents and publications from both men, for the Museum library. Eluard viewed the resulting financial windfall as "phenomenal."[20]

On June 25 Barr traveled from the studios of Paris to London to view the newly opened *International Exhibition* and make contact with the English Surrealists. Interestingly, this was the moment when Eluard was also in London for a lecture, although not Breton, who had already delivered his. They had broken in the spring and thus arranged to be in London at different times. Dalí was also there to present, though his words were overshadowed by his appearance in a diver's suit, which became infamous as a Surrealist performance.

Marga reported that Barr found Eluard more sympathetic than Breton, and they met again back in Paris on July 12, Breton being already out of town for the summer. Eluard himself left for the south the next day, writing from Avignon to demand the inclusion of certain artists, under the rubric "Exposition Surréaliste." Barr soon responded firmly to both Eluard and Breton, asserting his own right to decide the form of the exhibition, on behalf of the institution.[21] He also held out carrots, dangling the prospect of a tour to Philadelphia, Boston, and San Francisco and commissioning an essay from Breton on "the present position of Surrealist painting." Once they proved recalcitrant, Barr forged ahead and sent out loan letters toward the end of the first week of August. In them he acknowledged that he did not have the "approval" of Breton and Eluard. He flattered Man Ray, confiding his "wish to concentrate . . . upon the principal dada and surrealist artists without including much of the rank and file."[22] He subtly sowed other seeds of dissension, notifying Ernst that his *Elephant Celebes* from Eluard's collection couldn't be included. Thus he played on the varying vested interests of

1.5 Max Ernst works, *Fantastic Art, Dada, Surrealism* installation view, Museum of Modern Art, New York, December 7, 1936–January 17, 1937. At left: *Elephant Celebes.*

artists versus poets, for instance writing to Arp that he was "distressed but also surprised at their assumption of the right to dictate either to artists or to the Museum."[23] Barr then left for New York in mid-August, unreconciled with the two poets and not having seen them again. Only Wolfgang Paalen responded in writing that he could not lend while there was disagreement with Breton;[24] other artists either intended to cooperate or awaited further discussions, pending the October 1 deadline for the works to be assembled and shipped.

Back in New York Barr may well have consulted Duchamp, who returned there from the West on August 27 before again embarking on the *Normandie* on September 2. Meanwhile Marga Barr remained behind in Europe, returning to Paris from Italy in late August or early September. After Duchamp arrived there on September 7, she had him set up a joint meeting with Breton and herself.[25] She soon was able to telegraph of a September 21 "reconciliation dinner" with Eluard.[26] Mrs. Barr may well have been thinking of this moment when she recalled that Duchamp was "most helpful," "knows the currents and countercurrents of the art world, is interested in the problem as if it were chess, but is dispassionate about the outcome."[27] Mrs. Barr herself, with her fluency in French, played a central, unacknowledged role in securing the collaboration of Breton and Eluard by the beginning of October, which she herself did not commit to (preserved) paper but which is echoed in the comments of others. E. L. T. Mesens in Brussels had already heard of the rapprochement and offered his cooperation. On the other hand Tristan Tzara, with no love lost for Breton at this point, asked to withdraw his loans once the latter was on board.[28]

Most of the Parisian Surrealists, as well as Duchamp, never viewed *Fantastic Art, Dada, Surrealism* while it was on view at the Museum of Modern Art from December 7, 1936, to January 17, 1937. It was installed in spaces just previously devoted to *Cubism and Abstract Art*, and inevitably took on some of the character of the clean lines of a Bauhaus-derived approach to design. Some of the artists, including Duchamp, Ernst, and Fini, did receive installation photographs from the Museum, which gave some idea of the display, although usually of their own works only (fig. 1.5). More importantly, Man Ray and Dalí were in New York at the time, and both would be vital sources of description back in Paris. Dalí wrote Breton, "I'm doing my best for Surrealism," but of course also for himself.[29] Both artists were the subject of newspaper interviews in the vast outpouring of publicity surrounding the exhibition. Man Ray encountered fellow-exhibitor James Thurber at the opening, and part of their witty dialogue made the *New Yorker*'s "Talk of the Town." The nationwide tour assured that the show would bring Dada and Surrealism into the public domain, from advertising to department store vitrines, rather as the Armory Show had done for Fauvism and Cubism. As in 1913, it was not that these art movements were unknown; but their expanded public was new.

From the vantage point of our era's huge glossy publications, it is difficult to reconstruct the impact that Barr's delayed catalogue had until we attend to the chorus of praise he received by letter. Throughout the Paris group the catalogue loomed large as an impressive document, obviously supplanting the slim, unillustrated checklist produced in London. Simone Kahn thanked Barr for "the magnificent album, of the highest interest"; Eluard pronounced it "sumptuous" when he first saw it at Galerie Bucher.[30] Years later, Marcel Jean recalled that the historical dimension—precisely what Breton and Eluard had objected to—generated a lively interest. Barr's effort was "the most ambitious and the most successful attempt yet made to show the historical importance of poetical art. I must say that when it arrived in Paris the catalogue of the exhibition with its iconography ranging from Bosch to *The Marvelous Potato* . . . the Surrealists discovered that their genealogical tree spread farther than they themselves had imagined."[31] Similarly, the Vicomte de Noailles found the catalogue of "enormous" interest, and dropped the surprising aside that no less than Aldous Huxley had borrowed his copy.[32] The significance of such a catalogue as a historical document must have especially struck the Surrealist writers, who had long labored to produce the group's magazines. Barr had set an impressive, positivist example that Eluard and Breton soon were prodded to rival with the more antirational *Dictionnaire* of the Surrealist world view.

Not having been able to dictate terms to Barr, Eluard and Breton did come around in the end to cooperating with loans from their collections. Breton's commission for an essay was withdrawn, as it had become too late for publication in the catalogue. (Only Georges Hugnet's overview ultimately appeared.) Yet surprisingly the Museum brokered the sale of Picabia's *Catch as Catch Can* from

1.6   *Entartete Kunst* exhibition, Dada section, Munich, July 19–November 30, 1937.

Breton's collection to the San Francisco Museum for $280. At the same time Barr and the Museum also acquired a Miró and an Arp from Breton for $155. Indeed a considerable number of works were purchased for the permanent collection or on behalf of private collectors, in some cases the Museum's trustees. Aside from Breton, loan correspondence reveals purchases made from Valentine Hugo, Simone Kahn, Arp, Man Ray, Tanguy, and the collector René Gaffe.[33]

No doubt Breton took note of this blossoming market for Surrealism when hatching his own plans for a gallery. He and Eluard must have sensed that both the historical construction and the market for Surrealism were being set in the English-speaking world, and it was up to them to take steps to reclaim it for France.

Another forerunner exhibition that impinged on the Surrealist world view was the infamous "blockbuster" of the summer of 1937, the Nazi-organized *Entartete Kunst* show in Munich. Opening on July 19, it drew record crowds and international press, including a review in the first issue of the *London Bulletin*, alongside a discussion of the Paris Surrealist mannequins in relation to fashion designs. Though intended to bury modernism, not to praise it, its two million visitors over four months ironically made it the best-attended modern art exhibition.[34] Though focusing its disdain primarily on German Expressionist and abstract artists, "Degenerate Art" included De Chirico and Max Ernst. The latter's *Creation of Eve (Belle Jardinière)* of 1923 was removed from the Düsseldorf Art Museum, censured as degenerate, and apparently among the works destroyed following the exhibition. This most likely was a topic for discussion among the Parisian Surrealists. It certainly astonished Ernst's son Jimmy, who saw it in the traveling version in Hamburg.[35] It is a historical irony that part of the context for the Surrealists indulging in ideologically coded installations on the left was this Nazi forerunner. Neither side was subtle about expressing an ideological message via display. Quite a few elements, such as the crowded hanging, the large numbers of works by numerous participants, and the use of accompanying wall texts are in fact comparable between Munich and what the Surrealists would do in Paris. Or perhaps we should bear in mind what was happening in Paris on the Trocadéro grounds of the Universal Exposition that same summer. On the esplanade were the confronted pavilions of Germany and the Soviet Union, which many viewed as doing architectural and symbolic battle. As James Herbert has observed, "Despite the pacific intentions of its French organizers, [the Exposition Internationale] had become a forum for the expression of dangerous nationalist belligerence."[36] Thus when the Surrealists began planning their Paris show that autumn, they were most likely formulating a response to Hitler as well as to Alfred Barr.

2

The Origin of Surrealist Exhibition Space: The 1938 Paris Exposition Internationale du Surréalisme

There is no clear record of the factors that led the traditional Wildenstein firm to approach the Surrealist group about organizing an exhibition. Like others, the Galerie had tapped the more established French modern art tradition. It had an ongoing series of exhibitions publicized as "étapes de l'art contemporain" that had been organized by its director Raymond Cogniat. These began in the 1933–1934 season with Seurat and Neoimpressionism and went on to cover the movements of Fauvism and Cubism. Yet the only truly "contemporary" overview was the curiously titled *Peintres Instinctifs*, surveying the milder "Ecole de Paris" from Chagall to Utrillo. Seven artists were well represented with 172 catalogued works borrowed from a sizable group of dealers, collectors, and other artists. This *étape* number six was held from December 1935 to January 1936, and proclaimed as being of "an impartial and informative character." At the time of the Surrealism exhibition, some reviewers claimed that it followed in this series,[1] though it was not numbered as such nor was it organized by Cogniat. It was also noticeably separated by two years from the succession of *étapes*, and from the outset it did not pretend to "impartiality"; indeed it seemed to specifically counter such a notion. It probably was not initially planned as part of the series, though this became a post-facto rationalization. Most press critics were astonished that the Surrealists showed at the Right Bank gallery, completely overlooking the nature of the exhibition itself. One or two interpreted "the vulgar saleroom" as an indicator of the coopting of a formerly radical movement, "one more revolution that fades into that which it wished to overturn."[2] A similar few made the equally plausible argument that the Surrealists transcribed their innovative search for "convulsive beauty" and "the marvelous" in terms of display.

The most detailed insider's account appeared two decades later from the pen of writer and exhibitor Georges Hugnet. He postulates the possible significance of the connection between Kurt Seligmann's wife, Arlette, who was related to the Wildenstein family, owners of the Galerie.[3] Given Seligmann's substantial representation in the show, this seems a credible possibility. Note, too, that Seligmann designed the poster for the exhibition (fig. 2.1).

Wildenstein had also exhibited one of the Surrealists, André Masson, at its London gallery in February-March 1936. (Masson's painting *Daphne* [1935]was one of two loans to the 1938 show by Georges Wildenstein, the

2.1 Kurt Seligmann, poster for *Exposition Internationale du Surréalisme*, Galerie Beaux-Arts, Paris, January 17–February 22, 1938. Courtesy Ubu Gallery, New York.

Invitation: Galerie Beaux-Arts, Paris, January 17–February 22, 1938

2.2 Galerie Beaux-Arts: Seligmann adjusting his painting; Paalen's *Homage to Lichten-berg* (1937) at right.

other being Picasso's *Figure* [1929].) So the gallery had a limited investment in this area, though it was known primarily for its historical art. One artist-critic even dubbed it a "temple of the eighteenth century,"[4] its familiar position today.

Hugnet also tells us it was Cogniat who first approached Paul Eluard at the beginning of the fall of 1937 about the possibility of collaboration. It was undoubtedly with forethought that Eluard was asked and not Breton. It was the former who brought the whole group into the project, including the latter as coorganizer. If Breton had been approached first, he more likely would have set himself up as the sole head. Cogniat would have been aware that in 1937 Eluard was on closer terms with Picasso, whose participation would be much desired and who was represented by Wildenstein, jointly with Paul Rosenberg. (Wildenstein had approached Eluard the year before regarding a Picasso painting that had been damaged during its loan to an earlier Surrealist exhibition.)[5] Eluard in 1937 was likewise on closer terms with Dalí, in whom Georges Wildenstein was interested.

By November of 1937, exhibition plans were well under way, prompting Eluard to write to the Museum of Modern Art, which was considering purchase of his Ernst painting *Elephant Celebes*. Eluard asked that it be returned "as soon as possible, because it is probable that a large Surrealist exhibition (retrospective) will take place very soon in Paris."[6] Even though Eluard was not entirely certain about the exhibition, its "retrospective" character is confirmed in this request for a 1921 painting. Ernst would ultimately show five paintings and two collages from the 1920s, and the other early members of the group did similarly.

Hugnet believed that Cogniat took the project to heart. The latter even published a teaser in the house weekly paper he edited, *Beaux Arts*, announcing a forthcoming "total manifestation," if no revelation, "awaited with the liveliest curiosity." Cogniat concluded that "Surrealism is not a game, it's an obsession."[7] Yet his later review of the show after it opened, published in the premiere issue of what would prove to be an important periodical, *XXe Siècle*, is disappointingly tempered. Cogniat does concede the durability of Surrealism, still vital and cohesive more than ten years after its first manifesto. Yet the review also spoke, rather less favorably, of its hallucinatory and "nightmare" quality. He stressed that it is an art that confronts the spectator, provoking malaise, laughter, or anger, but left unsaid how he esteemed that art. Cogniat, though born in the same year as Breton (1896), was a more conservative critic who published largely on Impressionist and Postimpressionist artists. Much later he wrote a book on Duchamp's brother, Jacques Villon. Surrealism seems not to have been especially to his taste, given his descriptive, middle-of-the-road response to it, despite his role as the major spokesperson at the gallery for recent art.

At the same time *Beaux Arts* published the first of three intriguing reports on the exhibition, under the pseudonym "Grincheux Jovial." These lively articles by a magazine insider offer a contrast to Cogniat's noncommittal descriptions. The "jolly grinch's" preview stresses secrecy, while offering an apt description of the atmosphere: "of catacombs and roasted coffee." He jokes that the workmen are on the verge of becoming Surrealists by the hundreds.[8]

In the third column (s)he reveals that the editors of *Beaux Arts* are split between partisans of André Breton and of El Greco, with the latter group "mortified" at the success of the show,[9] not to men-

2.3 Marcel Duchamp, glass door for Gradiva gallery, 1937.

tion its radical format. Of course it was precisely the prestige of the Wilden-stein firm that the Surrealists sought to accrue. What the Wildensteins would gain from this unlikely collaboration is less obvious, though in later years they did point to the event as an example of their forward thinking.

An additional complication is that at the time Breton was running his Gradiva Gallery at 31 rue de Seine, so that inviting him as curator would effectively be promoting a rival gallery owner. Gradiva's small Left Bank space fronting on the street was essentially an ongoing Surrealist manifestation, including literature as well as art, that had opened in May of 1937. From the early part of the year, Breton had solicited his artist associates to lend works and contribute to the enterprise. In seeking Picasso's support, Breton perhaps unwisely stressed that he was opening this "boutique" of paintings, objects, and books to ameliorate his financial problems, yet it would not be an entirely commercial enterprise, as conferences and "spectacles" would be organized.[10] Significantly, Marcel Duchamp conceived a rare recent work and contributed his first work in glass in over a decade. It took the form of a door cut with the outline of an interlaced couple, perhaps suggesting that the bachelor finally wins the Bride, in a triumph of Surrealist *amour fou*? A series of snapshots taken outside Gradiva shows that Yves Tanguy helped to install this important yet little-known sequel to Duchamp's earlier experiments with a glass ground (fig. 2.3).[11] (At the same time, Paalen and others painted designs on the architectural borders.) With characteristic irony and sense of paradox, Duchamp had created a door that was always open, even when it was shut. It thus echoed a notorious swinging door made for his studio at 11 rue Larrey and later considered a "work." This amusing feature nonetheless presented the practical problem of exposing the space and its contents to the elements. Picasso was asked to sketch a Gradiva logo but did not comply. Nonetheless he was among the twenty artists announced for the opening exhibition, of whom sixteen would soon participate in the 1938 *Exposition*. Thus despite its modest proportions, Gradiva was clearly a trial run in exhibition-making.

One aspect of Gradiva, as well as the *Exposition*, is that these efforts underline the growing commercialization of Surrealism by this time. Michel Leiris referred to the *Exposition* in raising this complaint, claiming that "the Surrealist artists have always sold their works."[12] There had been short-lived attempts at a "Galerie Surréaliste" in the later 1920s. But Breton running his own gallery is a rather astonishing development, an episode played down in subsequent histories. It arises from a complex nexus including his self-avowed financial woes. To which must be added the prospect of success, stimulated by Barr's purchases for the Museum of Modern Art and its friends.

Another basic fact is that most if not all of the pieces in the Surrealist exhibitions were for sale, so the spectacular aspect of the installations was intended to attract not only critical but also commercial interest. Yet the shows also involved group bonding, something Breton recognized as a deep need (as was his desire to control the process). In fairness, Gradiva was actually a gallery-bookshop, billed also as a "paradis des livres" between utopia and reality. In short, Breton sought a place for like-minded artists and writers to congregate and for newcomers to be initiated, something akin to Alfred Stieglitz's gallery 291, which for similar reasons was not named after its director. It also grew out of the Surrealists' regular gatherings at nearby cafes, such as the Deux Magots. Another parallel is the agenda of text publication and presentation as part of Surrealism's presence in the public domain. Unlike Stieglitz, however, Breton was by all accounts ill-suited to direct day-to-day operations. A

Invitation: Galerie Beaux-Arts, Paris, January 17–February 22, 1938

year later, after being invited to lecture in Mexico, Breton liqui-
dated Gradiva.

Following the initial feeler from Cogniat, a small group of Surrealist "plenipotentiaries," headed by Breton and Eluard, carried
out discussions with the Beaux-Arts gallery representatives and arrived at an ambitious plan: some fifty artists from ten countries,
showing about two hundred works. Upon agreement, the proposal
was taken back to the general rank-and-file "membership," who
were only too happy to avail themselves of the "vast and respectable" locale at 140 rue du Faubourg Saint-Honoré.[13] Duchamp was soon agreed on by the two writers as the number three,
supervisor of the "mise en scène," both "generator" of ideas and "arbitrator"
of disagreements, probably including those of Eluard and Breton, whose
stormy relationship had already broken off for periods before. "Special ad-
visors" were announced as Dalí and Ernst. Meanwhile, Eluard and Breton
collaborated on the *Dictionnaire abrégé*, which gave equal representation to
a "retrospective" of the written word. While including the artists of the exhibition and certain of their works, techniques, and subjects, the *Dictionnaire* also defines and quotes from the major figures and themes of literary
Surrealism. As a publication it is less a catalogue than an "exhibition" of the
writers, a privileged few of whom additionally crossed media and created visual works, as we will see.

In the end the estimates were too modest, as 228 works are listed in the
separate checklist, not including books and documents. There were considerably more artworks than that, since numerous single entries such as "objects, sculptures, drawings, graphics" stand for multiple pieces. Add to this
sixteen mannequins and the installations, created by Duchamp and others,
and the total easily exceeds 250 items.

The writer André Thirion gives a rare glimpse of the preliminary discussions that animated the group on the terraces of their meeting place, the
Deux Magots, during the warm Indian summer evenings. He marveled at
the number of new ideas discussed for presenting their works, including
Dalí's vision of a dense field of grain which would obscure pictures from
view. Thirion admits he would have liked to insert himself as a participant
in this exciting prospect, but had to remain content to "assist from afar."[14]

Some of this was no doubt cafe chatter, but on another level the Parisian
Surrealists were uniting while they grappled with the serious issue of how to

convey their ideas in the exhibition sphere. Their problem was that of the butterfly collector: how to capture and display the marvelous without diminishing it. The plans took shape in a fashion analogous to other forays in the public sphere, such as the collaborative organization of magazines like *Minotaure*. Writers (Breton, Eluard, Hugnet) played a leading role in "publishing" essentially metaphoric or poetic concepts in the form of installation.

Hugnet notes the logistical difficulties that arose in putting verbal ideas into practice, particularly Duchamp's proposal to cover the glazed ceiling with hanging coal sacks. The gallery feared an explosion if a match was lit underneath, where a coal grate stood. Duchamp recalled, "The grate was electric, but the insurance companies said no. We did it anyway, and then they accepted it," indicating a certain defiance. In contrast, Hugnet remembered discussions proceeding until an underwriter agreed to accept the risk. Either way, this was recalled as a kind of turning point in the group mindset, spurring them on to various innovations, including the mannequins. The connections from Hugnet's family furniture business and his atelier "Livre-Objet" proved useful in borrowing the four beds and revolving doors, as well as fabricating some of the furniture-like objects.[15]

A number of private individuals are listed as lenders in the checklist, but no commercial galleries or institutions. Dealers like Kahnweiler and Pierre Loeb are thus credited as individuals, in the same form as collector-supporters like the Vicomte de Noailles or Etienne de Beaumont. The chief lenders were the coorganizers: Breton with twelve pieces and Eluard five. Max Ernst and Miró showed the most works, the former with fifteen paintings and more than three collages, the latter with twelve paintings plus objects. Kurt Seligmann is next with twelve (six paintings, two sculptures, and four objects), followed by Masson and Tanguy, with totals of eleven paintings and objects. Then Magritte and Wolfgang Paalen with nine works, De Chirico with eight (all borrowed and all from the 1910s), and Dalí, Domínguez, and Man Ray with seven each. Duchamp had only five, including a rotary demisphere of 1925. Apart from the prominence of Seligmann, there are no surprises here, only a reaffirmation of the primacy of the Parisian Surrealist masters. Despite an avowed goal that the show should not be just recent works of the main artists; it was that, yet more.

Invitation: Galerie Beaux-Arts, Paris, January 17–February 22, 1938

There was also a gesture toward internationalism, with representation solicited from the European capitals where the Parisian Surrealists had recently exhibited, or where Breton and Eluard had been invited to lecture. These local groups were given the autonomy to select their own pieces for the show, which usually ended up a token two per artist. Thus Eluard asked Mesens to put together the Belgian group. The checklist was to be submitted by December 15, 1937, with the works following before January 4; no further specifications.[16] Similarly, a member of the Copenhagen Surrealists said, "Breton considered us as a group, and it was as a group that we were invited to participate."[17] Following upon the vast Burlington Galleries show, the English Surrealists were apportioned the largest share after the French.

Almost miraculously by today's standards, the entire mammoth show, on the order of 250 or more works, was put together in less than four months.

 Visitors arriving at 140 rue du Faubourg Saint-Honoré entered a passageway which opened up onto a sizable courtyard ringed by massive stone buildings. Across the courtyard was a life-sized black taxi, perhaps mirroring one from which they had just disembarked. In the open air, most would not realize they were encountering the first work of the show, and one of the most popular, Salvador Dalí's *Rainy Taxi*. It was hailed, even by those who disliked the rest of the exhibit, as a "triumph," "la suprème trouvaille surréaliste."[18] Seen from a distance, it was not so remarkable. It has been well served by the photographers such as Denise Bellon and Raoul Ubac who focused on close-ups of its hallucinatory interior (fig. 2.5). Viewers saw a "car bedecked outside with ivy, the headlights full on, glaring with brilliant uselessness into the light of day. In the back seat a scantily clad female figure with a few pet snails crawling over her. Beside her is a sewing machine, and on the floor a mass of Pampas grass and other vegetation." Inside the cab, "the continuous torrent of water" struck a national chord to the English critic: "the motorist can carry his own weather with him,"[19] thanks to the perforated pipes along the ceiling. For the French the jetting water suggested rather a "piscine" or "un

2.4   Josef Breitenbach, *Dalí's Rainy Taxi* in courtyard, lights on, Galerie
Beaux-Arts, 1938. Collection Center for Creative Photography, Tucson.
(Opposite, top)

2.5   Raoul Ubac, *Dalí's Rainy Taxi,* detail, driver and passenger. Collection
Timothy Baum, New York.
(Opposite, bottom)

2.6   Raoul Ubac, *Dalí's Rainy Taxi,* detail, passenger with pipes spraying
water. Collection Timothy Baum, New York.

shampooing."[20] The water drained in the courtyard, "soaking the guests' evening slippers,"[21] during the vernissage. This life-sized sculpture represents a culmination in Dalí's explorations of the Surrealist object, while foreshadowing product-based object sculpture of recent times. Dalí himself prized it so much that he went on to repeat it twice, once the very next year for an American audience.

Among details not visible in photographs, but noted by approving reviewers, were the rider's bodice incorporating a reproduction of Millet's *Angelus*, the favored Dalían paranoiac-critical appropriation since the early 1930s.[22] On her lap, an omelette. Next to her, as mentioned, the Lautréamontian sewing machine, when clearly she would have needed its pendant, the encountered umbrella. (An umbrella was indeed found farther on in the show, as the basis for Wolfgang Paalen's *Nuage articulé*, but it, too, subverted its usual protective function, as we will see.) Ivy and foliage were for the snails' benefit, but they stimulated Simone de Beauvoir's appetite, "a sort of lettuce-and-chicory salad,"[23] she called it. All add to an overgrown greenhouse effect, mingled with revulsion at the sliminess of the snails. Dalí told one reviewer that he was inspired by the experience of waiting for a taxi during a downpour in Milan. The sudden cessation of rain once inside made him think, what if the shower had continued?[24]

Interestingly, Dalí's humid blonde mannequin is in several respects anticipated in the imagery of Louis Aragon's novel *Paris Peasant:* "This unfurled [blonde] hair had the electric pallor of storms, the cloudiness of breath upon metal. A drowsy animal of some kind, lolling in a car." The other main element turns up a few pages later, as a singer sings "Ah, if you only knew the details of the life of Burgundy snails."[25] These are exactly the type of snails dramatically photographed crawling over the mannequin's face. (The artist was said to be grateful to the person who taught him how to induce them to crawl.)

To ask whom she represents seems needlessly literal, yet Matta took the trouble to identify her as an opera-goer. Dalí's introductory sign placed on the car is addressed to the "lady snob," but it is unclear whether he means the passenger or the spectator. On one level she is both: a woman arriving by cab to see the exhibition! Another Surrealist nip at the hands that fed them.

This Dalí placard on the radiator announced the formation of an apocryphal "Ministry of Public Imagination" and prompted the spectator with the alleged details about the contents of the taxi.[26] The snails later rated their own news note indicating that the gallery assistant fed them lettuce hearts every day, and placed them back in the taxi at opening time.[27] They were slated to be eaten after the run of the exhibition, an actualization of the traditional expression "the artist's cuisine."[28] To add to the menagerie (and the closing menu of delicacies), Dalí had planned to add, fairy-tale-like, a dozen tiny frogs with gold crowns, but this was not carried out.[29] Still, such items fed the press's appetite for "strange" Surrealist doings.

The shark-jawed front seat passenger was photographed in its unclothed, headless mannequin state, carried by the artist. At the same time Dalí posed with the voracious teeth surrounding the separate goggled head, juxtaposed to the pretty face of his street mannequin (in her first, pre-Schiaparelli state; fig. 2.7). Several such camera tableaux, contrasting living and mute, were staged during the installation by Denise Bellon, with the handsome artist as effective actor. The shark teeth have convincingly reminded James Herbert of the "pearly" ones evoked in the verse to Bertolt Brecht and Kurt Weill's memorable tune "Mack the Knife." For those who made this association, Herbert notes, it "adds a savor of German Marxism to the exhibition's decidedly non-Francocentric mix."[30]

Dalí's presence as a headliner is somewhat unexpected, even if effective, given his earlier rifts with Breton, including the infamous trial of 1934. In response to an unflattering image of Lenin in a painting of his, Dalí was brought before a Surrealist mock tribunal, with Breton as presiding judge. Dalí cleverly managed to talk his way out of the charge. Only with the publication of Eluard's letters to Gala can we appreciate that it was that poet's continuing solicitude to his ex-wife's husband that helped pave the way for the painter's prominence in the movement.[31] Indeed for both Eluard and Dalí, the exhibition project represented a moment of reconciliation with the demanding Breton, a peace that in both cases did not last a year. Dalí was among the select number to decorate a mannequin, and was listed on the checklist cover as "special counselor" to the exhibition, along with Max Ernst. It would be his spectacular swan song as a participant in the Bretonian Surrealist group. Dalí's latest preserved letter to Breton is dated January 2, 1939, and makes apologies for not joining Breton's Fédération Internationale des Artistes Révolutionnaires Indépendants.[32] Nonetheless, several of the exhibition's most dramatic mo-

Escargots Surréalistes

2.7 Denise Bellon, Dalí with his mannequin (first state), holding *Rainy Taxi* driver head with goggles, Galerie Beaux-Arts, 1938. Documentation Musée Nationale d'Art Moderne, Centre Georges Pompidou, Paris.

tifs, including some from others artists, would be appropriated and restaged in Dalí's work over the next few years, as far afield as Queens and Hollywood.

In 1938 Dalí was already thinking of an encore for his sculpture in New York, writing Julien Levy to prepare a taxi with "inside rain" as a centerpiece of his March 1939 gallery exhibition.[33] The Manhattan audience would ultimately view it not at Levy's but rather at the World's Fair that summer, complete with a new, Spanish passenger, now male, designated as Christopher Columbus. This "portrait" identification does lend credence to specifying the "lady snob" of the earlier taxi: Aragon's humid female passenger.

Mannequin Street

Having studied the interior of Dalí's sharkish taxi out in the courtyard, viewers entered the Galerie Beaux-Arts beneath a sign proclaiming the International Exhibition. Inside they found themselves at the head of a corridor lined on one side with sixteen mannequins, each uniquely dressed by a different artist or writer. They were evenly spaced about two meters apart and stretched farther than the eye could see. An unexpected, more corporeal interaction thus replaced the usual encounter with pictures on a wall. Instead of the eye taking refuge in a pictorial space, the spectator's body was confronted by a series of kinesthetic equals, life-sized personages. With no other point of entry, the visitor had to pass the sixteen mannequins in the determined sequence in order to reach the main "body" of the display. This was and remains one of the most intriguing and commented features of the exhibition.

The "commentators" included a whole host of cameramen and women who made this the most photographed part of the show. The simulacra aspect of the mannequins was understood and exploited, from anonymous newspaper gag photos—the gentleman tips his hat to the lady mannequin—to publication in soft-core "model" magazines.[34] There were also more serious spreads that suggested a diversity of approaches with different examples: Eggarter's impressive suite in *Vogue,* or Gaston Paris's in *Marianne.*[35] The latter are arrayed in two groups of three head shots, cropped at the neck or midriff. They are seen close-up, mostly from below. In two cases Paris focused on a single eye from a partially obscured face, which eerily seems to fixate us in its return gaze. By contrast, few photos exist of more distant views down the hall or groups of mannequins. Instead, the bulk of the photos reinforce the impression that the fascination was with the one-to-one, lifelike encounter.

The choice of mannequins for this purpose was consonant with the rise of Surrealist sculpture and the use of readymade objects in the 1930s. More specifically, by that point mannequins were well established as a staple of Surrealist subject matter. From the outset, in the "Manifesto of Surrealism" (1924), Breton cites "the modern mannequin" as an example of the key concept of "the marvelous." (He probably had in mind the mannequins common in De Chirico's works of the teens.) As if in response, Man Ray the following year published a mannequin photograph from the fashion pavilion of the Arts Décoratifs exhibition in *Révolution Surréaliste.* Ray went on to shoot many more of the same for the fashion magazines in the mid-1930s.[36] Yet by the late thirties the tailor's dummy had a different presence than in the earlier phase, one that might be termed a shift from the De Chirican to the Bellmerian. Hans Bellmer's *La Poupée* series, disturbing photographs of a mannequin in various stages of alluring lifelikeness and/or dismemberment, first burst onto the scene with a two-page spread in *Minotaure* of December 1934. With these the Surrealist mannequin heated up sexually and overlaid misogynist violence and the crime story on the aura of the body double and dismemberment. At the same time the Bellmerian mannequin tended to undo the mechanistic automaton that had been an earlier fascination. To underline this, a group of Bellmer's photographs were hung near the beginning of the mannequin gauntlet and at the very end, as if a keynote to the enfilade.

Second, the mannequins were all women, confirming the long-standing Surrealist fetishization of the female body.[37] Since all but one of the artists dressing them were male, they were cast in the role of the adoring lover/boyfriend who brings his *amie* clothing, adornments, and other gifts (fig. 2.7). Hugnet emphasized this: "The Surrealist artists all felt they had the

2.8   Raoul Ubac, *Ernst's "Widow" Mannequin* with Miró's visible in background,
Galerie Beaux-Arts, 1938. Collection Timothy Baum, New York.

soul of Pygmalion. One could see the happy owners of mannequins . . . come in, furnished with mysterious little or big bundles,
tokens for their beloved, containing the most unlikely presents."[38] As Pygmalion sought to create the ideal beauty, so too these
Surrealist Galateas, once transformed to lifelikeness, are wooed
and made marvelous. Then again, on one level they are metaphorically put out to hustle the pavements. (So, too, is the spectator, no
sooner than having entered from the street.) Thus there appears
behind each a blue metal Parisian street sign, some real, some fictive, alluding to other Surrealist interests. With the exception of
Arp's, the mannequin streetwalkers are engaged in sexual provocation, being in various states of undress and/or allure. For one critic they
could only be "a species of whore."[39] There is even an explicit evocation of

2.9   Raoul Ubac, two undressed mannequins, Galerie Beaux-Arts, 1938. Collection
       Musée d'Art Moderne de la Ville de Paris.

2.10   Denise Bellon, Couturier mannequins with Lanvin gowns, fashion pavilion, 1937
       Universal Exposition, Paris.

the venerable *femme fatale* theme with Ernst's young widow who tramples a hapless man underfoot. The sexual level is confirmed in the terminology used by the participants. Man Ray said that the Surrealists "violated" their mannequins; Hugnet dubbed the artists "couturiers of eroticism."[40]

The artist as couturier suggests a third aspect of the mannequin, their close relation to the world of fashion. As Man Ray later wrote, they were "kidnapped from the windows of the Grands Magasins,"[41] and brought this association with them. As in the mid-1930s fashion designers increasingly used Surrealist props and even collaborated with Surrealist artists, so, too, the artists appropriated and "dressed" one of the basic tools of fashion display.[42] Man Ray is a crucial figure in this regard, very actively photographing both models and mannequins for *Harper's Bazaar* at this moment. One of his shots of a model with a strapless Lucien Lelong gown, seated in Oscar Domínguez's satin-lined wheelbarrow, even migrated from fashion magazines to the pages of the Surrealist periodical *Minotaure*.[43] At the same time Dalí was highly visible in producing a number of store windows, and collaborated with Elsa Schiaparelli in dress designs from 1937. Thus it is not surprising that Dalí introduced the one piece of true couture into the Surrealist exhibition: a recognizable "cagoule mauve de chez Schiaparelli" on the final state of his mannequin (fig. 2.25).[44] And a fashion magazine such as *Vogue* did not neglect to point to "Schiaparelli's shocking pink knitted helmet" as a vindication of fashion's status in the art world. Further, *Vogue* was the one source to mention the shop of the decorator Jean-Michel Frank next door to the gallery. When the crowds were delayed admission on the night of the vernissage, Frank opened his salon and welcomed the overflow "tout-Paris" to view Dalí's satin lip-sofa.[45] Such Surrealism in the decorative arts found an echo inside the show in Dalí's lobster-telephone within reach of his mannequin, a transformed yet functional chair by Seligmann, a second by Paalen, and other items.

It is noteworthy that the Surrealists were rather choosy about the mannequins they borrowed. The first group obtained were rejected as being too maladroit and unlifelike. Those finally used were quite realistic, with a range of hair colors and facial expressions. As such, Ubac even photographed them unadorned, composed in groups of two and three (fig. 2.9). In one, a confrontation of the mannequins to be dressed by Ernst and Marcel Jean plays on the classic juxtaposition of blonde and brunette. This recalls the

Mannequin Street

thematic of "les deux amies," a lesbian-tinged subject fairly common at the turn of the century, usually for the delectation of the male viewer.[46]

Mannequin design had its own history, within which the Surrealists chose their favorites. From the time of the 1925 Arts Décoratifs exhibition, quite stylized, tiny-featured mannequins were introduced. As their maker André Vigneux said, "the mannequin is no longer an exact copy of nature, it has more life."[47] Only months before photographing the Surrealist mannequins, Denise Bellon had shot the featureless female and rather De Chirican male ones used at the fashion pavilion of the 1937 Paris International Exposition (fig. 2.10). The artist Wols also photographed these widely discussed, tall and thin mannequins by Robert Couturier, "nymphs of a very special race." At the same time, portrait mannequins were in vogue, including those representing politicians and actors. One was even modeled after the painter Foujita. The Surrealists steered a different course, eschewing both the stylized and the specific for the simulacrum. Within the range of available and even up-to-date styles, the mannequins decorated by the Surrealists were rather conservative, the equivalent of the Dalían or veristic wing of the movement. As the writer Léo Malet put it, "Les poètes ont toujours aimé les simulacres,"[48] and so, too, the artists. Their lifelikeness was the foil for the artists to transgress or mutilate in an attempt to create a *frisson* in the spectator. They were also sexy, "delicious" in the words of one critic, "svelte stars" with lean bodies, in Hugnet's terms, "adorable puppets" abused by the Surrealists, according to a self-appointed "defender."[49] They are not mechanistic or stylized "others," but rather lifelike, active instigators/victims of an erotic or violent encounter with the viewer.

More than I would have supposed, mannequins also were classed and styled according to so-called national characteristics. After his winter 1936–1937 shoot in New York, Man Ray decided to import his own models, "taking with me a couple of charming mannequins whom I had recommended to the magazine to pose for me at French couturiers, to give an American accent to my photographs."[50] Likewise a critic at the Beaux-Arts exhibition spoke of "cette blonde Américaine en cire."[51] Such nationalistically tinged terminology is found all too often in the critical reception.

Within the Surrealist group a significant indicator of status lies in which artists (or writers) would be invited to prepare mannequins. Despite having major installations in the other parts of the exhibition, both Dalí and Duchamp also participated in the corridor "street." And the latter was apparently the source of the suggestion that some of the literary among the group be invited to dress mannequins. Thus the writer Malet prepared his model with a goldfish in a bowl "en guise de sexe." This somehow offended Breton, who asked for the goldfish to be removed the next day.[52] Evidently, although he did not spend as much time at the installation as Eluard or Hugnet, Breton still exercised a final approval. He cut Matta from the dressing roster, though his name was printed on the catalogue cover as a mannequinist. It is said that Matta wanted to take God, not woman, as his subject. Breton declared, "Look, my friend, we never speak of God around here."[53]

Perhaps it was Duchamp's benevolence that led to the appearance of Maurice Henry, Augustín Espinoza, and Sonia Mossé as mannequinists, the latter the only woman to dress one. They displayed alongside the well-known members of the group, plus a handful of new adherents like Domínguez and Marcel Jean (the category Matta would have fallen in). None of the foreign Surrealists was commissioned, since presence in Paris was a practical necessity.

The Parade

The controlled spectators viewed the mannequins in a particular sequence that has not been determined until now. This passage unfolded in time and had an initiatory or "running the gauntlet" quality. Indeed, the exhibition plan as a whole was not unlike a labyrinth, locale of the Minotaur of favored mythology. A ground plan of the exhibition would resemble Giacometti's horizontal sculpture, *Project for a Passageway (Labyrinth)* (1930–1931), itself reflecting an interest in Egyptian burial chambers and "primitive" art.

1. Jean Arp's mannequin was first, yet paradoxically least seen, as it is almost entirely covered. The black bag over the head and chest is printed *Papapillon*, suggesting "papa butterfly." Mounted to the wall to its left is an ad for the Mazda flashlights that the viewers were carrying to negotiate the dimness. The vertical box is a book-object by Georges Hugnet, his barklike binding for Roussel's *Locus Solus*, a prewar proto-science fiction novel. Hugnet's elaborate binding included insets containing dice and other objects.[54]

Propped atop its case was another ad, a plastic sign for "Mannequins PLEM," a credit line that had been requested by the manufacturer that furnished them, to the dismay of some of the artists.[55] These were actually the first items viewers saw and, significantly, they establish the poles of mid-1930s Surrealism: fashion and commercialism, on one hand, and the artist/writer collaboration, in the form of the Surrealist object, on the other.

2. To the right of Arp's were six photos from Hans Bellmer's *La Poupée* series, framed together, whose prime placement is noteworthy (fig. 2.12). Thematically linked, the dolls suggest the connection between Bellmer's aesthetics of dismemberment and the manipulation of the mannequins. Then comes Yves Tanguy's mannequin, which was finished before Arp's, its main feature the "mysterious spindles" yoking her shoulders. She is not "dressed" with any element of clothing except a belt. She wears a caged "headlight," which appears lit in one photo.[56] She holds a staff and treads on pillowlike fabrics. To her left are more pho-

2.11   Attributed to Denise Bellon, *Arp Mannequin*,
Galerie Beaux-Arts, 1938. Collection Getty
Research Institute.

2.12   *Tanguy Mannequin*, with Bellmer photos,
Galerie Beaux-Arts, 1938. Collection Getty
Research Institute. (Opposite, left)

2.13   Eggarter, *Tanguy Mannequin*, with light,
Galerie Beaux-Arts, 1938. (Opposite, right)

tos including, curiously, two views of Picasso's painted bronze *Glass of Absinthe* (1914). Breton had listed this Cubist sculpture as a Surrealist object in preparing a list of works for a 1936 show at Charles Ratton's gallery, where one cast *Glass* was exhibited in a vitrine.

3. Next, "a chalk white body with water-lilies here and there, a green beetle on her mouth, and tiny green lobsters on her body—the whole veiled in green tulle."[57] While the object on her stomach seems more like a scorpion, *Vogue*'s account does bring back the color involved in Sonia Mossé's mannequin, which is lost in black and white photographs. A press photo taken from a side angle shows wires connected to an extension apparently running the length of the corridor floor. It looks as if her lilies could be lit by tiny bulbs, though no reviewer mentions this.

As Mossé was the only woman to prepare a mannequin, one would like more information about her role, but she remains little known. She did not exhibit works in the other parts of the show, nor does she appear to have been a published author. Her name eludes even the detailed compilers of

2.14 Gaston Paris, *Sonia Mossé Mannequin*,
Galerie Beaux-Arts, 1938. Courtesy Ubu
Gallery, New York. (At right)

2.15 Raoul Ubac, *Duchamp Mannequin*,
Galerie Beaux-Arts, 1938. Collection
Getty Research Institute.

2.16 Raoul Ubac, *Duchamp Mannequin,* Rrose
Sélavy signature detail, Galerie Beaux-
Arts, 1938. Collection Musée d'Art
Moderne de la Ville de Paris.

Surrealist dictionaries, including the *Dictionnaire abrégé*. Her only other trace is as a model in the 1935 photograph *Nusch and Sonia* by Man Ray. There she appears youthful and blonde, cradling Nusch Eluard to her chest in a series of staged shots, another enactment of the "deux amies" theme.[58]

4. Duchamp's mannequin has not been regarded as one of his important works and is sparsely commented on. In Man Ray's account, "Duchamp simply took off his coat and hat, putting it on the figure as if it were a coat rack. It was the least conspicuous of the mannequins, but most significant of his desire not to attract too much attention."[59] Despite the apparent casualness of this entry, one should look beyond Man Ray's appraisal. He does not mention her vest, tie, or clunky oversized men's shoes, details that all magnify her absence of pants. He may underestimate the compelling economy of Duchamp's gesture, which could be appreciated by the Surrealists. It is unique among the mannequins in its cross-dressing, inevitably calling to mind the analogous gender crossing of Man Ray's Rose Sélavy photos of the early 1920s. Duchamp provocatively signed the latter's name on the lower abdomen, with two *R*s, thereby clouding the authorial function as well. That is, is Sélavy the (alter ego) "maker," as a signature would imply, or the identity/theme of the mannequin? Schwarz chooses the latter, listing it as a work titled *Rrose Sélavy*.[60] But the gesture is more complex, since we know that Rose Sélavy is credited with a number of artworks signed in her name in the early 1920s. And this mannequin is the first time she may be embodied in the three-dimensional "flesh" other than as an alter ego (i.e., Duchamp photographed in drag). Therefore, she clearly extends Duchamp's past themes, even as she foreshadows the salacious nude mannequin in *Etants donnés*.

By raising the issue of gender crossed with authorship, Duchamp calls attention to the other male artists' ultimately monotonous fetishization of the female body. In this way his work is both part of the exhibition and yet occupies a critical space separate from mainstream Surrealism, no mean feat. Duchamp allows for a favored Surrealist theme, sexuality. The mannequin's pubic area is not covered and drew the erotic gaze of Ubac, in a *frisson*-laden photo shot on his knees, pointed up to her crotch (fig. 2.16). The metaphor of camera/phallus is hard to avoid. More generally Rose implicates the rather token presence of women artists (usually with only one or two works) in this exhibition.

Mannequin Street

Duchamp also incorporated some wiring that is not obvious and has not been commented in the literature, for the bulb in her pocket is lit in one view down the corridor (Bellon photo #6696). This is confirmed by one reviewer who expressed annoyance that in place of a handkerchief was "une petite lampe rouge, moqueuse comme une blague." The critic thus sounds the canard of fakery long leveled at the avant-garde.[61] Did the "mockery" involve literalization of the street as a "red-light" district? At any rate, Duchamp's mannequin wears a visible wire that trails behind and between her legs in Ubac's full-length photo (fig. 2.15). Thus Duchamp (along with Tanguy, Masson, and most others) electrified his mannequin, perhaps a suggestion of erotic "charge." Yet for Duchamp there is a more mechanical association, recalling the energy source of his optical rotary machines of the 1920s, themselves among the earliest kinetic sculptures using electricity. The electrified mannequins clearly required effort and planning, especially for the source wire run along the floor for the length of the hall. The artists had some thought of self-illumination in the context of the notorious low lighting planned for the space. Duchamp himself may well have been responsible for the installing of the wire, as he also would electrically illumine the brazier in the first large room after the mannequin corridor.

5. Marcel Jean writes that "the greatest success was achieved by André Masson who had placed his mannequin's head in a cage, gagged her with a black velvet band, and, where the mouth would have been, set a flower: a pansy ('. . . pansies, that's for thoughts')."[62] Breton, too, praised this as the "most brilliant" of the mannequins, appreciating its linguistic turn, "its metaphor [for eroticism] in its pure state," what he also favored as the "veiled erotic." Breton had a prudish streak and was more comfortable with the "veiled" as opposed to the overt eroticism in Ernst's and Malet's original mannequins.

Masson seems to have formally titled it *Le baillon vert à bouche de pensée*, indicating the pun on *pensée*, meaning both the purple flower and *thought*. There is also a visual pun on the vulva, displaced to the oral, which is spelled out in Masson's sketchbook drawings.[63] By similar displacement, Masson covers the vagina with a circle of tiger eyes surrounding a mirror, adorning a G-string. It suggests the scopophilic stare, even as the viewer's gaze is returned by his or her own reflection in the mirror. This is thus the only man-

49

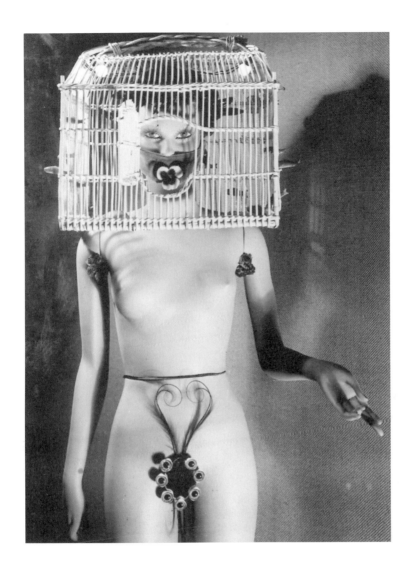

2.17 *Masson Mannequin,* Galerie Beaux-Arts, 1938. Collection Getty Research Institute.

nequin besides Arp's that makes an issue of, or resists, the viewer's taking possession by sight. With a similar sense of Masson's dualistic play vis-à-vis the spectator, Caws has pointed to "a double thrust of hiding and priding, as we might read in the peacock's eyes . . . with the curving plumes in the form of fallopian tubes."[64]

It is the wicker-caged head, however, that the reviewers and photographers—Bellon, Ubac, Eggarter—focused on. Bellon in fact took six shots, making this and Dalí's her most photographed mannequins. Close-ups reveal the goldfish as if swimming between the bars, and in her curls, "like waves," as Masson said. And this enclosure was something of a cliché, to judge from the similarly costumed participant in Caresse Crosby's "dream ball" staged for Dalí's first visit to New York, in 1935. There Mrs. George Crawford, "like a bird in a gilded cage," wore a red canary cage over her head. For her trouble, she was photographed in color for the Sunday *Mirror*.[65] Visitors to the exhibition could easily make this connection to fashion and masquerade in high-society costume balls, for the earlier *Mirror* clipping was posted nearby. Dalí himself

2.18 Duchamp seen from behind, Rrose Sélavy mannequin, full view, wire visible, Masson mannequin at right with wire visible. Collection Bibliothèque Historique de la Ville de Paris.

probably was responsible for tacking it to the wall to the left of his mannequin, among his exhibition announcements and other clippings!

Masson arranged a pile of salt with traps set with red pimentos at his mannequin's feet, but these went unnoticed, or at least unremarked. So, too, did the small stuffed birds nestled in her armpits, often misidentified from photos, and the red cord at her waist, intended to evoke a bloody gash. Woman as nature (birds, fish), and as victim of assault, are both clichéd Surrealist themes. Masson left one of his most detailed accounts of this work, revealing that he, too, found inspiration in that favored Surrealist site of chance encounter, the flea market. He went to the one at the Hôtel de Ville. For his unusual materials he also visited a naturalist on the Boulevard Saint-Germain.

Masson underlined the "emblematic value" of the street signs behind the mannequins. He felt proud to have rue Vivienne, "a capital of Surrealist myth, important in the *Chants de Maldoror*;" and where its author Lautréamont lived. Likewise, the author Gérard de Nerval lived on the evocative rue de la Vieille Lanterne, the sign behind Espinoza's mannequin. Rue Nicolas-Flamel, the first sign on the corridor and an actual street, refers to a medieval alchemist who interested the Surrealists. Perhaps the Porte de Lilas, the sign behind Tanguy's mannequin, alludes to another flea market, or to the well-known literary café Closerie de Lilas.[66] Other blue plaques, such as "Blood Transfusion" (Domínguez; fig. 2.30) or "All the Devils" (Seligmann), were clearly fictive and reinforced a macabre mood. Whereas Passage des Panoramas (Dalí; fig. 2.7) is poetically evocative and an appropriate title for the entire row.

Masson did not mention, nor did the critics, that the cage was wired with two small bulbs in the upper corners. Eggarter's photo clearly shows them lit, like eyes of an oversized head whose mouth is the open door of the cage. And side views show the tell-tale electrical cord again (fig. 2.18), indicating that this puppet also was "wired" and perhaps dangerous.

6. Kurt Seligmann's mannequin is one of the most ghoulish: a dagger-pierced egg is fixed to the top of the laurel-crowned head. The rest of the body is draped in white, nunlike, except for the hands, which are loosely tied with an excess of tubing. There are four candles plus a displaced length of wavy hair incongruously issuing from a bell attached to the draping. Given Seligmann's interests in magic and the occult, elaborate symbolism is possible. He

2.19 Raoul Ubac, *Kurt Seligmann Mannequin,* Galerie Beaux-Arts, 1938.
Collection Musée d'Art Moderne
de la Ville de Paris.

2.20 Raoul Ubac, *Kurt Seligmann Mannequin,* front view, Galerie Beaux-
Arts, 1938. Collection Getty Research Institute.

probably alludes to an alchemical allegory, "the philosopher's egg," which is illustrated in a seventeenth-century text that he knew. It shows an oversized egg about to be cloven by a man with a sword heated in a fire. The initiate is bidden "learn about the egg and cut it with a flaming sword."[67] The two elements of oversized egg pierced by a blade, atop Seligmann's mannequin, together seem beyond coincidence. The cowl is draped so that from straight on, as Ubac captured it, a single eye returns our gaze (fig. 2.20). Together with the unsmiling expression, a mesmerizing, somewhat uncanny effect is produced. Denise Bellon took a more prosaic shot of it from the side, which also records the presence of Paul Eluard during the installation process.

7. Max Ernst's display was the only one to have two figurines interacting (fig. 2.8). The lion-headed man on the floor at the widow's feet, associated with "the Lion of Belfort, already celebrated in [Ernst's] books,"[68] also suggested an artist, given his paint-spattered clothes. His position was aligned closer to the wall in the later view of the corridor with the protective cord in place.[69] Also his hand seems headed under her skirt, belying the reading of one journalist who thought the man was a corpse that had been murdered by the widow.[70] The only male on the street, albeit so covered that we cannot be sure what's underneath, he recalls the rather De Chirican masculine mannequins used at the fashion pavilion of the 1937 Paris International Exposition.

Ernst's "widow whose genitals are replaced by an electric bulb" also scandalized the fastidious Breton, who insisted it be modified.[71] The light was removed, or perhaps it migrated to the pocket of Rose Sélavy? At least figuratively it did, so Duchamp's pocket bulb may signal covert support for Ernst, against Breton's interference.

8. After Ernst's, Miró's mannequin is disappointing, partly because it is too pictorial. Sprightly line, a feature of many of his canvases, is less telling when rendered in wire, though it might be claimed as an early "drawing in space." Likewise the drawing and sheet music of a love song at her feet are tacked-on pictorial elements. The woman's large handlebar moustache suggests Miró's humor, evoking both Duchamp's *L.H.O.O.Q.* and the staples of popular graffiti. At this moment Miró's mere presence is remarkable, reflecting underlying efforts to marshal past masters of the Surrealist group who had meanwhile opted out.

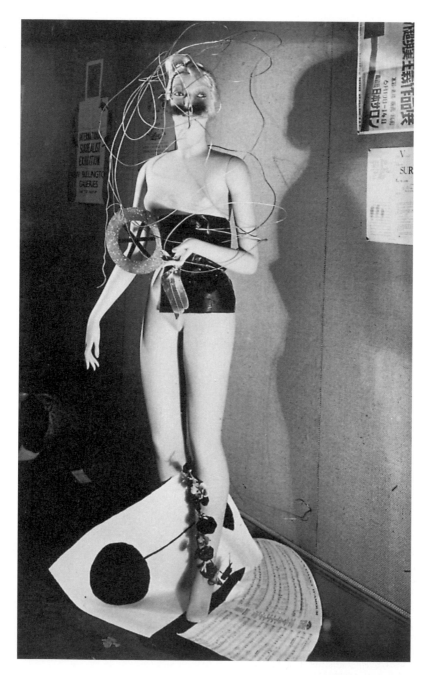

2.21 *Miró Mannequin*, Galerie Beaux-Arts, 1938. Collection Getty Research Institute.

2.22 Raoul Ubac, *Espinoza Mannequin*, Galerie Beaux-Arts, 1938. Collection Timothy Baum, New York. (Opposite)

9. A lesser-known fellow-Spaniard follows. Augustín Espinoza, born in 1897 in the Canaries, was one of three underwriters of the 1935 Surrealist exhibition in Tenerife. His macabre novel *Crimen* (1934) was "a grisly anthology of sex, murder and mutilation."[72] After this, his mannequin seems relatively tame; perhaps PLEM's rental agreement forbade their dismemberment. She sports an animal-skull "hat" and various other small items, including a butterfly and a tiny male doll attached to her waistband. One reviewer speaks of "a lit up sheep skull," so it seems this, too, had an electric bulb. There is a hint of bondage in the black fabric wrapping her body and wrists, however, and sadism in the pins stuck in her nipple, upper thigh, and arm. Together with Seligmann's, and Paalen's following, this anchors the "Gothick" section of the "street," where the female body receives its most macabre treatment.

10. Wolfgang Paalen, Austrian-born, was appreciated by Breton for a German romantic quality to his works. Her body encrusted with mushrooms and a spread-winged bat atop her head, Paalen's mannequin seems to have wandered out of the forests of *Nosferatu*. Most likely this prompted

2.23 Denise Bellon, *Wolfgang Paalen Mannequin,*
Galerie Beaux-Arts, 1938. Courtesy Ubu Gallery,
New York.

2.24 Raoul Ubac, *Wolfgang Paalen Mannequin,* hand
detail. Collection Musée d'Art Moderne de la
Ville de Paris.

the writers who criticized "les laboratoires du romantisme allemand et russe."[73] Such nationalist terms were intended negatively, in comparison to proper "French" qualities. Another critic associated the mannequin with the old woman fiancée in Dickens's *Great Expectations*, whose veil would crumble to dust at a touch.[74] Touch is indeed emphasized by Paalen, who transformed her extended hand into a clawlike appendage. One of Ubac's best photographs is a disorienting detail of this claw protruding from the moss and mushrooms (fig. 2.24), misidentified as a detail of Dalí's taxi mannequin.

11. Dalí's street mannequin is the only one photographed and even described in two distinct states, suggestive of the pains he took. Janet Flanner imaginatively wrote of "orange Aztec feathers for her feet and Poe's raven for her hat." This first state was photographed at least five times by Bellon, sometimes with Dalí present (fig. 2.7). Still in the course of preparation, the mannequin wears a handsome fabric turban and a scrolled sheet wrapped around her waist like a dress. In a later photo by Bellon (#6739), the birdlike aspects are diminished. She appears more menacing, sporting long gloves and with her ideal face covered by "Schiaparelli's shocking pink knitted helmet," topped, *Vogue* continues, "by a penguin," plus "a broken egg on her chest and tiny coffee-spoons all over."[75] (Another critic identified them as salt spoons; either way, they were noticed.) The critic Guetta got lathered up by these "little spoons of kleptomania," and haunted by visions of a thousand where there were actually about four dozen. The hallucinatory quality of a field of small objects recurs from the "veston-aphrodisiaque" exhibited in London in 1936, and then at Ratton's. There Dalí had covered a man's jacket with a like number of liqueur glasses, meant to be filled with peppermint. Here the gender difference takes us from the drinkable to the edible, the female body consumed as banquet.

The mannequin holds the ubiquitous lightbulb in the hand that reaches toward a version of the infamous lobster-telephone on a wicker table (see fig. 2.41). The still life setup includes a liqueur bottle and glasses, six full, one empty. Behind are invitations and reviews from Dalí's shows at Julien Levy Gallery, as well as the long handwritten text that had earlier been wrapped around the mannequin. Like Ernst's, Dalí's figure is developed into a narrative tableau.

The fashion industry paid Dalí the ultimate flattery by commissioning a variant of his mannequin, somewhat overly spooned, in an actual shop window during the course of the exhibition. (If primarily Dalían, the pastiched store mannequin also sports an oversized Mossé flower and Duchampian men's shoes.) This vitrine in the same tony Right Bank street as the gallery, Faubourg Saint-Honoré, is further evidence (if any were needed) of fashion keeping a watchful eye on developments in the "fine" art avant-garde, and quickly appropriating its more spectacular aspects.

12. Maurice Henry was the only participant for whom a sketch for the mannequin survives (fig. 2.27). Henry was also the only one to publish an article contemporary with the exhibition, illustrated with photos by Gaston Paris. In it he pointed to the democracy of objects: "If you don't know how to draw, don't know how to write, you can make a Surrealist object" (or a Surrealist mannequin, one might add).[76] In fact Henry primarily did the two former. He joined the Surrealist group in 1933 and is

mainly known for his cartoons. It is no surprise that his mannequin closely follows the sketch. Her breasts are covered by two strainers, below which is a tiny hourglass over a small board inscribed with a text. Cloudlike cottony wool is attached to her head, her neck is covered with black tulle, and she wears a clothespin collar. Her long dark skirt is covered with ears of grain, and her feet covered with sticks. Thus she metamorphoses in part into a woman of earth, of nature, an old cliché.

2.25 Dalí mannequin head with Schiaparelli facemask, Galerie Beaux-Arts, 1938. Collection Getty Research Institute. (Opposite, left)

2.26 Store window based on Dalí mannequin, rue du Faubourg Saint-Honoré, Paris, from *Voilà*, January 1938. Documentation Musée Nationale d'Art Moderne, Centre Georges Pompidou, Paris. (Opposite, right)

2.27 Maurice Henry, drawing for mannequin, ink and pencil on paper, 1938. Documentation Musée National d'Art Moderne, Centre Georges Pompidou, Paris.

Mannequin Street

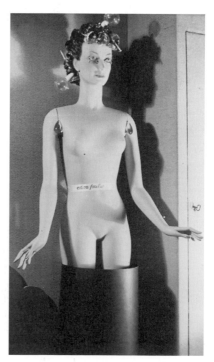

2.28 Raoul Ubac, *Maurice Henry Mannequin,*
upper detail, Galerie Beaux-Arts, 1938.
Collection Timothy Baum, New York.

2.29 *Man Ray Mannequin,* Galerie Beaux-Arts,
1938. Collection Getty Research Institute.

13. Her "clouded thoughts" relate to the adjoining background for Man Ray's mannequin, the *Portemanteau esthétique*, listed as a separate work in the exhibition checklist (no. 189). Again, the beginnings of a narrative tableau are evoked. A rack in cloud shape is hung with men's coats, implying the antechamber of a brothel, with the men already inside. Did Man Ray intend to refer to Duchamp's *Trébuchet* (Trap), also a coat rack, nailed to the floor of his New York studio back in 1917? The mannequin's head is developed from two of Man Ray's own earlier artworks. Her hair contains two of his glass bubble pipes, an object entitled *Ce que manque à nous tous* (1935). Though this is a phrase that stems from Engels, Man Ray associated it with "imagination"[77] and thus effectively depoliticized it. Glass tears also appear on her face (and larger tear-shaped glass at her armpits), reprising his striking crocodile tear photographs of the early 1930s.

Her legs are enclosed in a cylindrical container, making her immobile. And she extends her hand, as if toward the key in the adjacent small door, an effect increased in one photo made by Man Ray himself. She wears nothing else but a ribbon around her waist, inscribed with the enigmatic phrase "adieu *foulard.*" It relates visually to the kind of ribbon found on new mannequins. Man Ray appropriates the space and format of advertising for his own idiosyncratic expression, perhaps a farewell to scarves, clothes, and, by extension, a hello to nakedness.

Man Ray also made a now well-known series of photographs of the mannequins (fig. 5.5), all but Arp's, and apparently none of any other part of the exhibition. He is an extreme case, yet most other photographers also focused on the mannequins. When a questioner later asked if these shots were just "reportage," Man Ray would not agree. But he did stress their "straight" quality: "there is no philosophical idea or artistic idea behind it."[78] He recalled only printing up a few at the time, for himself or artists he was friendly with, like Duchamp.[79] There was no attempt to publish them until after World War II, when the fifteen negatives left behind in France were refound. With the publisher Petithory, Man Ray ultimately arranged for a limited-edition reprinting of these negatives. At that time (1966) he made a provocative introductory statement, clearly analogizing his 1938 photo session as a marathon sexual encounter with the mannequins. "So inspiring to . . . Man Ray that he unbuttoned his pants and taking out his apparatus proceeded to record the event without giving any further thought to the happening but that of his immediate pleasure."[80] This use of the camera/phallus cliché is calculated to shock, even as it relates to 1960s sexual liberation.

14. The photographer Josef Breitenbach's caption records that Oscar Domínguez's mannequin has an iron spiral around its head, apparently topped by a small light. A siphon elevated on a stovepipe emits a jet of light blue curtain material, the color of water. She otherwise wears only the wrapping of rope around her arm, which extends to depress the button of the siphon.

15. Like Domínguez's, Léo Malet's mannequin is prominently hatted, in this case with a paraffin cooker.[81] She is made a passive object, blindfolded with a cottony material. Her right hand has been removed, making her the only mannequin who is amputated, and anticipating the grisly murder mysteries Malet would pen in the 1940s. This brings to mind the Surrealists' fondness for crime stories, Souvestre and Allain's Fantômas series in particular, as represented by Magritte's *Menaced Assassin* (1926), as well as the aesthetics of violence and dismemberment—an unappetizing aspect of the Surrealists' fascination with the female body. The supports that formerly held the censored goldfish bowl hang limply. Malet also mentions the spring attached to the chest, which was to be manipulated interactively by the viewer.[82]

16. The last, Marcel Jean's mannequin, is described in his own important history of Surrealism as "a water nymph enmeshed in a lead-weighted casting-net."[83] The weights seem to include magnets and sponges. Jean's mermaid at the end of the corridor is visible when looking back from the next (coal sack) room (fig. 2.33). That large room contained Jean's more interesting body double: the dressmaker's dummy *L'horoscope*, a torso elevated at the foot of a bed and painted with both maps and internal bone structure (fig. 2.36). These last three mannequins, by lesser members of the group, seem rather perfunctory, and are less engaging than those in the middle section. That area may have been calculated as the high point of the enfilade, while the novelty value and talent wore thin by the end and the viewer was transitioned to the next space.

As with Picasso's *Demoiselles* over thirty years earlier, there is an implicit choice to be made by the spectator among the sixteen streetwalkers. One London paper sanitized this aspect by positing "a competition for the Ideal Mannequin."[84] This is cast in terms that recall the beauty contest. The next

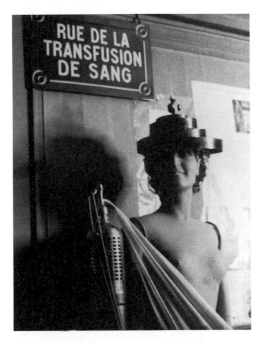

2.30 Josef Breitenbach, *Oscar Domínguez Mannequin*,
Galerie Beaux-Arts, 1938. Photo courtesy Sotheby's,
New York.

step after selection is all too obvious: one enters a large room, an
"interior" installed with four beds, one in each corner. Some called
them "lits de vaudeville," but "brothel bed" was Breton's term. Next
to each was an "aphrodisiac night table."[85] Each bed was wide, with
two pillows pointedly designating the implicit number of inhabi-
tants. At the outset they were carefully made, with clean silk sheets
that were rumpled in the course of Hélène Vanel's opening night
performance. They could be seen as inaugurating a seam of "active" bed iconography stretching from Robert Rauschenberg
through Felix González-Torres to Maureen Conner.[86]

After the show, the mannequins were apparently deinstalled
and returned to PLEM, for there is no indication of their being exhibited later. Thus they comprised a site-specific installation,
which by all accounts utilized a narrow space quite effectively. By
starting from a common base, the participants ingeniously pre-

2.31 Josef Breitenbach, Léo Malet mannequin (center), with Bellmer photos, Jean
mannequin (right), Galerie Beaux-Arts, 1938. Collection Getty Research Institute.

sented a suggestion of unity through shared group activity, with permutations of individualistic creative diversity.

It was an installation that effectively neutralized traditional art expertise; the one mannequin "expert," Bellmer, participated only with his photographs. Most of the painters were as inexperienced with figurative sculpture as the writers. Only Dalí had worked with mannequins before. Nonetheless, it was the major visual artists—Masson, Dalí, Paalen—who produced the most acclaimed examples. It is not known who suggested this mode of display, though Malet attributes it to Duchamp. Certainly it was congenial to the majority, including Duchamp, who could have appreciated the "ready-made" aspect of the assignment, as well as the fact that a nontraditional, nonpainting medium was the basis. There is a performative aspect to the whole project, with the participants called upon to come up with a catchy concept and enact it within the given, somewhat malleable parameters. This would suit the "theatrical" wing of the veristic Surrealists.

The public and private spheres were fairly mingled on this "rue Surréaliste," as it is sometimes called. The metal street signs behind each mannequin are public, yet the wall is treated as a page collaged with various gallery announcements, posters, and reviews, a spectacle of reception, as it were. The scantily clad mannequins, suggestive of erotic encounter, read as private. Only Ernst's is plausible as a streetwalker outdoors. They are more separated than they would be in a vitrine; otherwise most address the spectator in a similar fashion.

The choice of the nude female body as central fetish was backward-looking and did not reflect the latest experiments in automatist techniques among the painters. Its simulacral figuration could only be disfigured and/or eroticized in so many ways without becoming repetitive. This applies equally to the one female *mannequiniste*, Mossé. Despite a growing presence of women artists in later Surrealism, they had only this token representation. It was left to Arp and Duchamp to resist the monotonous fetishization of the female nude. Arp's covering effectively negated the spectator's gaze, a denial that would have been more pointed had it been situated farther along in the file. Duchamp used the occasion to embody his Rose Sélavy concept born in 1920, retaining its cross-dressing feature and thus throwing gender into doubt.

Mannequin Street

2.32 Gaston Paris, *Marcel Jean Mannequin,* Galerie Beaux-Arts, 1938.
Courtesy Ubu Gallery, New York.

2.33 Josef Breitenbach, view back at Marcel Jean mannequin from coal sacks room.
Courtesy Ubu Gallery, New York. (Opposite)

The success of the mannequins assured that they would continue to appear in a variety of Surrealist forays in display. Hugnet got his chance to arrange one when a reduced version of the Beaux-Arts exhibition traveled to Amsterdam. In the next year Dalí had mannequins both in the vitrines of Bonwit's department store and in a World's Fair pavilion. Also in New York, Duchamp would utilize a headless mannequin in the bookstore window display for Breton's *Arcane 17* (1945). Recently grotesque and deformed mannequins have appeared in the photographs of Cindy Sherman and the sculptures of the Chapman brothers, indicating an ongoing *frisson* to be wrung from the uncanniness of the body double.

A Central Grotto / Dante's Inferno / A Space of Dream

 The spectators dramatically passed from the constriction of the mannequin gauntlet to the vastest space, big enough for four beds, one in each corner, dimly lit by a brazier in the center (fig. 2.33). One could barely see that its walls were lined with numerous, closely hung works in all media. Smaller works such as Ubac photographs were stacked on the wooden frames of two free-standing, fixed revolving doors (fig. 2.34). Yet most striking was the room's dropped ceiling of burlap bags, hanging just above the spectator's heads. The *1200 Coal Sacks* were the installation concept of Marcel Duchamp, the largest "piece" of the 1938 show, and the locus of attention and response. Participant Marcel Jean said it well; Duchamp "had succeeded in transforming the central hall into a space in which the marvellous coincided— at the level of humor . . . —with an essential disorientation, a fantastic metaphor in which the spectator found himself plunged, whether he wanted or not."[87] Duchamp thus combined two hallowed Surrealist concepts, *le merveilleux* and *dérèglement*. He collated Bretonian awestruck wonder and the Dalían call for "systematic confusion" and reversal of the senses. This in order to undermine the world of appearance, not to mention the expectations of the spectator or the gallerist.

2.34 Thérèse LePrat, coal sacks, revolving door with Ubac photos, bed, and Paalen's *Ivy Chair* (1937). Above the bed, Man Ray's *L'orateur* (1935), and at right paintings by Paalen, Ernst, Seligmann, and Paalen. Galerie Beaux- Arts, 1938. Archives Wildenstein.

2.35 Marcel Duchamp, *1200 Coal Sacks,* view with Penrose, Ernst (?), by bed Domínguez's *Jamais,*
Galerie Beaux-Arts, 1938. Collection Bibliothèque Historique de la Ville de Paris.

2.36 Thérèse LePrat, bed and Marcel Jean's *Horoscope* at Paalen sand pool, Galerie Beaux- Arts,
1938. Archives Wildenstein.

2.37 Josef Breitenbach, spectator with flashlight looking at De Chirico paintings, Galerie Beaux-Arts, 1938. Collection Center for Creative Photography, Tucson.

2.38 Eluards, Magritte, and Léo Malet with flashlights, viewing Breton object-chest, Galerie Beaux-Arts, 1938. Collection Bibliothèque Historique de la Ville de Paris.

"If provocatively anti-institutional," this installation was furthermore a "visual and 'aesthetic' statement of a kind."[88] More
specifically, of an anti-aesthetic kind, which was kinesthetically uncomfortable, even disagreeable, to many spectators. Indeed, the
critical responses generally describe it as "oppressive," even "sinis-
terly erotic"; one felt the need to flee the "choking" claustrophobic
atmosphere.[89] In several ways Duchamp reversed the visitor's normal experience of this room, which had a glass-windowed ceiling.
Instead of openness and natural light, there was opaqueness and
darkness, a "nightmare of a low ceiling" that "just missed your
head."[90] The choice of coal sacks perhaps had an element of expe-
diency, as Hugnet reported that other materials, including open umbrellas
(Lautréamont's or Magritte's?), were originally contemplated.[91] What remains consistent is the intention to cover the ceiling using ordinary, readymade objects that had no associations of beauty. The coal sacks do strike a
somewhat different note for Duchamp, distinct from the industrial, mechanistic feel of his materials of the teens such as metal and glass. I also suspect
there was a provocative aspect to the choice, intended to cause a certain ir-
ritation or even sneezing. Some reviewers reported complaints of dust in the
air at the opening. Masson remembered that although the sacks were empty,
they were "still able to shed a little black powder on the visitors."[92] This
helps clarify the point behind Duchamp's similar recollection: "There was
coal dust. They were real sacks, which had been found in La Villette. There
were papers inside, newspapers, which filled them out."[93] Apparently their
sootiness was a cultivated effect, planned to discomfort the viewers, especially at the outset. How else to explain the *Dictionnaire abrégé*'s knowing
emphasis on *black* air: "dans l'air beau et noir (Lautréamont). Ma faim, c'est
les bouts d'air noir (Rimbaud)."

As O'Doherty has described, there is also an element of surprise in that
the ceiling, normally an unnoticed inactive zone in exhibitions, becomes a
focal point that is apparently massive and sculptural in presence, "totally ob-
trusive psychologically."[94] (It was not generally known that the sacks were
stuffed with paper, as Duchamp remembered, and thus lighter than they
seemed. Thus one reviewer even calculated that they must comprise three
thousand kilos of coal as a "sword of Damocles" menacing the spectator.
Another spoke of the possibility of opening the sacks so the "English" coal
would fall.)[95] Their apparent weightiness and all-pervasiveness, coming

from overhead, became a metaphor for aerial danger in more suggestible minds: "On attendait avec angoisse le hurlement soudain de la sirène annonçant le Zeppelin!"[96] Some extra sacks were placed around Domínguez's eroticized record player called *Jamais*, and recorded in a well-known Denise Bellon photograph. (Similar sacks would appear, sandbagging the city, after the declaration of war the following year. Fashion models were photographed, rather incongruously, sitting on or in front of such sandbags around the Place de la Concorde and the Place Vendôme.)[97] Analogous to the mannequin street, the 1,200 sacks induce the metaphorical suggestion of the interior as exterior. In this case Duchamp evoked "a central grotto,"[98] no doubt a response to the stalactite-ness of the sacks. Yet another reviewer found it a correlate for the inside of the mind, thus "a space/cavern of dream." This may be the most poetic of the many metaphors that accrued to the simple rows of burlap.

The floor, covered with "six inches of sand" and dead leaves of "a forest in autumn," reinforced the "outdoor" setting.[99] Though sometimes credited to Duchamp, they were introduced by Wolfgang Paalen, whom the catalogue lists for "waters and brushwood."

The brazier "which illuminated not at all" (fig. 2.33), by or of Duchamp, suggested to one participant "the terraces of the Parisian cafes, round which the Surrealists had foregathered so often in wintertime So the brazier represented friendship."[100] Given fire regulations, it was not actually burning but artificially illuminated, casting a reddish glow and thus Duchamp's second electric red-light "work" in the show. Still, reviewers reported that they feared a fire during the show. The brazier also is a neat conceptual completion of the ceiling, being the "consuming organ" of the fuel above.[101]

By allowing the brazier to remain the one fixed illumination, director of lighting Man Ray essentially set the stage for his old friend's mise-en-scène. And Man Ray took the heat for his related plan to distribute flashlights for viewing at the opening: "Needless to say, the flashlights were directed more to people's faces than to the works themselves. . . . The painters were quite angry with me, but I assured them that for the following weeks the gallery would be well lighted, when people came with the intention of seeing the works."[102] The flashlight feature was the most widely mentioned in the papers, even generating one headline. Two photographs by

A Central Grotto / Dante's Inferno /
A Space of Dream

Breitenbach give the best idea of the general murkiness. They show a man peering closely at the De Chiricos, the pocket lamp in his palm barely effective in lighting one canvas at a time (fig. 2.37). Likewise a UPI press photo shot from above documents the Eluards, Magritte, and Léo Malet in an adjoining room with the same sort of small hand light (fig. 2.38). These photos lend credence to the complaint that the two-volt lamps were insufficient. The dimness was undocumentable, with photographers using their own light sources to increase the wattage during their shoots. In any event, most of the loaned flashlights were not returned at the exit, so the practice could not be continued. Man Ray recalled that he had from the outset installed banks of lights for use after the opening. Yet only one later reviewer mentioned that lighting had been "secured." This and the "deflating" of the coal sacks were said to be "easing" the "weighty atmosphere of the first days" of the exhibition.[103] Perhaps few of the opening night crowd came back to see the show better lit, and hence it is universally remembered for its initial murkiness.

By exhibiting works in a space where it was difficult to see them, the Surrealists were again reversing expectation and essentially obstructing spectators. The flashlights were a clever index of vision, for the beam would trace the direction of visual attention. Man Ray surmised that the opening was more about seeing others and being seen than viewing the works, and the beams would confirm this. Gaze is thus made more conscious, and ritualized as an act. On one level the Surrealists were echoing a founding moment in their history, the opening of Max Ernst's first exhibition of collages at Au Sans Pareil bookstore in May 1921. It was held in the basement with the lights out. Instead of flashlights, the visitors "received" strange sounds and insults from members of the group. (Ernst was not present.)

What is remarkable is that the other participants tolerated being subsumed in this dimness created by Duchamp and Man Ray together. The former's ceiling literally overarches the rest, including major paintings by Dalí and Tanguy that were far less visible once the photographer's lamps were turned off. Most artists were not mentioned by name in any review, whereas few if any commentators failed to weigh in about the astonishing coal sack ceiling.

Breton's admiration for Duchamp's work, especially the *Large Glass*, was astute. His leadership allowed Duchamp to be convincingly installed as "générateur-arbitre," as the checklist indicates. His capacity as arbiter stems more from Duchamp's absence from the original 1920s group, his detachment from any faction, indeed his detachment in general. By the mid-1930s most of the early group around Breton, notably Aragon and Eluard, had been banished, leaving room for some new blood.

For his part Duchamp made the most of his opportunity while still managing to avoid the charge of overambition. The Surrealist exhibition provided a context for him to continue provoking the spectator, to trap a larger public than would visit his studio. One suspects that Duchamp anticipated that at least the avant-garde public would applaud its provocateur.

Other Rooms

Georges Hugnet took a leading role in carrying out ceiling decor in the two smaller rooms adjacent to the main one. These areas are less documented, as they drew less photographic and critical attention. One was notable for a fixture of "un pantalon blanc de jeune fille, mode 1830, orné de rubans cramoisis et de jupons en corolles, [qui] pendait en guise d'abat-jour!," which the critic Guetta found "charming."[104] Hugnet credits Breton with the orignal idea of "pantalons de french-cancan" meant to suggest the lower half of a giantess.[105] The London *Times* critic thought of the "frilly drawers" of a Victorian circus giantess, but most did not respond in terms of scale. Rather the associations were to nightlife and entertainment, such as dancers of the Bal Tabarin, or to the absurdly dated, "the underwear of their grandmothers."[106] Below it was another revolving door used to hang pictures. Guetta was one of few to comment further, detailing favorably three Dalí paintings hung in this room, one a vast desert landscape that made him thirsty!

The critic had to pass back through the "haunted rotunda" to reach the final room, which contained Domínguez's satin-lined wheelbarrow. This object had already served as a settee for a model sporting a Lucien Lelong gown, photographed by Man Ray (published in *Minotaure* the previous year). Along with the other Surrealist objects there were Miró paintings, including *Corps de ma brune*. The objects included "André Breton's really beautiful exhibit—an antique Spanish chest standing on women's legs," "a laquered and gilded cabinet called 'the exquisite corpse.'"[107] It went unnoticed that Breton had only actualized a similar tripartite *cadavre exquis* drawing published in the *Dictionnaire abrégé*.[108] It also made the same pun on "legs" as Seligmann's *Ultrameuble*. By including two artificial hands, one in a gesture of benediction (as Hugnet recognized), Breton seemingly accepts and humorously plays on the supposed epithet "Pope of Surrealism." Between the upraised arms is a metaphorical "head" of stuffed hummingbirds covered by a glass bell. One wonders if Breton's sculpture was seen by the young art student Louise Bourgeois, who was in contact with some of the Surrealist circle in Paris. It certainly amounts to a forerunner to her

2.39 Eggarter, *pantalon* on ceiling, opening crowd, Galerie Beaux-Arts, 1938.

similarly bifurcated *Femme-maison* works of the 1940s. Breton's personnage was flanked by Arp's relief *Mutilé et apatride* (1936) and a concretion sculpture. To the viewer's right are two major paintings by Magritte, including *Le thérapeute.* The cage-body of the latter is echoed by the caged "clouds" object just visible hanging at the upper right. Such pairings suggest the care taken in the installation to bring out analogous themes. The ceiling was decorated by Hugnet with a trompe l'oeil skylight completely unremarked by critics and photographers captivated by Duchamp's menacing burlaps.

2.40 Josef Breitenbach, André Breton object-chest, with Arp relief at left, Magritte paintings, Arp sculpture at right, Galerie Beaux-Arts, 1938. Courtesy Ubu Gallery, New York.

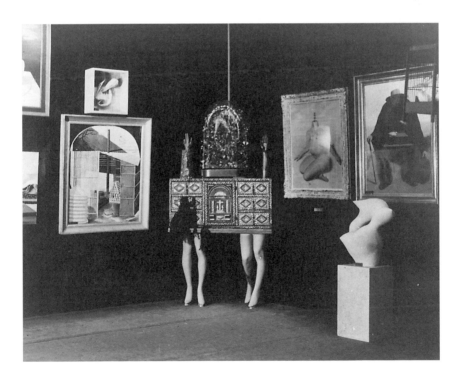

Situation of the Surrealist Object

 Breton's *cadavre exquis* and Domínguez's satin-lined wheelbarrow were among the notable Surrealist objects featured in the last two rooms. While concentrated at the end, objects appeared in each area of the Galerie Beaux-Arts. The mannequin street itself, while marking a long-term Surrealist fetishization of the female body and of sexuality, can also be seen as "the culminating point of the researches on the Surrealist object," begun as a group project in 1932.[109] In this apotheosis the body is treated as an object. This current also signals the impact of Dalí on the group, as his writings and practice were central in launching this major development of Surrealism of the 1930s. It starts with his essay delineating six categories of Surrealist objects, published in *Le Surréalisme au Service de la Révolution* in December 1931.

The Surrealist object became a growing focus in the early to mid-1930s. To cite a little-known instance, it was the fourth and concluding topic of a cycle of subscription lectures the group announced for June 1935. Breton and Dalí were to be the main speakers, along with Hugnet, on "L'objet usuel."[110]

This foreshadowed the marshaling of objects in the landmark exhibition at Charles Ratton (May 22–29, 1936), the subject of a special issue of Zervos's *Cahiers d'Art* that greatly expanded the audience over the number who made their way to Ratton's apartment-gallery during the brief run of the show. Essays by Breton and Dalí in the magazine are joined by an extensive discussion of Duchamp's readymades by Gabrielle Buffct. There were also numerous reproductions, including many of the works exhibited. Installation photos attributed to Man Ray show dozens of objects ringing a single small room (fig. 2.49).[111] Surrealists are exhibited on an equal footing with the "magical" power of non-Western artifacts and even natural finds. Thus Giacometti and Paalen objects flank one from the Pacific islands, while a Picasso guitar relief shares wall space with African and Northwest Coast Indian masks. The glass vitrine was the main display unit, one with connotations of the practices of both the department store and the natural history museum. Three floor vitrines and two wall units are visible in the photographs, each with three glass shelves. Atop one vitrine is a twisting olive root "found and interpreted" by Magnelli, also pictured in *Cahiers d'Art*. Such items are both based on and extend the notion of the Duchampian readymade. The mingling of Western and non-Western as well as natural and found objects recalls the same practice of display in Breton's apartment. Surrounding himself with such things, for Breton, could unlock glimpses into the unconscious: "Every piece of debris within our reach should be considered a precipitate of our desire."[112]

It was mostly urban debris that was within reach, castoffs of consumer society, as the Surrealists transformed flea market shopping into a voyage of discovery.[113] Matta recalled spending New Year's Eve of 1937 at Breton's apartment, discussing flea market finds. Masson and others clearly raided these open-air markets in preparing their mannequins. Indeed, Masson found materials at the same Bazar de l'Hôtel de Ville where Duchamp had singled out his bottle rack more than two decades earlier.

Such "readymades" comprised a category in Breton's systematic analysis of types of objects. Breton's essay "Crise de l'objet," published in *Cahiers d'Art*, mentions only three specific examples: Dalí's objects of symbolic function, Ernst's interpreted found objects, and Duchamp's readymades. The definition of *objet* subsequently published in the *Dictionnaire abrégé* is essentially a gloss on

Situation of the Surrealist Object

the latter part of this essay, with the notable exception that Duchamp's readymades are rather remarkably claimed as "the first Surrealist objects." No doubt authored by Breton, this definition does not necessarily reveal Duchamp's own attitude toward the readymades, but rather his rising position among the Surrealists.

In the *Exposition Internationale*, "objects looming up out of the carefully contrived semidarkness," as de Beauvoir described them, played a major role.[114] In the press they were often featured, and perhaps lent themselves to verbal evocation more than paintings did. One pictorial spread was entirely devoted to "Surrealist Furniture." More than 37 objects are listed in the checklist, about one-seventh of the overall number of works. Their main makers are the non-French painters recently brought into the group: Domínguez, Paalen, and Seligmann, each with four. They are followed closely by Duchamp, Hugnet, and Masson, with three each. This is a very different list from that of the featured painters, in fact including one writer, and underlines how the object became the growth area and wild card for later Surrealism. It democratized or "deskilled" Surrealist production, as Maurice Henry had pointed out: art training was not needed, in fact might be an impediment to the pure play of free association and the unconscious. As a corollary, writers could more readily participate. Indeed Henry, along with Péret and Breton, joined Hugnet in presenting writers' objects, which often punned on or objectified their words.

Hugnet and Breton even apparently divided a mannequin between them, with the latter's *cadavre exquis* supported by two pairs of legs (fig. 2.38) while Hugnet incorporated the mannequin's bust atop a table for his object *La table est mise*, setting it with a fetishized female body (fig. 2.42). It was shown near one of the beds and included inset pools of mercury in which floated a hand, perhaps the one severed from Malet's mannequin.

Along with writers, women artists also found a noteworthy, expanded role in object-making. One, Meret Oppenheim, fabricated one of Surrealism's signature fetishes, the remarkable fur-lined teacup and spoon. It is another token of Surrealism's strong connection with fashion, as it derived from her previous fur-lined jewelry for Schiaparelli. The concept came to her in the Café Flore in a conversation about this jewelry with Picasso and Dora Maar, when they opined that anything could be fur-covered.[115] The teacup was specifically made for the objects exhibition at Charles Ratton. Later it was one of the sensations of *Fantastic Art, Dada, Surrealism*, was widely reproduced, and even drew the censorship of the Modern Museum trustee A. Conger Goodyear, who wanted it removed from the traveling version of the Museum's show.[116] Alfred Barr did not yield, however, and ultimately succeeded in acquiring it for the museum's collection (yet only in 1946). It does not seem to have been included in the 1938 *Exposition Internationale* among Oppenheim's unspecified "objects," as there is no mention of it in the press.

One historian has analyzed a gender distinction in Surrealist objects, with the male artists more erotic or "disturbing by means of violent juxtaposition," while "those by women artists tend toward the more personal and more gently associative."[117] Yet Oppenheim's teacup, at least, crosses over to better fit the former description. Perhaps more typical is Ann Clark's contribution to the *Exposition*, a construction entitled *Parallel Reality*. She described it as "a box with silver Christmas tree balls—like a mask." They were arrayed to reflect like a mirror.[118] As a young artist Clark felt that she was invited because she was newly married to Matta. In retrospect she felt she was too "intimidated" by the better-known artists to pursue painting.[119] Thus she found only in objects, as well as in her sketches for Surrealist fashion designs, sufficient "space" to create.

While Surrealist objects found favor with many, a vocal minority of critics saw the pursuit of a Lautréamontian juxtaposition of heterogeneous items as all too facile. François Fosca felt that the object could produce a shock to the spirit, or a brief aesthetic pleasure, but that it was too "thin" to found a whole aesthetic. And this approach risked becoming monotonous and formulaic. Others focused on the use value of the objects. "The most prominent [Surrealist mechanism] consists of diverting objects from their customary use. Since the umbrella serves to protect one from water, a person will make an umbrella of sponges; since an iron must slide on the linen, a person will make an iron with nails . . . and a person will then believe that he has discovered the peculiarity, the magic character of these 'gratuitous' objects."[120] The critic evokes two of the most striking objects in the show: Paalen's *Nuage articulé* and Man Ray's *Cadeau* from 1921 which, despite the dismissal, were clearly memorable pieces. As here, typically the object itself is described for public amusement, while the artist's name is omitted.

Situation of the Surrealist Object

Paalen's "open umbrella, beautifully made from sponges," is smaller than it seems in dramatic photos by Ubac, more a child's than adult's size. It drew the tellingly rain-conscious comment of the English critic: "Presumably the bearer is less concerned to shelter himself from the rain than to ensure a steady wetting, neither too great during heavy showers nor too small in the intervals."[121] Amusing as it is, this comment underlines the insistence on functionality as a criterion for the objects, which then can be condemned as "gratuits" or "inutiles." Of course it is the artworks' very defunctionalization that distinguishes them from their utilitarian brethren.

Surrealist objects were present from the very outset of the display, with the wall placement of Hugnet's *Locus Solus* book-object next to Arp's mannequin. Two others were incorporated in the mannequin "street": Dalí's *Aphrodisiac Telephone* (fig. 2.41) and Man Ray's *Aesthetic Coat Rack*. Both in-

2.41 Raoul Ubac, *Dalí's Aphrodisiac Telephone*, detail, 1938. Collection Timothy Baum, New York.

volve what Breton termed the "perturbing" of utilitarian objects nominally in use. Dalí's lobster-telephone is on a table near the hand of his mannequin, while Man Ray's cloudlike coat rack is behind his. The undertone is that two men have shed their coats in a brothel with the mannequin/prostitute.

More objects, like Hugnet's woman-table, were shown in the coal sack room near one of the beds (fig. 2.42). There Hugnet's table is joined by a tripodlike branch construction, an easel for a board inscribed with the word *moi* and an arrow. It is apparently Paalen's *Le moi et le soi* (1937). Another Paalen, an ivy-covered chair, is placed at the foot of a second bed (fig. 2.34). This forerunner to Lucas Samaras's chair transformations is listed as owned by the Vicomte Charles de Noailles, a prominent patron of the Surrealists. Nearby, Domínguez's *Jamais*, which had already been exhibited at Gradiva. One of the most-remarked items in the show, it combined the female body and a mechanical device: a Victrola with horn, painted white. This juxtaposition was most striking in the parts that combined aspects of body and machine. Thus its arm became a human hand hovering over the breast-platter which actually turned, evoking the tactile sense and the erotic, along with implicit sound. During the opening, in fact, there were real sounds, "recordings of hysterical laughter by inmates of an insane asylum, coming out of a hidden phonograph." Perhaps these seemed to issue from the "ghost" player of *Jamais*.

In addition to sound, the multisensory installation included smell, as Man Ray recalled: "The poet Péret, who had lived in South America, installed a coffee-roasting machine, whose fumes assailed the nostrils of the visitors."[122] One of these was Simone de Beauvoir, who emphasized, "The whole place smelled of Brazilian coffee."[123] From the later perspective of conceptual art, this may be the most intriguingly dematerialized "piece." Except for taste (or were there drinks at the vernissage?), all the senses were engaged, as the Surrealists sought to fully engage or confront the spectator.

Seligmann's *Ultrameuble* was another of the most commented objects, "un trépied à quatre pieds." A stool supported by four female legs covered with pink stockings and black and pink shoes, it looked especially striking when a stockinged woman sat in it (fig. 2.44).[124] The multiplication of legs was a disorienting sight that at least two photographers sought to document. Seligmann also made a *Soupière* covered in goose feathers. Despite his dislike for these

Situation of the Surrealist Object

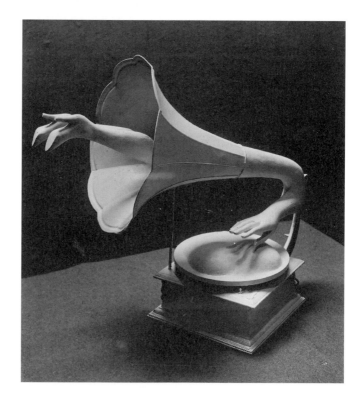

2.42 Bed with Paalen and Hugnet objects, and (left to right) paintings by Ernst, Hayter?, Miró, and Dalí, Galerie Beaux-Arts, 1938.

2.43 Oscar Domínguez, *Jamais* (1937). Collection Getty Research Institute.

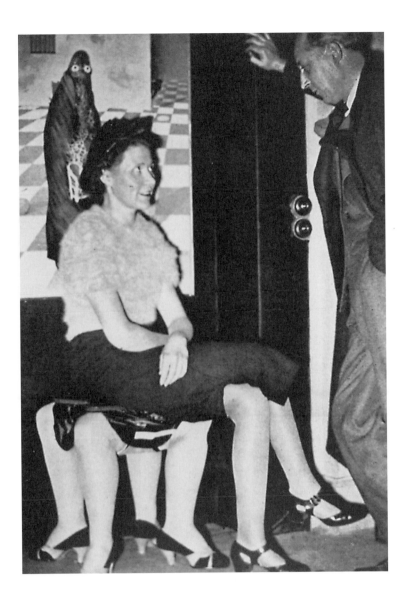

2.44 Kurt Seligmann, *Ultrameuble* with sitter, Galerie Beaux-Arts, 1938.

defunctionalized objects, the critic Colombier nonetheless found this tureen "ravishing." (Hérault used the same word for Domínguez's satin-lined wheelbarrow.) And Seligmann's *Cage* related to Magritte's and other cages in the show, though its nonavian contents of hands and fingers effectively gave Guetta a feeling of "torture."

Aside from sound, provision was made for dance, too, to be represented at the vernissage. (Various other events were promised, including the appearance of an automaton, which did not take place.) Hugnet tells how he, Breton, and Eluard auditioned Hélène Vanel at her Montmartre studio.[125] She presented a more sincere than talented potpourri of mime and dance. Dalí, who knew her, offered to advise the "disheveled sorceress." Her "acte manqué" was prepared in time to be announced on the opening invitation card. Vanel burst forth around midnight in the coal sack room. She moved dramatically, splashing in a small pool encircled by reeds and leaping up on the adjacent bed. By some accounts "nude swathed in chains," she apparently made a costume change and reap-

2.45 Hélène Vanel dancing by brazier, Galerie Beaux-Arts, 1938. Archives Wildenstein. (Opposite)

2.46 Hélène Vanel conjuring at brazier. Archives Wildenstein.

2.47 Hélène Vanel bewitching group, from left: unidentified man, Georges Hugnet, Man Ray, Paul Eluard, Dalí, Paalen. Collection Bibliothèque Historique de la Ville de Paris.

peared in a chemise, or "torn nightgown." At the outset she brandished a live cock; later she "gave an only too realistic impression of a hysterical fit."[126] One reviewer glimpsed through the crush only feathers, a pillow, and cries of hysteria; another described her lying in the bed, and then suddenly springing up, throwing off the covers.[127] All agreed that she splashed vigorously in the water and wet and muddied the fancy evening clothes of her surrounding audience.

As much as the setting prefigured recent installation art, her "dance" foreshadows performance art. Yet Vanel vanishes from the annals of Surrealism, leaving behind only a cryptic definition in the addenda to the *Dictionnaire abrégé:* "L'iris des brumes." Press photographers alone have preserved her image; indeed a variety of suggestive tableaux were staged for their "greedy cameras." One shot of her atop a bed, scantily clad and apparently acting out the Freudian staple "hysteria," has been most often reproduced. Press archives yield quite a few others, unpublished at the time. In one dramatic shot she gestures, witchlike, over the glowing brazier (fig. 2.46). In a related pose, with upraised eyes and hands, she casts a spell over the supporting cast of assembled males (fig. 2.47). Of these, only Man Ray acts convincingly in her thrall, as opposed to Wolfgang Paalen, bemused, who happens into the scene from the right. This enacting of woman as sorceress whose role is to enchant men, Circe-like, seems rather clichéd from today's vantage point.

The presence of Dalí is suggestive, for he had staged similar types of "events" in London in the summer of 1936. The first was his own lecture clad in a diving suit, in which he nearly suffocated. The second was a collaboration with Sheila Legge who appeared, covered in a long white dress, black gloves, and a lettuce-like "rose" headdress, in Trafalgar Square. This performance was called the "Phantom of Sex Appeal," though the main spectators in the documentary photo were the Square's pigeons. Vanel, also young and attractive, was similarly deployed as a kind of "Phantom of Sex Appeal." These also can be related to Dalí's efforts in the thirties to theatricalize the masked ball into a Surrealist "happening," effectively blurring the lines between art and life. The wonder is that Dalí's theatricalizing bent played such a considerable role in this group exhibition, given his already strained relations with Breton.

Duchamp and Breton

One of the greatest indicators of Duchamp's tact is his long association with André Breton, who had an ongoing string of breaks with artists and writers in his circle. Their dual collaboration included coorganizing the Surrealist exhibitions of 1938 and 1942. Breton's admiration for Duchamp was profound, and extended beyond his art to his lifestyle. Breton even gave him the predominant credit for the 1938 show, in glowing terms: "Its principal organizer and director was Marcel Duchamp, who had always enjoyed an unmatched prestige in the Surrealists' eyes, particularly my own, owing both to the genius that all his artistic and antiartistic interventions demonstrated, and to his exemplary emancipation from every servitude and every misery that are the price of artistic activities properly speaking."[128] Breton at first reveals his esteem for the oeuvre and then, at the end, for how Duchamp seemed to glide above material considerations. This was in sharp contrast to how Breton eked out his own living during the Depression years. This point, not without envy, was made more than once.

The two met in 1919, through Picabia, but had little contact in the early years of Surrealism. Duchamp later pointed out that he was of a different

2.48 Breton, *Au lavoir noir* with Duchamp's *Bagarre d'Austerlitz* (Paris: Guy Lévis-Mano, 1936).

2.49 Surrealist exhibition of objects, vitrine with Duchamp's bottle rack, Galerie Charles Ratton, Paris, May 22–29, 1936.

generation from the formative group: "I was fifteen years older than those young men."[129] Duchamp begins to turn up in *Le Surréalisme au Service de la Révolution* with a chess article and, in May 1933, with a reproduction of the unbroken *Large Glass*. This was accompanied by a short preface by Breton, foreshadowing the major article he was soon to write.

Their collaboration was essentially made possible by Breton's inspired essay, "Phare de la Mariée," in the December 1934 *Minotaure*. Paradoxically, Breton had responded sympathetically not to an artwork, but to Duchamp's writing: the recently published notes of the fabled *Green Box*. Of course these notes relate to Duchamp's *Large Glass*, which Breton in fact had not yet seen in the original. He responded more to Duchamp's quality of mind and the complexity of his theme and its iconography. In signaling the *Large Glass* as a beacon "to guide future ships," Breton anointed it one of the most important works of the century.[130] This essay was doubtless what Duchamp recalled in gratitude as Breton's "comprehension at a time when he was the only one to unveil [*dévoiler*] me to myself."[131]

Their relations became closer in the mid-1930s, especially in the context of Surrealist publications and exhibitions. Only two months after the *Minotaure* article, in February 1935, Duchamp wrote to Breton in order to be included in the Copenhagen group show.[132] That September Breton approached Duchamp for an unpublished artwork that could illustrate a short story. Duchamp offered the *Bagarre d'Austerlitz*, and spent time that fall and winter working with a printer on an elaborate double-sided reproduction, brick wall on one side and interior window on the back, sandwiching the clear plastic painted window. When it was finished in January, Duchamp congratulated the writer on his refound health, his new-born child, and a "window," "les 3 à votre goût,"[133] an oddly leveled set of felicitations. Their *Au lavoir noir* appeared that month in an edition of seventy, the sixth *repère* in a series of twelve published by Guy Lévis-Mano. Each paired an important Surrealist artist and writer, beginning with Eluard and Dalí in the first (1935). There was no doubt discussion behind these matches, so the collaboration of Breton and Duchamp is a significant, though often overlooked, signpost in their friendship.

For his part Breton's story of a butterfly included details that allude directly to specific works of Duchamp. Above all, there is a prominent *fenêtre*, a generic reference to *Bagarre*, which is open and closed at the same time. This unusual feature recalls Duchamp's door installed in 1927 at 11 rue Larrey. And Breton describes a pharmacist's flanked green and red glass containers, a pointed reference to Duchamp's *Pharmacy*, which appeared in the London and other Surrealist exhibitions of this era. These may have functioned largely as an inside allusion; nonetheless it is remarkable that Breton took the trouble to pay subtle homage in his prose.

In the same congratulatory letter Duchamp speaks of the selection of objects for the forthcoming exhibition at Charles Ratton (May 1936). His reselected bottle rack appeared there in one vitrine, apparently its earliest documented public exhibition (fig. 2.49). In the special issue of *Cahiers d'Art* on this exhibition, Breton theorized a prominent place for the readymade in the pantheon of the Surrealist object. Apart from the *Fountain* controversy, Duchamp's readymades were little known and in many cases not even preserved until they began their public life under the aegis of the Surrealists. Thus in the mid-1930s, Breton had managed to focus attention on both the *Large Glass* and then the readymade, the two creations that have dominated writings on Duchamp ever since.

After his return to France in September 1936, Duchamp was enlisted by Marga Barr to heal the breach between her husband and the Surrealists. Duchamp immediately arranged for a lunch between her and Breton. What

2.50 Cover of *L'Usage de la Parole*, no. 1 (December 1939), design by Man Ray.

2.51 Marcel Duchamp, *Boîte-en-valise* (1942), ad in *VVV*, no. 2–3, p. 137. (Opposite)

transpired has not been recorded, but accord was reached by October. This is the first token of Duchamp's position as a mediator for the Surrealists as a group, which would expand with his role as organizer of their exhibitions. Duchamp also backed the Surrealists' efforts at commercialization in the form of Breton's Gradiva Gallery, opened in May 1937, for which he designed the door. When queried about his association, Duchamp later remarked, "I had been borrowed from the ordinary world by the Surrealists. They liked me a lot; Breton liked me a lot; we were very good together. They had a lot of confidence in the ideas I could bring to them, ideas which weren't antisurrealist, but which weren't always Surrealist either."[134] So a fine line of independence was walked and, like Picasso, Duchamp became "hors concours" in Breton's mind. He was never asked, for instance, to sign the various Surrealist political manifestos. Soon after Gradiva Gallery opened, Duchamp was preparing a cover for Breton's *Anthology of Black Humor*. Then in December 1937, he became the only artist invited to the new Surrealist editorial board of *Minotaure*, at the same moment as he was actively helping organize the *Exposition Internationale*.

After the *Exposition* collaboration, Duchamp wrote Breton in Mexico that he was at work on the *Humor* cover. After a dinner at Breton's in January 1939, there is a one-year gap in their correspondence. Duchamp at that time seemed to gravitate toward Georges Hugnet, who with Eluard

founded an anti-Breton, "post-Surrealist" group. Benjamin Péret exulted in this "beautiful dissidence" among the Surrealists, while attacking the Hugnet group as "avowed and unavowed Stalinists" only interested in art for art's sake. (In these groups the personal and political were closely intertwined.) Péret noted, too, that they were seeking to manifest themselves in the exhibition arena, and had already had discussions to this end with the "maison de culture."[135] In December 1939 Hugnet and his collaborators brought out the first issue of *L'Usage de la Parole*, to which Duchamp also contributed a brief wordplay, "SURcenSURE" [RErePROACH].[136]

This disconnected collection of clichés offers a kind of business form letter, the blanks to be filled in. Until the latter part, that is, with its reference to Jarry's Père Ubu. Still, as a submission to the first number, the symbolism of Duchamp's contribution should not be overlooked. As before, joint productions of magazines and exhibitions by artists and writers were the means to stake out a group identity. The outbreak of war in 1940 shut down *L'Usage* after only three issues, curtailed the group's exhibition plans, and effectively obscured this Surrealist schism in the sweep of larger events. Breton was able to regroup those dissidents who emigrated to New York after the occupation of Paris, where the apostate Hugnet remained. In a sense the New York exile facilitated an artificial extension of the Breton group's active life.

Duchamp was a relatively late arrival in New York. Breton later recalled in interviews that his contacts with the artist were one of the few bright spots of the émigré years: "I encountered brief but intense joys in New York, such as the ones afforded by my occasional lunches . . . with my admirable friend Marcel Duchamp."[137] Enrico Donati recalled that Breton excitedly welcomed the appearance of Duchamp among the group that had gathered at Larré's French restaurant in midtown. Their curatorial pairing was revived to organize the *First Papers* exhibition, a project that was launched quite soon after Duchamp's arrival in New York, as elaborated below.

The college freshman poet Charles Duits came into the group shortly after the exhibition and provides a striking witness to their interaction. Duits was frankly "surprised" that his hero Breton "abdicated" in the presence of Duchamp. "Before him Breton became strangely smaller. He was naturally in the center as Duchamp was naturally peripheral. But when he was present Breton refused to take his place. All others looked to him and listened to him;

whereas he looked to Duchamp and listened to him. A strange humility."[138] No doubt this seemed "strange" to Duits as he had never witnessed the cantankerous Breton defer to others. But it does mirror the kind of deference Breton extends in his fawning correspondence with Picasso. Duchamp preferred to attribute this to his generational seniority, which may have been a factor, but surely Breton made a calculated sacrifice to affiliate these prestigious figures for the benefit of the group's reputation. In America, as Duits noted, the Duchamp of *Nude Descending* Armory Show renown was as famous as Picasso. The displaced Surrealists could clearly benefit from Duchamp's network built up in previous sojourns in New York. They soon did so, to judge from the list of Duchamp-derived benefactors of *First Papers*, or from the stories of advertising revenues solicited by Duchamp for the periodical *VVV* (fig. 2.51).

What has previously been less clear is what Duchamp gained from his association with the Surrealists. I would say that it was no less than a very respectable platform from which to reemerge in the art world of the 1930s, while at the same time not becoming overly associated with or merged into it. As indicated above, Breton extended both critical and exhibition frameworks in which Duchamp significantly participated, yet from which he claimed independence. Breton's praise and support weighed heavily in these years.

As to why Duchamp would have wanted to reemerge in the art world, part of the answer is suggested by developments in the world of chess. When he began competing intensively in the mid-1920s, the chess world was booming. International tournaments were frequent, with substantial prize money. But the Depression soon ended that. Meanwhile, Duchamp's results had been fairly middling. Thus it is no coincidence that in the early 1930s he veered away from chess toward other ways of making a living.

Duchamp continued to collaborate with Breton on organizing exhibitions in the postwar period. Though there was a falling out the year before Breton died, Duchamp attended his funeral. A subsequent interview underlined the regard he maintained for Breton's ideas on love, and for the man himself.[139] So their interaction was significant and long-standing, if unexpected, even if biographers of both have tended to minimize it.

 The extensive and wide-ranging critical response to the Surrealist exhibition is a fascinating index of how the show was interpreted. At the beginning of "Devant le rideau" (1947), Breton looks back on a number of reviews, "glancing with keen satisfaction at the articles in the press in 1938." He emphasizes their critical negativity and cliché pronunciations of the death of Surrealism. And he points to the setting, particularly the coal sack room and the street signs, as prescient: "all this has since assumed only too much meaning, proved with what clairvoyance, alas, it saw into the future."[140]

Yet Surrealism's present at the beginning of 1938 already included the Spanish Civil War and the Nazi *Entartete Kunst* exhibition (seen by over two million visitors in Munich in the summer and fall of 1937, then reopened in Berlin and other cities). A general sense of foreboding in Europe was widely commented in the same illustrated magazines that reviewed the show. Nationally, several critics mentioned that the vernissage occurred in the days of political crisis after the Popular Front government was dissolved; in this context, what some perceived as merely Surrealist high jinks fell flat. Thus for one critic the *Exposition* "offered a curious comparison with the tragedy and incoherence of the present."[141] Given these foreshadowings, the striking installations were less prophetic than Breton cared to remember, and more of their moment.

This is well illustrated by one satirist, who tells of strolling and thinking that France has had no government for the last four days. Suddenly he has a "chance" encounter with a pressing crowd, attended by police agents. He thinks of three possibilities: a political demonstration, a clandestine arms depot, or a nest of right-wing terrorists, "two steps from the Elysée!" In the end none of these: rather, the vernissage crowd for the *Exposition*.[142] Likewise a taxi driver arriving with an English Surrealist assumed the crowd was another antigovernment demonstration.[143] Another prematurely expected a celebration for the forming of a new government. Thus, merely staging such a high-profile exhibition at this moment meant that it would be politicized.

There was also the prominent discourse not so much on the death of Surrealism as of a revolution that was losing its revolutionary character. Thus in Jacques Lassaigne's terms, success in itself is necessarily compromised, "ideas that have triumphed do not continue to ferment . . . we judge its lack of fermentation by the extent of its success and the ease with which it wins support." He added that Surrealism had become for the bourgeoisie a pleasurable *frisson*, "an adorable violence."[144] *Ce Soir*, the Communist daily edited by Breton's former ally Aragon, predictably disliked the evening dress of the opening and, more surprisingly, the "charm" of installations, both insufficiently revolutionary.[145] Yet it was only our satirist Rouletabille who applied class terminology in imagining a political angle to the "elegant crowd" rendered sheepish by these "mystifiers": "To organize the leisure time of workers is good; to supress that of the idlers and rich amateurs is better."[146] Another suggests that the avant-garde "loses its intensity as it enlarges its audience," raising a point that remains relevant in the expanded art world of recent years.[147] Similarly, another saw Surrealism as "art without danger" whose popularity with high society meant that it would devolve to the province of "the decorator, the advertising executive, the hairdresser, and the grand couturier."[148] This, another critic elaborated, is the life cycle of the avant-gardes: disconcerting yesterday, today pleases without being understood, tomorrow will be monopolized, without being assimilated, by fashion and commercial decoration. He goes on to predict that Surrealist mannequins would be in the windows of the large department stores in a few months.[149] As it turned out, it was more a matter

Adorable Violence

of a few weeks: another source soon reported two couturiers' pseudo-Surrealist vitrines. One involved a skeleton, another plaster sculptures with odd garnishings.[150] Surrealism and fashion intertwined in the blink of an eye, almost indistinguishably; a variation on Dalí's mannequin was vitrined while the show was on nearby. So, too, the mannequins attracted the satirical cartoonists. Takeoffs on those of Dalí and Masson were drawn by Serge for *Paris-Midi*.[151] Karzon's visitor "leaving the Surrealist exhibition" has turned mannequin-like, foot and hand changing places (fig. 2.52). A la Rose Sélavy, he is also gender-crossed, with pigtail, plucked eyebrow, and stocking calf. Likewise with the satirist's concision, Issaiev sites the whole show in one room, not the coal sacks but the pantalons on the ceiling (fig. 2.53). Pygmalion-like, the mannequins come to life and run wild, including those derived from Domínguez and Masson, again, as well as Breton's legged *cadavre exquis*. Domínguez's objects also are featured (the phonograph and the wheelbarrow), as well as Paalen's *Moi*.

Breton essentially ignored or criticized such applications in popular culture, holding fast to Surrealism as "high" art. As instances piled up, his

2.52 Karzon, *Leaving the Surrealist Exhibition*, 1938, press clipping, Seligmann archives.

2.53 Issaiev, *At the Surrealist Salon*, *Le Rire* 44 (February 4, 1938), n.p.

response was the founding, later in 1938, of FIARI, the Fédération Internationale des Artistes Révolutionnaires Indépendants. The undeniable spectacle of the installation won adherents, more than Breton in 1947 was comfortable admitting. While he vaguely lauded "certain aspects of [the exhibition's] structure intended by us to suggest as widely as possible the zone of agitation which is situated at the confines of the poetic and the real," he curiously claimed that these aspects are "not that of art."[152] It was precisely in "the zone of agitation" that this exhibition was most innovative, in embodying for the first time the revolutionary ideology of Surrealism in the shaping of the gallery space. To an extent this innovation, what Breton sees as pushing to the verge of the unreal, gained critical recognition. For some "the zone of agitation" *could* be "that of art."

This space—of disorientation, dimness, of *détournement*—was what appealed to a handful who were ready for its overt subjectivism. Janet Flanner notably found it the "best exhibition for showmanship, for humor, and for paintings, that the Surrealists have ever given anywhere."[153] Cogniat similarly argued for showmanship: a Surrealist exhibition had to be more than pictures on the wall; it would embody a position, a "parti-pris." Therefore, absurdity, provocation, and paradox become potential means of expression.[154] Even the critical Lassaigne allowed that the staging was "un succès aussi extraordinaire."[155]

Among self-conscious critics of the avant-garde, there is often a flurry to name the latest *nouveauté*. So quite a bit of effort went into coining phrases like "synthetic manifestation" for the presentation, or "cavern of dream" for the central room.[156] These attempts to name the "mise-en-scène" indicate a sense that it constituted something in itself. Altogether, Breton's image of universal opposition should be qualified, then, as part of the myth-making of "embattlement," which he apparently thrived upon.

It should be noted, too, that it was mostly partisan daily papers that slung the most outrageous headlines and opinions. The weeklies and monthly magazines were more reflective and generally treated Surrealism more favorably. Breton knew this, as he would have followed the reactions closely, and they would be fodder for group cafe gatherings. The fact that he later quoted numerous reviews suggests that he subscribed to a clippings service, as we know Picasso and Seligmann did. Though the latter's files are quite

Adorable Violence

extensive, still one cannot account for all the barbs cited in Breton's 1947 "Devant le rideau." One article, however, is revealing as the source of the singular phrase that Breton quotes, unattributed, at the beginning of his essay: "Never did society people tread so hard on each other's feet since the fire at the Bazar de la Charité." While its author Guy Crouzet, the critic of *La Grande Revue*, does lampoon the crowded opening, he also gives a fair overview of the history of the Surrealist movement, including some of its literary manifestations. True, he is among those who find the Surrealist object gratuitous. Yet he favors the "taste for the absurd," and interestingly links it to Freud's concept of slips of the tongue and their relation to the unconscious. In conclusion, Crouzet feels that the Surrealists exemplify "the lines of rupture of a civilization" and are thereby "the most authentic and the most lucid of the spiritual tendencies of today."[157] Rather strong and well-considered support. One would not surmise that this was one of the most thoughtful reviews from the one sound bite the petulant Breton quotes out of context, nor in his sweeping dismissal of journalistic opinion.

In part the vaunted internationalism of the *Exposition*, with representatives of 14 countries listed in the checklist, was just quid pro quo for groups of artists who had recently hosted the Surrealists for lectures and/or exhibitions. Thus one or two paintings or objects were allowed by artists from Copenhagen, Prague, Tenerife, Tokyo. Some of the English Surrealists, recent hosts and collaborators, fared a little better, averaging three, above all Paul Nash, listed with six paintings plus collages. But this so-called "internationalism" was in fact essentially Europeanism. Thus the United States was barely represented. Apart from the expatriate Man Ray and Matta's young bride Ann Clark, only Joseph Cornell was truly imported, probably through the auspices of Julien Levy's gallery or from locally owned works. But of course many of the Paris-based Surrealists were born abroad; thus, "the catalogue, happily international, hardly contains any French names."[158]

Here we reach a discourse that merits Breton's disdain. A rather foreboding emphasis on nationality was carried further by a few French critics, who used "foreignness" to dismiss Surrealism as a whole as insufficiently "French." One snidely described the opening as packed with Czechs, Germans, Japanese, and "even a few Parisians," while another stereotyped the crowd as "pretty American women, German Jewish men, and crazy old English."[159] Others likewise stigmatized the installation: "Its bad taste is not very French."[160] Lecuyer traced Surrealism's roots to "romantisme allemand et russe," and then ghettoized it as impure: "This type of romanticism can scarcely be called French. A way of thinking is needed that the people of our race can never properly acquire"[161]—the obvious implication being that the French were above acquiring such sensibilities. Reenacting the World War I-era objections against "kub-ism" as "boche" and foreign, the critic uses nationality as a crude stick.[162] *La Croix*, the official daily of the clergy, carried this nationalist bias toward racism, castigating Surrealism as "no more French than a Hottentot or Poldève."[163] The Surrealists were thus stigmatized by identification with the non-Western objects and cultures that intrigued them.

The other flag waved against the Surrealists was red. Apparently some journalists had heard that Breton had joined the Communist party, but not that he had left it in 1933. One felt that some of the Surrealists had probably started as blaguers, but the problem really was that most of them were Communists.[164] The *Nouvelle Revue Française*, in finding them "false revolutionaries," conceded that Surrealism had lasted longer than Lenin, or the Commune.[165] But not longer than Stalin, one might add, whose policies and show trials drove Breton from the party and also divided him from his old friends Aragon, then Eluard. These distinctions were too subtle for those of the popular press who accused the Surrealists of joining the "anti-Fascist front," forming soviets all over and winking at the masses instead of activating them.[166]

The Market

In contrast to the polarized polemics of the press, the reception of the market was all too quiescent. The Surrealist exhibitions of the mid-1930s were a sign of the movement's spreading influence and internationalization. In a sense each show was a manifesto, staking out a public position on the Surrealists' latest interests. Each also was a barometer of the group dynamics and competitive positioning. Yet the artists presented themselves in the public sphere to generate attention, including purchases. Making a living became one of the vital concerns for Surrealist artists (and writers) in the economic downturns of the 1930s.

It is unclear who assumed the costs related to staging the exhibitions, such as shipping. The settlement of costs for frame damage to a Picasso painting sent to Tenerife in 1935 reveals that the works were shipped uninsured. Man Ray reported a strong positive response to the Surrealist exhibition in London in 1936, yet Roland Penrose recalled "virtually no sales."[167] All indications are that the Wildensteins put no ceiling on, and picked up, all the costs for the 1938 exhibition. Interestingly, these included a 1,000-franc fee to Breton as organizer.[168]

To some extent the market improved with the arrival on the scene of Alfred Barr (and by extension, New York collectors). The summer before the Museum of Modern Art's two big historical shows, Barr was soliciting loans as well as making purchases for the Museum's collection. Paul Eluard reported to Gala that Barr purchased 2,000 francs' worth of art from him, mostly works by Max Ernst, plus another 350 francs' worth of Surrealist documents. He also reports that Breton sold twice as much; we can only imagine that reaction.[169] In response to Barr's interest, artists (and writers) suddenly scrambled to locate old works held by former friends, spouses, or lovers. Barr purchased from Breton's ex-wife Simone Collinet, as well as buying Magritte's "eye" from Man Ray, a Tanguy from Valentine Hugo, and so on. Eluard's disaffection with Surrealism would enable Penrose to purchase his fine collection at a low price.

As had the London show, the *Exposition Internationale* carried an admission charge that generated significant revenue. The principal memoirs pass over this feature in (embarrassed?) silence, and only one reviewer happened to complain about the charge. "Grincheux Jovial" reported up to 500 visitors per day, far more than at the Galerie Beaux-Arts' previous El Greco exhibition. He rhetorically asks, can all these visitors be true Surrealists?[170] Clearly many came out of curiosity, all increasing the daily receipts.

By the time the Surrealist exiles reached Manhattan, the art market was in a wartime tailspin. As one of their leading dealers put it, "In 1941 business was not only terrible, it was non-existent."[171] Early in 1942 Breton wrote that painting was selling poorly, with no sales at Masson's or Ernst's shows.[172] Nonetheless, plans went ahead for *First Papers* that fall, with works on sale. There was also an admission of $1.10 for the preview, 50 cents thereafter, as well as a catalogue for sale, with profits going not to the group but for the benefit of war relief. Masson sold his major submission, the large canvas *Il n'y a pas de monde achevé*, to an established collector of his work, Saidie May of Baltimore, for one thousand dollars. The bill was drawn by Buchholz Gallery, and it does not appear that any of the price went to the benefit cause.[173] There is no other indication of works directly bought from this show, and the Surrealists did not try another until the war was over.

The Market

Surrealism Goes to the Fair: Projects for an American Surrealist

Display at the 1939 New York World's Fair

Julien Levy and Dalí
(the Carnivalesque meets Lunatic Narcissus)

 The impact and notoriety of the 1938 *Exposition Internationale* prompted a number of efforts to repeat or expand upon experimental Surrealist installation. First, a reduced version of the *Exposition* circulated to Amsterdam and Brussels. The Amsterdam show at Gallery Robert was carried out by Georges Hugnet, who took the opportunity to create his own mannequin wielding a whip.[1] The environmental aspect of the Paris installation, however, was not reattempted.

New York gallery owner Julien Levy was one of those who, inspired by the Paris example, moved quickly to bring such a display to these shores. Levy was a natural for this project, having been the first to exhibit Surrealism in New York and thus having many contacts with the group. But now he thought beyond his gallery to envision newly theatricalized Surrealist installation in broadly public space, on the grounds of the upcoming and much ballyhooed New York World's Fair.

Within days of the astonishing Galerie Beaux-Arts vernissage, Levy was at work on a proposal for a Surrealist pavilion. But his initial sketchy application for a concession, a "Surrealist 'walkthrough,'" was returned by Fair officials for further details. Undaunted, he joined forces at this point with the young architect Woodner Silverman (today known as Ian Woodner), who, in soliciting for architectural commissions at the Fair, had approached Levy as the leading Surrealist dealer in New York. (Woodner was working on a number of commissions, including the Pharmacy building.) In less than two months they produced a substantial project that garnered preliminary approval.[2] In the proposal statement, Levy proclaimed that the "*Surrealist House* for the World's Fair shoul[d] far excell [sic] in quality the present Surrealist exhibition in Paris, and should be adopted and modified to satisfy American taste."[3] Levy wanted to blend native amusements with the *Exposition*'s bold use of Surrealist display, thereby appealing to the carnivalesque aspects of American popular culture. Thus the deployment of a so-called Surrealist "fun house walk," a modified "house of horrors," and a "human kaleidoscope," which all sound more like an amusement fair than an art exhibit. Expanding on the circuitous aspect of the *Exposition*, Levy's project would have proceeded as a kind of passage through discreet encounters. Levy's "Surrealist walk," with its three-dimensional "exhibits" by artists and "waxwork" figures, was particularly reminiscent of the street of mannequins in Paris. Other features clearly derived from American popular culture: the

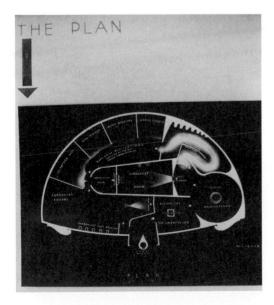

3.1   Julien Levy and Woodner Silverman, variant ground plan, Surrealist House, New York World's Fair proposal, 1938. Private collection.

Page 105: Detail of figure 3.27.

penny arcade, the peep show, the fun house. These often had the individual spectator peering into a dark space, experiencing what Dalí elsewhere heralded as "a systematic confusion of the senses." This would have been a vivid instance of Surrealism's broader dilution and reception in 1930s America. "Drained of its political content and reconstituted as entertainment, Surrealism was frequently cast as the close cousin of cartoons and popular culture."[4]

Within Levy's Surrealist House was embedded a conventional group exhibition of unspecified size, to include both European and American artists. This would have been the first Surrealist show where American artists were substantially represented. (The only names specifically mentioned, however, are the familiar Europeans Dalí, Ernst, Magritte, and Duchamp, the latter the most striking inclusion in this "Surrealist" context.) Duchamp had already appeared in Levy's pioneering study *Surrealism*, which discusses the *Large Glass* as a Surrealist work. It is worth noting that Levy knew the artist well, for Marcel was his first guide to the Parisian avant-garde.[5] The Surrealist House would also contain Coney Island-like nickel slot mechanical viewers, an illustration of Surrealist methods applied to popular culture. Thus the exhibit was to mix fine art freely with commercial and entertainment forms. The official Fair reviewers responded favorably to precisely this blending of "great mass as well as class attractions." The latter, it was frankly hoped, would bring in the "Vogue and Harper's Bazaar set," while the former drew the hoi polloi.[6] Clearly Surrealism was perceived as glamorously linked to the worlds of upper class chic and fashion.

The round exterior was amazing, being largely composed of a Magrittian (or Buñuelian) large eye, whose iris would frame changing color projections.[7] This, too, was promoted for the "shock value in its design." The eye would have been most appropriate, for vision was the main sensory appeal. The spectator's gaze brought him or her into the realm of the marvelous or the stupefying. To stimulate the other senses, Levy would have inside a microphoned "Audible Staircase" and malleable architecture: "rocking floors, pneumatic walls," kinesthetic aspects very much in the fun house mode, yet also echoing Dalí and Matta's architectural proposals of the mid-1930s.[8] Levy was aware of and meant to exploit Surrealism's recent moves into three-dimensional space.

Levy's three-page typescript is lent substance and visualization in a recently rediscovered binder that contains Woodner Silverman's original renderings of the elevation and the interior ground plan. Also entitled "Surrealist House," it most likely accompanied the written proposal to the Fair officials. Most strikingly, it begins with the architect's gouache of a round building encasing a bloodshot eye, dramatically set in a dark purple-black night. The cornea reflects items "seen" by the eye, including a small image of Botticelli's renowned Venus rising from the sea. A photographic print of the same monumental eye structure on the second page has different reflections in the iris, including the words "New York." The *Birth of Venus* reflection is altered to two people on the shell, most likely a primordial first man and woman (fig. 3.2).

On the verso of these elevations follows a red ink rendition of the ground plan (fig. 3.1). This shows a rounded, shell-like structure, with a succession of encounters arrayed counterclockwise. The first was to be a documentary section, which would display the historical background of Surrealism, followed by the "Photographic Booth" and the "Kaleidoscope." As the proposal elaborates, there were to be three of the latter, one human-

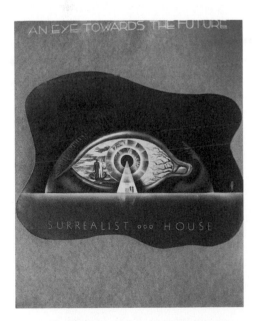

3.2 Woodner Silverman, eye pavilion, rendering,
Surrealist House, New York World's Fair proposal, 1938.

sized, to throw off multiplied reflections of participants who entered. Next followed a "peep window" view of a "Surrealist room," a mode of controlled spectatorship that anticipates Friedrich Kiesler's peep-type designs for the mechanized section of the Art of This Century gallery in 1942. This led to a curved "persecution corridor," probably the space for Levy's modified "fun house walk." Here would have been the "Audible Staircase" and malleable architecture, or "hallucinations" based on dreams. Most of the width of the pavilion was then devoted to four individual artist's rooms, (Dalí, Ernst, Duchamp, and Tanguy in place of Magritte). Without giving details, it was suggested that these were to show three-dimensional paintings, including "Surrealist waxworks." These surreal spaces would have an interactive aspect—"the public will participate in the decor of the room itself"—not unlike the row of mannequins at the Galerie Beaux-Arts.

In a variant ground plan, represented by a photographed rendering on page three, Magritte replaces Tanguy among the four artists of "Dark Room Realizations." (Dalí's first name is still misspelled "Salvatore.")

These rooms were followed by a larger open space labeled "Gallery." Here presumably Levy's more conventional group exhibition would take place. Again, no indication of contents is given, but the room did present the prospect of a curving wall, even more so than the one in Levy's midtown gallery. The final station featured slot machines in the form of Surrealist-designed nickelodeons. Spectators would there complete the circle and exit where they had entered.

The photographic variant of the ground plan also incorporated a "Song of Songs" display in the midst of the historical documentation section. This pet project of Levy's was intended to suggest that Surrealist metaphor operated even in the Old Testament. A glass woman was to have been constructed that literalized the poetic description in the biblical text. This rather didactic display would out-historicize even Barr's forerunners to Surrealism.

It appears that the processional stations of the display were Levy's concept, with the architect Woodner providing the innovative container for them. Levy's ideas were wide-ranging and freely adulterated Bretonian Surrealism with amusement house and other modes of spectacle. The texts supporting and elaborating on the drawings admit to a "combination of dime museum and industrial display."

Levy had planned to travel to Paris in the summer of 1938 to enlist the support of the artists, but protracted negotiations with Fair officials dragged on through this time, and it is not clear whether he made the voyage. A contract was drawn up, dated May 27, for plot AM-14, fronting on street no. 3 in the Amusement area. It had 120 linear feet of frontage on the street and a total of about 9,700 square feet, to contain a building 50 by 90 feet. All of Levy and Woodner's proposed rooms and corridors were included as approved. The space charge was $6,240, of which one quarter ($1,560) was required as a deposit. Riders specified a 25 cent admission fee and granted permission to "sell photographs, Surrealist-type souvenirs and novelties." In the meantime Levy and Woodner consulted Billy Rose, a songwriter as well as colorful promoter of his fiancée Eleanor Holm's aquatic show at the Fair. Rose persuaded them that the 20 percent of the gate that they had agreed to pay was too high. Negotiations apparently resumed, for in late August Levy and Woodner were threatened with the loss of the space if they did not sign and submit the deposit. From October 15 there is a gap in the official record until the following April, when comes a rush to complete the building dubbed "Dalí's Bottoms of the Sea." At some point between the fall of 1938 and early 1939, then, the more elaborate Levy/Woodner Surrealist House was dropped. As Levy blithely recounted, he was persuaded by no less than William Morris, founder of the talent agency, that the recently Bonwit's-bathtubbed Dalí was more fundable than Surrealism, and he voluntarily decided to yield to the former's presumed drawing power.[9]

If Levy could not recruit a wider group in Europe, the arrival of Salvador Dalí in New York in February 1939 would take on magnified significance. Already *the* Surrealist in the popular American imagination, thanks to the "Bal Onirique," Levy's exhibitions, and his appearance on the cover of *Time*, Dalí had the highest name recognition here, a factor that all involved could appreciate.[10] Indeed, in his most developed preliminary study for the World's Fair pavilion, Dalí immodestly topped the building with the apotheosis of his own name, framed, in huge, three-dimensional letters. Inside, Dalí's eventual transformation of the display included even more direct appropriations of the 1938 Paris exposition than Levy's proposal.

Meanwhile his exhibition at Levy's gallery from March 21 to April 15 was a resounding success, with 21 paintings sold for a reported $25,000 plus. Even *Life* hailed its popularity. And it was immediately preceded by Dalí's infamous fracas at the Bonwit Teller store, best evoked by the *Daily Mirror* headline, "Bathtub Bests Surrealist Dali in 5th Ave. Showwindow Bout."[11] Disputing Bonwit's changes to his display centered on symbolic figures of Day and Night, Dalí attempted to overturn its "hairy" bathtub, which slipped and crashed through the vitrine's plate glass. Dalí walked or fell through the hole in the window, was arrested, and thereby provided all the daily papers with a field day reporting this "happening." Even at the time, there were those who suspected the apparent accident was a publicity stunt, including *Art Digest*.[12] This should not obscure the fact that there was a lively interest among the art world in what Dalí had wrought. Artists Peter Busa and his friend Jackson Pollock had come uptown to see the window on opening day. (The uptown stores unveiled their new displays on the same day, something of an event.) The two arrived just in time to see shattered glass and Dalí on the Fifth Avenue side-

3.3 New York *Daily Mirror,* "Bathtub Bests Surrealist Dali," newspaper clipping, Friday, March 17, 1939, Dalí scrapbook, Museum of Modern Art Library, New York.

walk, a sight that amused Pollock for days.[13] Another coincidence: Jimmy Ernst was passing on a Fifth Avenue bus and witnessed the fracas, as did the detective next to him, who took Dalí into custody. As he was led away to the police station, Dalí spotted Julien Levy and told him to summon a lawyer. All in all, quite a cast of art world characters in the midtown neighborhood at that moment, suggestive of the connections between fashion and art gallery display. Later Levy noted that the contretemps stimulated interest in the show which opened shortly thereafter: "With the publicity of the Bonwit window, [Dalí's works] sold like hotcakes."[14] Then the artist turned his attentions to the Fair.

Already in 1936 Dalí had titled a painting *Suburbs of a Paranoiac-Critical Town: Afternoon on the Outskirts of European History*, which seemed to anticipate the Flushing location, in the "suburbs" of New York, as well as the fact that an afternoon visit confronted the spectator with (the downfall of) the old world. Nazi Germany refused to participate in the Fair. As a result of the German invasion, the Czechoslovak pavilion tragically lost its basis. "They put in a fine supply of Prague ham and Pilsen beer before there wasn't any Czecho-Slovakia anymore."[15] Thus events in the European theater hung over spectators' experience of the pavilions.

Levy recalled that Dalí marshaled English collector Edward James's financial support to obtain a controlling interest, and also hired James's lawyer Philip Wittenberg. (Dali was under contract to James for a monthly stipend in exchange for all his art, an agreement that was about to expire on June 1.) After discussions, they agreed to join forces with a "rubber man" from Pittsburgh who wanted to fund an aquarium with rubber-tailed mermaids. According to the *New Yorker*'s report, William Morris apprised Levy of a new type of cast rubber that could be used for underwater displays, and this possibility intrigued the artist.[16] The collaborating parties formed the "Dali World Fair Corporation," signing a contract on April 10. Dalí was paid $2,500 plus 20 percent of the profits "to create facade and interior designs, costumes, incidental scenery and souvenirs for the exhibition . . . tentatively named 'Bottoms of the Sea.'"[17] This must have seemed to Levy like the fulfillment of his original proposal to illustrate Surrealism in advertising. Yet this eleventh-hour attempt to wed art and commerce was problem-ridden from early on.

Julien Levy and Dali

3.4　George Platt Lynes, *Model, Lynes, Julien Levy, Salvador and Gala Dalí,* 1939.

3.5　George Platt Lynes, *Salvador Dalí,* April 1939, gelatin silver print, Collection Metropolitan Museum of Art, New York.

The "Corporation" turned to photography to generate some racy publicity stills for the project. Most likely Levy marshaled the group to the studio of a photographer that he represented, George Platt Lynes. A sequence
of prints owned by Levy begin with a group shot of the Dalí entourage, including the photographer and the model, still clothed in fur (fig. 3.4). Then
follow several shots of her nude, with Dalí and a suited man attaching a lobster shell to cover her crotch. This was the setup for an inspired portrait of
Dalí grasping her legs, her head and arms cropped at the top (fig. 3.5). His
head emerges from behind her, on a level with the lobster fig leaf, as if he is
carrying the upright body like a mannequin. The final print involved
Lynes's collaboration in double-exposing Dalí's hand, so that it appears to
emerge from a gash in her leg.[18]

The same model also appeared solo, arms akimbo, wearing Gala's metal
star necklace. Dalí drew over this print in ink, metamorphosing a fairly ba-

3.6 George Platt Lynes, nude model with Dalí overdrawing, 1939, ink on gelatin
silver print, 24.1 x 19.1 cm. Collection Baltimore Museum of Art.

nal shot into a fantastic mermaid with two fish-tailed feet (fig. 3.6). Fish tails also sprout from her shoulders and head, as does a unicorn horn. Dalí also converted the setting into an arid beach, with a wrecked hull and two tiny figures before a distant horizon. In modified form the horned mermaid, arms raised, was drawn as a vignette on the press reception invitation card for the pavilion's opening. Less sublime are a group of awkward shots of a taller model cradling or simulating breast-feeding a fish. These were apparently not further used or published at the time.

Dalí also tried out the seafood props in two other studios sessions. At the fashion photographer Horst's, he appropriately focused on costumes for the liquid ladies. The lobster reappears as a fig leaf and as a hat, a nice irony on fashion (fig. 3.7). The most astonishing prop was a beaded necklace attached to six large hooks piercing mussels. The slimy shellfish on her bare breasts and the barbs menacing her skin make this one of the most effectively chilling sadoerotic images in Surrealism. It prompted one interpreter to remind us that "Venus in mythology is connected to castration, since she was born of the foam of the genitals of the

3.7 Horst, *Model with Seafood Dress*, 1939. Courtesy Staley-Wise Gallery, New York.

castrated Uranus."[19] He also suggests a possible pun between the necklace and the French slang for hymen (*la perle*) as part of the erotics of the image. Dalí also tropes the photographic itself, by the use of trompe l'oeil. The cutout bathing costume is not actual, but again rather carefully inked in on the photo of the nude. Dalí also clearly added linear detail to the lobster. A photographer, perhaps Horst, apparently participated in a collaborative exchange, and illusionistic complication, by rephotographing the ink-drawn print. Subsequently made prints entered a number of collections; the original was kept by Levy until its purchase for the Israel Museum. Meanwhile, two of the ink-drawn photographs were displayed for a time in niches in the facade of the pavilion itself, to the left of the entry, as an eroticized lure to paid admission. The actual rather frilly mermaids' costumes were nowhere near as innovative or free-form as Dalí designed, although there was one with a much simpler heart-shaped opening exposing the wearer's breasts. It is interesting that Dalí collaborated with both photographers to produce manipulated prints, adulterating the verism of the photographic to his own "marvelous" ends. The other props included oyster shells, traditionally associated with aphrodisiac qualities. There is also an eel, which becomes a slithery belt in the Israel Museum print. While the lobster hat satirizes fashion in a variant photo, a crustacean at the crotch is a more complex metaphor. On one level the masked model becomes an anonymous yet edible ground for a seafood feast.[20]

Most of the same props were used again in photographing a different, long-haired model, her head topped with a sponge (fig. 3.8).[21] She is surrounded by the clothed group: Dalí and Gala, Edward James and Levy seated below. But for all the tableau posturing, or because of it, this photograph lacks the *frisson* of Horst's sexualized close-ups. This and further shots of the long-haired model issued from a "more mass than class" third studio, that of publicity photographer Murray Korman. He was located in Queens and did other work for the Fair and especially for Billy Rose, including alluring shots of Eleanor Holm published in the Aquacade souvenir program (fig. 3.9).[22] Holm poses with the same block and rope that appear in Dalí's vaguely nautical tableau. In the latter, the nude model, hands apparently bound, wears the familiar lobster G-string, while Dalí and Gala rather superfluously stand nearby (fig. 3.10).[23] Another shot shows the same blonde model, like a self-displaying *Demoiselle*

3.8   Murray Korman, *Tableau with Edward James, Dalí, Model with Lobster,*
Gala, and Julien Levy, 1939. Private collection. (Above)

3.9   Murray Korman, *Eleanor Holm,* Aquacade brochure, New York World's Fair,
1939. (Below)

3.10   Murray Korman, *Model with Lobster, Dalí, and Gala,* 1939.
Weingrow Collection, Hofstra University Library. (Opposite, left)

3.11   Murray Korman, *Model astride Trylon and Perisphere,* 1939.
Weingrow Collection, Hofstra University Library. (Opposite, right)

astride a miniature Trylon and perisphere, all too obviously placed between her legs as a phallic symbol (fig. 3.11). Dalí again eroticizes the Fair's trademark, just as he had done, in premonitory fashion, for his February 1939 Levy exhibition announcement.

In three more Korman photos the same long-haired model is necklaced with shellfish on hooks and holds up three open oysters (fig. 3.12), as had Horst's masked model. Their traditional association as an aphrodisiac heightens the mingling of edible and sexual. The isolated nude again sports a lobster as fig leaf, an unusual item further elaborated in Dalían iconography in these years, from telephone to dress design. The crustacean, its main shell phallic, but also suggestively fallopian in shape and placement, could be a metaphor of fertility. On the other hand, its large claws have been seen as castrating, even as it is protective and shielding. The three Korman photos vary mostly in lighting, and do not achieve the charge that Horst's convey.

As the self-appointed publicist, Levy successfully placed some Dalí preliminary drawings in tony magazines before the pavilion opened. The *Vogue* sketch for the pavilion, although set in a vast landscape, suggests a subterranean grotto, with a Medusa-headed mermaid swimming through it (fig. 3.13). Draping and spikes ring the outside, along with tumescent forms sup-

ported by two typical Dalían crutches. The pointy protrusions are longer, including those around the vaginal slit of an entrance, to the right of the sideshow platform. Two spikes support golden balls sprouting streaming hair. Halfway between this spiky version and the tentacled built one is the large study with collage, elaborately signed and dated 1939, showing his own name framed in three-dimensional, reddish-pink letters atop the facade (fig. 3.14). This immodest feature was replaced in the built version by the title "Dream of Venus."

Ending up in the collection of the architect Woodner Silverman, this collage seems to be Dalí's final working plan for the exterior. It appears in situ on an easel behind Dalí and James, with additional small drawings pinned to it, in a photo of the workshop on the Fair grounds. It is clear from examining the original that someone ruled in the rectangular proportions of the structure with a straightedge, and Dalí then embellished. The sheet is most strikingly colored, with pink as the main tone of the plastered exterior. This unusual choice recalls Schiaparelli's promotion of pink in her "Shocking" perfume line and as a general signature hue. Dalí had already adapted this unusual color on a stuffed bear with drawers that he loaned to Schia-

3.12 Murray Korman, *Model with Seafood Dress,* 1939.
Weingrow Collection, Hofstra University Library. (Opposite)

3.13 Salvador Dalí, *Exterior of the Dream House,* June 1939,
drawing reproduced in *Vogue.*

3.14 Salvador Dalí, Dream of Venus pavilion study, New York World's
Fair, 1939. Tempera, pencil, and pasted paper on illustration
board, 30 x 40 in. Collection Dian and Andrea Woodner, New York.

3.15 Salvador Dalí, zipper chamber, *Town and Country*, June 1939. Dalí scrapbook, Museum of Modern Art Library, New York.

3.16 Salvador Dalí, studies for "Seaweed Figures," Dream of Venus pavilion, 1939. Pen and ink and watercolor on printed paper, 9⅜ x 12½ in. Woodner Family Collection, New York.

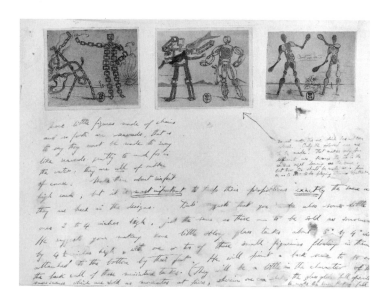

parelli for her display window, as well as in his Mae West lip-sofa.[24] Dalí's facade is also self-conscious about other art, perhaps in dialogue with the official art exhibitions elsewhere in the Fair.[25] Thus he appropriates via collage both a black and white reproduction of the face of Da Vinci's *Mona Lisa*, tilted and linked to the body of the hermaphroditic *John the Baptist* in the Louvre. *Art Digest* and a number of subsequent publications misidentified the figure as only the *Mona Lisa*! Apart from his renown, Leonardo's significance here is obscure, though in Dalí's mind the mermaids and their costumes were linked to "ideas of Da Vinci."[26] More relevant to the goddess theme is Botticelli's famed Venus rising from the sea. She is metamorphosed into a reversed mermaid (fish head instead of fish tail), floating on a seaborne shell. These Renaissance masters are joined by a newer archetypal image: a Dalían limp watch hanging over one of the tentacles. In the other inset views, the green mermaid swimming through is joined by the carefully painted, harshly modeled grisaille torso of a nude woman. At the front left Dalí includes a bright red and yellow platform for a *parade*, a traditional theme in French art. In this case the sideshow is a colorfully costumed couple bearing a pole supporting a sea urchin that contains a tiny mermaid. Behind the bearers is a spiky, rather vaginal-looking entrance to the pavilion. The skirted purple legs appear to the right, as if seated on a gilded wooden chair projecting in front of the facade, a visual pun on two pairs of "legs." Both the apparent black holes in the facade and the illusionistic detailed cracks in its surface suggest the structure's metamorphosis and entropy. The favored Dalían theme of rotting and decay is now imaginatively applied to architecture. Of course such suggestions of destabilization were not practical for the final structure, though an attempt was made to suggest illusionistic cracks on the irregular plaster surface.

Two additional sketches published in *Vogue* indicate Dalí's attention to interior details like the seaweeded piano and the eyelashes terminating in telephones. Another appeared as a two-page color spread in *Town and Country*, showing how the "living liquid ladies" would enter their chamber beneath the sea through a zipper entry in the wall (fig. 3.15). They passed through a harp, probably inspired by the artist's positive exchange with Harpo Marx in Hollywood the previous year. Then after warming at an illusory underwater fireplace, their exit would be equally dramatic: "through

Julien Levy and Dalí

a mirror."[27] Here the omnivorous Dalí clearly hoped to adapt the striking mirror passage scenes of Jean Cocteau's film *Blood of a Poet* (1932), although technically it seems (and apparently was) unrealizable. This eye-catching publicity reached those tastemakers the Fair officials had already targeted. Yet one wonders whether reaching for the "smart set" worked against a broader popular appeal, leaving the uninitiated baffled.

Three tiny studies also in the Woodner collection (fig. 3.16) shed light on Dalí's working process as well as his rocky collaboration with Gardner Displays (the firm of the "rubber man" from Pittsburgh). They prove, surprisingly, to be "readymade" images, which the artist has "assisted" by drawing in his typical spatialized low horizon and tiny figural details. But the imaginative personages are appropriated from the seventeenth-century Italian artist Giovanni Battista Bracelli's series of fifty engravings called *Bizzarie* (1624). In these, figures are conjured out of shapes or common objects: diamonds, ribbons, links, boxes, or, as in the right-hand image, paddles. Dalí scissored the latter out of the Museum of Modern Art's *Fantastic Art* catalogue, number 53, where Bracelli was included among the forerunners of Surrealism. Dalí watercolored the figures and added a smaller horseman and standing person in the distance. He also altered the collector's stamp to become his crested signature. Thus one Surrealist exhibition literally feeds off another, a microcosm of Dalí's synthetic approach. The other two images are also from the same Bracelli *Bizzarie* but are from a different printed source, as they are not reproduced in the Modern's catalogue. These Dalí transforms into underwater scenes by drawing mermaids swimming through the chain personages. The one on the left also reprises the *Vogue* eyelash-telephones in the distance. These are working sketches, as the accompanying inscription by Edward James makes clear. The figures are to be fabricated in rubber, six feet high, unfixed, "made to sway like seaweeds." The text also relays Dalí's suggestion of producing miniature three- to four-inch versions, to be sold as souvenirs. Dalí utilizes appropriation as a shortcut here, revealing that he is far more interested in conception than the practicalities of fabrication. Thus these tiny sketches are all the specifications the manufacturers had to work from. Small wonder that Dalí later found himself disappointed in what they produced.

On May 9 Levy notified Fair officials that the name "Bottoms of the Sea" had been changed to the mythological and higher-toned "Dali's Dream of Venus." For the preview gala scheduled for late May, a full month after the Fair itself opened, he requested permission to sell higher-priced tickets and serve liquor, both requests apparently turned down. The building would not be ready for the projected premiere of May 31, not surprisingly. The public relations firm hired wittily attributed the delay to the "complexity of [the] subconscious."[28] In fact about half of all Fair amusements did not open on time, so that the area had the character of a "frontier town" during its first weeks, with buildings and roads unfinished.[29] Thus Dalí's conception actually made its public premiere in the pages of the June 1 number of *Vogue*.

The Dream of Venus had its postponed inauguration on June 15, with various changes in the intervening two weeks including the appearance of a "Lunatic Narcissus" instead of the "countless small bicycle riders" that Venus in bed was to count instead of sheep. Dalí evidently formulated an image more reflective of himself in those frantic days of final preparation. The "Lunatic Narcissus" also embodies the mythic image of the "mad" artist that Dalí hoped would generate big box office success with a curious public. In fact his press agents issued a related release, no doubt with his assent, entitled, "Is Dali Insane?" It is widely echoed in the press. One subsequent listing neatly summarized this cultivated image of eros and craziness as spectacle: "Frankly a girl show, but pepped up into something by the Surrealist madness of Salvador Dali."[30] *Time*'s reviewer perceptively perceived a Hamlet-like pose: "A writhing plaster castle on the outside, it shrewdly

3.17 Dream of Venus invitation card, 1939.

combines surrealism with sex, inside, proving that there is plenty of Broadway method in Dali's madness."[31] The terms *Surrealism* and *madness* are thus fused as elements of publicity.

It is said that the day before the press preview, Dalí, having withdrawn from the project, sailed for a Europe on the brink of war. His departure is usually ascribed to disputes with Gardner over the manufacturing, but a recent biographer has suggested, more pragmatically, that he was overdue in Europe to produce commissioned ballet designs needed for a mid-September performance.[32] And Levy recalled that Dalí planned to leave once Venus opened anyway; thus his departure probably depended on ocean liner schedules. As it was, Levy and James were left behind to make the best of it. The latter cabled Dalí that the press preview had been a "slight fiasco," as the uncirculated water in the tank got cloudy from the running dye oozing from the mermaids' gloves,[33] which were soon abandoned. James omitted that he was embarrassed to be found partying in the tank after hours. According to Levy's account, W. M. Gardner used the so-called "drunken orgy" as blackmail to force them to sell him their share.[34]

Though Dalí attempted to straight-facedly appropriate 1930s leftist ideology in his statement "I paint for the masses . . . for the people,"[35] the people didn't come. Attendance was disappointing, as it was for the Fair as a whole. It certainly was not helped by the fact that the pavilion was not listed at all among the 57 amusements described in the first two editions of the official guidebook. In July there appeared Dalí's last word, a protest manifesto "Declaration of the Independence of the Imagination and the Rights of Man to His Own Madness," in part distributed by being dropped from an airplane! This was a calculated appeal in its reference to (and pastiche of) two historic documents of the American founding fathers, as well as a reprise of the insanity theme and a "calling upon the artists of America to rise up against the forces of cultural tyranny." In it Dalí justifiably complained that his fish-headed Venus was vetoed by Fair bureaucrats (and by Gardner). He also indicted the corrupting influence of "the lofty airs and superior quackings of 'middle-men of culture.'" Despite its calculated appeals, the "Declaration" did not draw a groundswell of support from a summering art world, or even much publicity.[36] A *succès de scandale*, apparently hoped for, did not materialize. Dalí's "Declaration" has not been taken seriously in the literature. Yet given the evidence of defacement evidenced in Carl Van Vechten's

3.18 Anonymous, "20,000 Legs under the Sea" pavilion, 1940. Smithsonian Institution.

photos discussed below, his complaints seem more than justified. By this time Levy and James were so in the red that the project for them had become a nightmarish "Dream of Minus," and they abandoned it to Gardner's management, perhaps with some relief.[37]

In late August Gardner's concessionaires started to demand cuts in the Fair's percentage, along with reductions in the hours and the admission fee. By then Jungle Land, the Parachute Jump, and Rose's Aquacade had emerged as the top moneymaking amusements, while the $300,000 Cuban Village and the Savoy Ballroom concessions had already failed and closed.[38] The first two weeks of October were the best attended of the season; still, the Fair shut at the end of November with a little over 25 million visitors, a hefty sum but only half of what had been predicted. Fair officials began to negotiate with Gardner to reopen a modified pavilion in 1940. It would reopen, without Dalí or Venus but with many of the same props, and with a more prurient, punning title: "20,000 Legs Under the Sea" (i.e., the return of the not entirely repressed "Bottoms of the Sea" concept). This title replaces "Dream of Venus" on the fa-

Julien Levy and Dalí

cade, and the Da Vinci and Horst photos were also removed. In their stead were blowups of sexy photos of an underwater diver that had appeared in *Life*, a tie-in to a more populist mass media promotion. Signage proclaimed the entrance price reduced to twenty cents.

All this had nothing to do with Dalí, or with Levy, who in December 1939 had filed an "involuntary petition in bankruptcy" formally dissolving D.W.F., Inc. Figurative Surrealism, even as tirelessly promoted by a colorful "Lunatic Narcissus," his backer, and his dealer, was not able to outshine the other attractions of the truly carnivalesque midway.

An Afternoon on the Outskirts
of European History:
Salvador Dalí's Dream of Venus Pavilion

This sort of thing belongs to what the Germans call '*panop-tikum*' and which used to be called Eden Musée, Madame Tussaud's Waxworks, and in less dignified cases, a side room for men only.
— Marsden Hartley[39]

Dalí did preserve Julien Levy's concept of a building that would exemplify Surrealist architecture, while establishing a spectacle to attract public attention. As the Fair's general manager assessed it in the planning stage, "the building has shock value in its design."[40] For other officials it was more schlock than shock. George Smith, Co-Director of Amusements, found it "weird," and took Dalí's later departure as an opportunity to campaign for changing the "very peculiar looking front" before reopening it for a second year.[41] Yet a standard text on the buildings of the period deems it "the most architecturally arresting and certainly the most bizarre attraction in the amusement area."[42] This is especially true of the pavilion at night, as seen in the view Dalí chose to illustrate his autobiography *Secret Life* (1942). Spotlights highlight the looming, partly handlike forms and create ominous shadows on the irregular surface (fig. 3.20).

Dalí opposed the contemporary geometries of the Bauhaus and favored the earlier Art Nouveau or organic architecture, as delineated in his 1933 essay "On the Terrifying and Edible Beauty of Modern Style Architecture." Thus his facade is generically organic, analogous with Gaudí's buildings or the hand-made look of Facteur Cheval's "palace" celebrated in the pages of *Minotaure*. For the interior Dalí insisted on "palpitating" walls and zipper doors, in his flow of unrealizable ideas.[43] *Vogue* called the pavilion a *cabana*, painted pale pink (an attempt at flesh color?) and decorated "with sirens and sea-urchin's spikes."[44] This hints at our perception today, with the development of underwater photography, of a resemblance to coral reefs. Still Dalí conveyed an underwater association to most observers, consonant with the interior. This unified theme also aligned with promoter Billy Rose's advice which so struck Julien Levy: "The theme for this year will be water, WATER. . . . Anything writ in water will succeed."[45] Thus far, Surrealism and commerce were hand-in-hand.

The Venus theme of the pavilion is clichéd, and the original Greek myth was not one of the Surrealists' favorites. Still Dalí had already produced a related Surrealist object, a cast of the Venus de Milo inset with drawers, in 1936. That classical fragment in the Louvre also inspired Man Ray,

3.19 Anonymous, general view of the Dream of Venus pavilion with Sun Valley pavilion
behind, after mid-July 1939. Smithsonian Institution. (Opposite)

3.20 Eric Schaal, *Dali's Dream of Venus,* exterior night view, 1939. Eric Schaal Estate,
courtesy Jan Van der Donk Rare Books.

3.21 Carl Van Vechten, *Dali's Dream of Venus,* entry booth, August 3, 1939.
Museum of the City of New York, Print Archives.

3.22 Anonymous, general view of the Dream of Venus pavilion with Water-Bugs ride
behind, before mid-July 1939. Smithsonian Institution.

Magritte, and others. Interestingly, like the Shocking pink color planned for the pavilion exterior, the classical theme also has close parallels in the world of couture. Schiaparelli had used a Venus figure in her "pagan" (*païenne*) theme fashion show in autumn 1938. The models were garlanded with wreathes and leaves to "look as if they had come out of a Botticelli painting."[46] Of course Dalí had worked for Schiaparelli, most intensively just then, producing his infamous shoe-hat. He was a constant caller at her boutique, and she competed with Chanel to dress Gala. Dalí's design for an illusionistic "torn" chiffon dress had been featured in her February 1938 collection.

As mentioned above, Botticelli's *Venus* already figured in the eye of Woodner Silverman's planned pavilion exterior. Meanwhile, the original Botticelli *Venus* was stirring up its own publicity in Manhattan. Plans were afoot to bring it from the Uffizi to New York for an exhibition. The famous canvas was eventually on view at the Museum of Modern Art's *Italian Masters* exhibiton from January to March 1940. Thus there are several possible sources for Dalí's evocation of the goddess of love and beauty.

To enter Venus's "prenatal" interior, the spectator purchased tickets at a fish-headed booth, with windows for eyes and a toothy mouth. There is some resemblance to an angler fish, which lures with a tentacle extending from atop its head, even as the tentacle appears from the side to be an armless Nike statue. Dalí told one journalist that the booth represented a dolphin. One passed into the entry between red and blue striped and gartered stockings, and beneath a short frilly pink slip, in other words between the spread legs of a giantess. (This enlarges on Breton's idea of gigantic bloomers overhead in one of the small rooms at the Galerie Beaux-Arts.) The Botticelli reproduction aligned directly above implies that the viewer enters the very womb of Venus herself. This is what Dalí spoke of as "the symbolic conception of the maternal complex," a dark safe watery place,[47] in an analogy between amniotic fluid and the deep sea. At the same time, entry through a female figure updates display practice at Coney Island from the turn of the century. The Creation goddess at Dreamland, in particular, was an over-life-size nude who welcomed visitors to enter beneath the arch of her spread wings. As one historian has observed, she "was intentionally and unavoidably a titillating nude first, and only

3.23 Carl Van Vechten, *Dali's Dream of Venus*, facade detail, June 26, 1939.
Museum of the City of New York, Print Archives.

second and superficially an ostensibly religious or allegorical figure."[48] This dual characterization applies as well to Dalí's female forms.

To the left of the entrance, a massive female torso with ludicrously over-sized breasts and irregular patterning on the skin swells out from the niche (fig. 3.23). As a soft material sculpture, it does not appear very Dalían, anticipating instead a 1960s look. The torso is erotically grasped by long dark bands, apparently the eight tentacles of an unseen octopus. Is this the mannequin *Vogue* reported "girdled with eels"? Ivy appears, as well as numerous hair whisks. Higher up is a featureless mermaid, her face and body painted light blue with a spotted pattern, the outstretched arms and forked tail striped red. With the red bunting above, there is a note of patriotic American flag (or French tricolor) hues. She reaches through an adjacent hole in the facade, demonstrating the premeability of the architecture.

Harlem Renaissance maven Carl Van Vechten was a frequent visitor to and documenter of the Fair. A writer, theater and music critic, in 1932 he began a new career as a photographer when he acquired a hand-held Leica camera. Among his portrait subjects are Man Ray and Dalí, taken outside the former's studio in 1934.[49] Van Vechten looked upon the Fair as a documentary challenge: "The Flushing World's Fair was the first project I ever went into very extensively . . . I have a very complete record of that Fair."[50] He visited regularly, sometimes several times a week, so that by August he could announce, "On the whole I've done everything at the Fair, except a couple of tricks on the midway."[51] A lifelong quasi-ethnographic interest in black culture led him to focus on the Seminole Indians and other ethnic group exhibits. And like most, he spent time at the Aquacade water show. But he did snap at least the outside of Dream of Venus, and his photos document changes apparently made by the managers after Dalí departed from the project. His earliest, dated June 22, 1939, only a week after the pavilion opened, shows the oversize Botticelli Venus photomural in the niche over the entry stockings. By August 11, this 25-foot-high Venus had migrated to the flat wall around to the side of the pavilion (fig. 3.24). Her photomural is now inset in a rather ineptly painted seascape, and is visible at quite some distance to strollers on the midway. An earlier photo taken from the Water-Bugs ride shows the long side unadorned, but the scaffold rising which would support the pastiche mural.[52] Because of the low adjacent popcorn concession stand, this side wall re-

Dalí's Dream of Venus Pavilion

3.24 Carl Van Vechten, *Dali's Dream of Venus,* side view of exterior,
August 11, 1939. Museum of the City of New York, Print Archives.

mained visible, as opposed to its opposite side, which was abutted by the higher, chalet-like spires of Sun Valley. And the concessionaires decided to exploit this visibility, no doubt another effort to boost disappointing attendance. Van Vechten's first photo also reveals an inactive barker. There are only two prospective customers stopped to watch the two bathing beauties trying to attract some attention by waving from the lap above the entrance.

A slightly earlier group of photos, taken August 3, show a plainer typographic "Dream of Venus" sign added to the mid-facade; the original Botticelli Venus niche has been occupied by photopanels of two smaller bathing beauties amidst a tentacle (see figs. 3.25, 3.26). Their beaming visages and more realistic style does not fit with Dalí's figures, and are at the opposite pole from his original plan for a fish-headed mermaid. Gardner took over control on or just before July 15,[53] and apparently lost no time in redesigning the pavilion as he pleased. The result is that most visitors that summer saw only a censored and defaced version of the artist's original vision, which was in place only for about a month.

Inside were two 11-meter-long glass tanks, one actually filled 2 meters deep with water, the other dry. In the first and most noted, the viewer is implicitly underwater, recalling Dalí's dressing in a diving suit to present his lecture at the 1936 London Surrealist exhibition. Apart from the theatrics, on that occasion Dalí suggested that his costume was appropriate to descend literally to the "depths" of the unconscious. Here, likewise, he proclaimed that the bottom of the sea could be likened to the unconscious "bottom" of (and the bottoms on) men's minds. Thus the male spectator's id was directed to gender-specific objects of desire: the alluring young Venuses and mermaids, a changing cast of female models who swam the tanks.

The 17 Venuses hired were reported "mostly intelligent," with "a Portuguese" even studying a copy of Levy's recent book on Surrealism.[54] *Time* magazine assured its readers that all were "comely" and most "able surface swimmers" who had been thoroughly coached. "Some were plucked out of Greenwich Village dives, some were recruited from strictly amateur ranks through friends of the management."[55] The accompanying titillating publicity photos show only young women, some topless or wearing mesh tops rendering them effectively bare-breasted.

There is a striking Surrealist forerunner to these mermaids, in the popular soft-core entertainment found in nightclubs and mu-

Dalí's Dream of Venus Pavilion

sic halls. The Coliseum music hall in Montmartre featured such nude "dancers" in a water tank. One such was the young Jacqueline Lamba at the time she met Breton in 1934.[56] The latter, unabashed, took his friends to see her act (was Dalí among them?). And soon after he romanticized her as "ondine" in *L'Amour fou*, complete with a nude photo by Rogi-André.[57]

Photographic Venus costume studies were prominently displayed to the left of the entry. Dalí drew fantastic swimwear in black ink or gouache over the Horst nude photos, apparently unproducible, but so convincing in their trompe l'oeil that the suits seem actual. Both these facade photos actualized the promise of eroticized mermaids within, usually reinforced by the appearance of actual bathing beauty shills in the lap above.

Similarly, the press release unsubtly promised "living mermaids clad in crustacean fins, long gloves and little else." Levy remembered them scantily

3.25 Anonymous, Dream of Venus pavilion, altered front, after mid-July 1939. Smithsonian Institution. (Opposite)

3.26 Anonymous, swimmers in lap, Dream of Venus pavilion, 1939. Smithsonian Institution.

dressed, sunbathing on the pavilion roof and waving to passengers on the nearby elevated IND 8th Avenue subway.[58] Luring patrons, as sirens of the ticket booth, they tried to boost attendance. Once inside, the degree of nudity depended on the prevailing atmosphere and the vice squad. Media "uncoverage" ranged from *Time*'s somewhat surprising bare-breasted diver, in "little Gay Nineties girdles and fish-net stockings," to *Life*'s more modest swimmer. Both had the areas around their eyes made up to suggest an illusory mask. A vintage newsreel shows yet another attire, closer to the Horst photos, as far as can be seen in the rather murky depths. To judge from the group of pavilion-top snapshots by Levy, there was one costume with a heart shape cut out of the chest area, while the other swimmers had ordinary suits. This risqué attraction was one lure that spanned class lines. Lady Duff reported difficulty in prying her Viscount away: "It took a lot of beating. . . . When you get in its dark except for a dimly-lit tank full of organs and rubber corpses of women. Ceaselessly a beautiful living siren, apparently amphibious, dives slowly round her own bubbles, completely naked to the waist. She fondles the turtles and kisses the rubber corpses' mouth and hands. In the dark I could see Duff's face glowing like a Hallowe'en turnip."[59]

3.27 Richard Wurts, *Dali's Dream of Venus,* diver in costume under water,
chained cow, 1939. Museum of the City of New York, Wurts Bros. Collection.
(Opposite)

3.28 *Dali's Dream of Venus,* piano-body mannequin in tank, 1939.
Edward James Foundation.7

Time cleverly labeled the sirens "Lady Godivers," actually a historically apt pun, for the landmark in seminude "entertainment" at the world's fairs was Sally Rand's Lady Godiva act at Chicago in 1933.[60] It prompted many attempts to replicate its success, including rival Amusement Area pavilions at the New York fair such as Norman Bel Geddes's Crystal Lassies, discussed below. Another, John Ringling North's show, ended with a multiplied Lady Godiva ride: sixteen topless equestrians.[61] Many amusements fetishized the female body in various pseudo-representations. Among the most relevant were the Living Magazine Covers, which adapted artistic conventions of framing and sculptural pose purporting to be the quotation marks of "art." Topless models were to hold a statuelike stillness, inside the cutout frame of an imagined "Romantic Life Magazine" of 1949. This feeble attempt to project a decade in the future was placed close enough to the audience that spectators attempted to make the near-nudes laugh.[62] (This form has reemerged in contemporary performance art, as in the living tableaux of Gilbert and George, and others.) Most today would agree with Rydell that such displays were exploitative, although the architect Rem Koolhaas bends over backward to find a liberated aspect in these "representatives of American womanhood—lean, athletic, strong, yet feminine and seductive."[63] In this he echoes *Life*'s rather strained rationale for a suggestive photo spread in their family magazine.

The tasks the "Godivers" performed underwater were likewise stereotypically gendered. They could play milkmaid or secretary, typing on floating keys, or chat on the telephone.[64] Their attractive presence as living mermaids also was juxtaposed to the uncanny, lifelike rubberoid one supplied by Gardner Displays, a contrast pointedly made in Lady Duff's account of the nonawakening kiss of the swimmer. This rubber mannequin is chained to the piano underwater, her body colored white with black stripes to simulate a keyboard. This suggests that her nude skin is to be "played" like an instrument in the fantasy of the (male) viewer. She simultaneously extends the 1938 Surrealist mannequins, prompts the desire of the spectator, and advertises the lifelikeness of the latest commercial rubber mold display techniques. This was the high point of the Gardner collaboration.

The other rubber props included the cow wrapped in bandages, "a man made of rubber ping pong paddles" and the similar chain-link figure (visible to the lower left of the piano mannequin), a fireplace, and "a wavering duster

of rubber telephones" (probably the telephone-eyelashes of the sketch).[65]
Tiny studies for the male figures composed of other objects have emerged
from the collection of the architect Woodner (fig. 3.16). Annotations indicate their size as six feet, and their construction as nonrigid: "they must be
made to sway like seaweeds gently to and fro in the water." The square-
linked man was intended as an homage to the seventeenth-century figures
of Bracelli, but reminded *Vogue*'s reviewer more of Disney's Pinocchio. The
cow produced by the manufacturer looked rather toylike, so Dalí apparently
decided on the Surrealist device of covering or wrapping to render an object enigmatic (fig. 3.27). As he left the face showing, however, this effort
was to no avail. It was probably such feeble results that led Dalí to withdraw
from the pavilion and denounce the manufacturer as a half-hearted collaborator. He probably had hoped for the *frisson* of the steer's hollowed-out car-
cass fitted with a phonograph that was a sensation at the "Bal Onirique" of
January 1935.

A sequence of casual snapshots owned by Julien Levy reveals the
preparatory activity in Dalí's workshop.[66] In one the artist poses as a cruci-
fied figure on the "cross" of the chain-link figure. (Such tableaux recall the
more haunting photos of Dalí by Denise Bellon in 1938.) In others he is
busy making armatures for the individual Arp-like plaster tentacles on the
facade. One even shows Gala helping pull the mesh around these armatures;
in another she is pitching in with sewing. Likewise a knee-deep Edward
James lent a hand in affixing underwater props such as the typewriter and
chain-link man to the floor of the tank. Eric Schaal also documented the
frantic weeks of construction, including a group portrait of Dalí,
Gala, and ten workmen.

Dalí is said to have utilized assistants to paint parts of the background vistas visible through the tanks. The first, oddly Italianate
or De Chirican, was to suggest a ruined submerged Pompeii (although Atlantis would have been more appropriate). It included a
redundant pool, a mausoleum-like structure, and columnar statues
in spatial recession. The second, "a Surrealist vista of limp watches
in a stark landscape" (fig. 3.30), is a monumental variant of the already familiar *Persistence of Memory* (1931). This serves as the contrasting dry background for an elaborately staged scenario inside
the waterless enclosure, which appropriated and combined several
elements of the 1938 *Exposition*. First, mannequins "whose bodies

3.29 Richard Wurts, *Dali's Dream of Venus,* lion-headed mannequin, umbrellas,
painted backdrop, 1939. Museum of the City of New York, Wurts Bros. Collection.

3.30 Dalí painting his mural backdrop, Dream of Venus pavilion, 1939.
Edward James Foundation. (Opposite)

are birdcages or are faced with small glasses." The former copies the imagery of Magritte's painting *Le Thérapeute II* of 1937, shown in the *Exposition*, while the latter reprises the covering of Dalí's *Aphrodisiac Jacket*,
exhibited in 1936. Second, the ceiling, "hung with enough umbrellas to re-
capture the spirit of Munich"; in other words, it carried out Duchamp's original idea for the ceiling of the Galerie Beaux-Arts, which Dalí must have

known. As the quote indicates, however, by this time the Lautréamont umbrella had also become associated with British Prime Minister Neville Chamberlain, who had returned from Munich in September 1938 with a pact of appeasement toward the Nazis. It functioned likewise for Dalí, who included what he identified as Chamberlain's (rolled) umbrella hanging on a line in the painting *The Enigma of Hitler* (1938).[67] An umbrella is also carried by Dalí as a prop throughout a sequence of publicity photographs by Eric Schaal.[68] Third, the Surrealist object, such as the plaster re-creation of Domínguez's embodied gramophone to the left, or the round diving helmet from Dalí's London lecture. Here these flotsam of prior shows are washed up on the "Beach of Gala Salvador."

Both Schaal's and Richard Wurts's contemporary photographs record this "Beach" tableau as featuring an over-life-sized, glass-bodied mannequin with arms outstretched and a tiger's head, dubbed "The Aphrodisiac Vampire" (fig. 3.29). Just above are the downward points of numerous open, and two closed, umbrellas. The oversized mannequin is placed as if in the foreground of the enlarged backdrop variant of *Persistence of Memory*, four panels totaling 240 by 480 centimeters. If the broad areas of the background were laid in by assistants, Dalí seems to have added his typical motifs such as the burning giraffes visible at the right. Several "action" photos show him painting in the details of the blocked-in old man with drawers (fig. 3.30). This "Beach" was viewed through a glass window set in wood paneling, clearly analogized to the Fifth Avenue department store displays Dalí had done.

Just inside the vitrine was the foot of the bright red cover of the "Ardent Couch." This 36-foot bed, with a mattress of apparently glowing coals, is covered in red and white satin, ivy, and foliage. It reprises the beds amidst brushwood of the 1938 show, which had already been re-presented in Dalí's Bonwit's "Day" vitrine display. The bed supported the dreaming Venus, as well as luxury edibles: lobsters and champagne. An accompanying sound track identified it as "a bed eternally long, [for] dreaming the longest dreams ever dreamed, without beginning and without end."[69] The oval cutout in the plush red headboard allows a glimpse of the adjacent wet tank. Thus the underwater "unconscious" is figured as a dream in a cartoonlike bubble over Venus's head. Next to her hangs an oversized "aphrodisiac telephone" covered with liqueur glasses, like those at the hand of Dalí's mannequin at the

3.31 David E. Scherman, Dalí dry-tank tableau, sleeping Venus, 1939.

Galerie Beaux-Arts. She is also accompanied by "her bird," the dove.[70] (The word in French, *colombe*, puns on the explorer Columbus, who later appears, as discussed below.)

Sometimes other resting swimmers appeared in costume, one "helmeted with a hood of flowers." This rose-headed woman from Dalí's paintings had already been enacted by Sheila Legge in Trafalgar Square. A hugely elongated bed as banquet table, fusing metaphors of the oral and genital, had been broached the previous year in Dalí's sketch for a scenario for a Marx Brothers film.[71] There the attendant diners were rendered; here they are implicitly the (male) spectators who "feast" with their eyes. If the dreamer opened her eyes, she faced the uncomfortably desiring gaze of the spectators, multiplied by the oval mirrors encircling her. Thus one "liquid lady," Betty Kuzmeck, expressed her preference for the more arduous wet tank, where the divers couldn't see the audience, to the dry tank's male stares "like hungry wolves" which made her tense.[72] This despite the fact that the "Ardent Couch" amounted to a break from swimming and holding one's breath underwater.

3.32 Eric Schaal, *Dali's Dream of Venus,* interior, Gala sewing Columbus mannequin, 1939. Eric Schaal Estate, courtesy Jan Van der Donk Rare Books.

3.33 Dalí and Gala with taxi of Columbus, Dream of Venus pavilion, 1939.
Edward James Foundation.

Beyond the glass tanks were other sights unrelated to Venus, though as there are only sketchy journalistic accounts, it is difficult to reconstruct the exact layout. The relatively long and narrow shape of the lot probably dictated a fairly linear gamut. Schaal's photograph of Gala sewing is an important document (fig. 3.32). To the left edge is the face-lamp at the end of the vitrine "Beach of Gala Salvador." To the right is a perpendicular barrier, behind which we glimpse the front of the ivy-strewn taxi. This is the reprise of the highly regarded *Rainy Taxi* from the Galerie Beaux-Arts courtyard. Dalí's *New Yorker* profile began with this as an inspiration that came to him one day at Levy's gallery. Instead of a soaked female rider, however, Dalí proposed for his potentially civic-minded Fair audience the more chaste and historical personage of Christopher Columbus as the passenger, bearing a sign "I Return." He is represented by the hermaphroditic mannequin at Gala's feet, with the head of a bearded man and the torso of a woman. The 300 Burgundy snails were also to encore. The sponsor reportedly balked at the $150 estimate for the roof piping, but eventually capitulated, so that Columbus would be continually sprayed with interior rain, as had been done in Paris.[73] The success of the first *Rainy Taxi* had been very much on the artist's mind, as Levy recalled. Dalí already wanted a replica hoisted into the gallery for his spring show. The Fair site became a more expeditious alternative, though the outcome was disappointing: Columbus's reconfigured V8 Cadillac was little match for the mermaids; indeed, it was seen as incomprehensible.[74] One of the better tableau photos (fig. 3.33) strikingly has Dalí seated on the taxi roof, umbrella in hand, pointing (as Columbus did inside). The mermaid theme is echoed in the life-sized fishtail projecting through the front windshield. Suggestively, the devouring shark-toothed driver is replaced by the formidable Gala, in what some would call type casting. A quaint echo of old New York: the taxi rates posted on the door, twenty cents for the first quarter-mile, and a nickel for each additional one.

In his "Declaration," Dalí explicated the taxi scene at length as an improbable "nightmare of the American Venus," an enigma that he himself did not fully grasp: "Why, with his index finger, does he point toward Europe? ... Why is a somnambulistic Spanish girl attached to the steering wheel of his deluxe Cadillac with golden chains? Here are still more impenetrable Dalian mysteries, heavy with obscure and far reaching significance."[75] At this moment it was obvious enough to posit some relation between uneasy America and Europe, as the latter moved into war. After ambiguous prediction comes showmanship: Dalí concluded his "Declaration" by linking himself and Columbus as Catalans, and as explorers of new (American) worlds. Perhaps, too, both were motivated by the riches they expected to discover.

Clearly the 1938 Surrealist show was Dalí's frame of reference for this display. He even appropriated André Breton's idea of a sculptural "exquisite corpse" incorporating furniture. Described as "head and neck a curved umbrella handle, its chest a wooden chest, its thighs made of saucepans, its curved piano legs made of chocolate,"[76] Dalí's sculpture merely transposes into three dimensions the illustration for "Cadavre exquis" in the *Dictionnaire abrégé*. Such pastiche highlights of the 1938 *Exposition Internationale* recall Levy's original overview proposal, yet, appearing unattributed, they moreover suggest Dalí forwarding *himself* as Surrealism. Such grandstanding would not have gone over well in Paris, and may have contributed to his seemingly inevitable final excommunication from the Surrealist group just at this time.[77] Nonetheless, by all accounts the "Lady Godivers" stole the show, although they reinforce a gender-biased, figurative basis for Surrealism. Dalí was unable to move beyond recapitulating this bias. Like the Beaux-Arts mannequins come to life, these Galateas embodied Levy's vision of a literally watered-down, popular-culturized "surrealism" for the American audience. This is the sense of the prediction that the divers, "seen at close range and a trifle water-magnified, should win more converts to surrealism than a dozen high-brow exhibitions."[78]

The erotics of the "liquid ladies" is less astonishing if we consider context: where they were displayed at the Fair. As Levy recalled, "the girls . . . [were] usually allowed to be semi-nude because our location, the Midway at the Fair, was intended to be sexy."[79] This amusement zone, literally on the margins of Flushing Meadows, occupied a distinct, separate space, thematically disorganized, less didactic, with a perceived mandate for a degree of licentiousness. Levy's words are borne out by rival pavilions, such as Norman Bel Geddes's Crystal Lassies, a self-avowed "glorified peep show." *Time* opined that "for peepshows, in spite of police threats, [the area] contains more public nudity than any place outside of Bali."[80] For American society as a whole in 1939, it seemed, "soft-core pornography is arguably more acceptable than it is today. In fact pornography was a mainstay of the World's Fair. The Amusement Area was loaded with it, and some of the fair's best talents devoted themselves earnestly to the very finest in girlie shows."[81]

Indeed, the very words "Amusement Area" could be seen as an innuendo of sexual signification, as made clear by the eponymous phrase covering the crotch of Bel Geddes's Crystal Lassies. These dancers became the target of a Brooklyn minister as "among the places in the Amusement area which I had reason to believe were violating the laws of common decency and proving a menace to morals."[82] Debates over morality in public art are not unique to our own era.

Before the Fair opened there were conflicting signals from officials. Entertainers "couldn't be sure what size of fig-leaf would pass muster."[83] The first arrests came in June, of two contestants at a "Miss Nude of 1939" in the Cuban Village, along with the promoters. For the sensational trial, Mayor LaGuardia took the unusual step of acting as magistrate. It was widely reported that he lectured the Miss Nudes, then suspended sentences. After that publicity, all such shows did increased business and even garnered the praise of an Indian maharaja who made it his mission to visit every one.[84] Despite protests, things got even raunchier during the second year of the Fair. What we look back on as a more prudish age was perhaps not so in some ways, though it certainly lacked the consciousness and terminology of current debates on pornography. Few if any seemed to realize that such "techno-porn extravaganzas" routinely "targeted women's bodies as commodities to be purchased and as sites for 'the pursuit of happiness.'"[85] At the time, an ostensibly celebratory rhetorical tone was more typical, as one newspaper waxed: "the female form divine is represented in almost every concession."[86]

The Amusement Area was situated east of the main Fair area, with its national and corporate pavilions, and was separated from them by a major roadway, Empire State Boulevard. At 270 acres its total area was larger than the entire 1937 Paris exposition, and it is often presented as one of the most popular parts of the Fair. Yet two of three repeat visitors had never or only once visited it. Typically, it is listed last in guidebooks and maps and was presented by the organizers as secondary, merely a respite from the serious "real" Fair. Yet "however highminded the aims of the Fair Corporation . . . the timeless and universal aura of carnie and Coney were all-pervasive."[87] Albeit "timeless," the specific forms of these appeals are quite revealing of their era. They included typical carnival games, like Guess Your Weight, and updated ones, such as Water-Bugs, gas-powered bumper craft in a large pool. This "dodge 'em" was the western neighbor of Dream of Venus. Also nearby was Children's World, the other space where fantastic architecture, along with miniaturized sphinxes and towers of Pisa, was sanctioned. Here small Gimbel's Flyer trains transported children through a mélange of building styles on an imaginary voyage around the world.

Even Dalí's overlay of a fine art veneer to the mode of popular entertainment had its parallels in other pavilions. Bel Geddes's Crystal Lassies created multiple points of view seen simultaneously, fragmented images of a shimmering dancer that shuffled illusion and reality: all attributes of the popularized definition of Cubism. In fact a Cubist offshoot—the "Vortographs" by Alvin Langdon Coburn, quasi-abstract photographs done in 1917—are a precise precedent for the use of mirrors to multiply and refract images. Yet Coburn's photos tend to generalize and abstract form, while the Crystal Lassies were meant to provide legible access for the desiring gaze from all sides and points of view. As the *Nation* detailed, "One stands on a platform just outside a huge crystal polygon while nude dancers, deliriously multiplied by reflection, dance on the mirrored floor. The girls are young and pretty, one of them wears absolutely nothing except one gardenia." Spectators are overheard retailing the fine art justification of the nude: "Well, it's art. You see the same thing in art, don't you?"[88] As Rydell points out, the fantasies of the predominantly male viewers, segregated in

3.34 Norman Bel Geddes, Crystal Lassies, New York World's Fair, 1939.
Smithsonian Institution. (Opposite)

3.35 Skating show, Sun Valley, New York World's Fair, 1939.

individualized viewing booths, were encouraged. Less ambitiously, the mirrors around Dalí's "Bed of Venus" nonetheless functioned similarly. Closer still, though minus the nudity, would have been Levy's idea for "kaleidoscope" booths, suggesting the pervasiveness of such popular offshoots of Cubist-inspired multiplied vision.

On the same day that he photographed details of the erotically sculpted mermaids on Dalí's facade, Carl Van Vechten also shot the nearby alluring The Ice Girls. Here was Billy Rose's theme of water again, only in frozen form. Swimsuited, "self-hypnotized" young women were suspended in a large, 1,400-pound block of it, for six to eight minutes, until they signaled for release. The "erotic frigidaire" is literalized in this display. The models seem comparable to the "liquid ladies"; perhaps they were only non-swimmers.

Cold also was the appeal of Sun Valley, the eastern neighbor of Venus, and one of the biggest of all the amusements. As such it charged forty cents for admission, as opposed to the quarter for Venus and most other exhibits. Its winter wonderland's spires and timbered walls were highly noticeable (fig. 3.19), as were its two entrances flanking a rustic Rheingold Inn, situated at the north end of a pedestrian street. Like Dream of Venus, it promoted a fantasy image through imaginative architecture, here an Alpine ski lodge effect. Its themes were also announced by an exterior figure, in this case a snowman. Inside were twelve daily ice skating performances, a toboggan run, and ski jump shows. It became a landmark, as the Dream of Venus's own opening invitation acknowledges, describing its location as "north of Sun Valley."

Across the street the Crystal Palace's "Museum of Changing American Taste" offered a permeable veil of history, rather than temperature. It also evoked the trappings of the art museum and its array of changing styles, spectacularized in "reenactments of famous girls in fair history." One Stella, "the breathing painting," imitated artwork itself, and a simulacrum of Sally Rand reerected her 1933 Chicago daring fan dance. "As a climax it presents a new attraction in Rosita Royce, who performs clad in a fluttering covey of doves."[89] Not exactly "new," however, for Rosita, a "former bubble dancer," had already performed at the Chicago and San Diego fairs. One reporter enjoyed her finale, "which ends in purple shadows and a lightning-quick strip," while another wondered what would happen if birdseed was scattered. Nothing, quipped Ms. Royce, "these birds are serious about their careers."[90]

The *New Yorker* sounded a more cynical note, but still paid lip service to the "Museum's" aura of history: "a revue . . . of the peepshow aspects of other fairs down through the ages."[91] What this display really had to do with the concept of "Museum" is never articulated.

Similarly, the small "Artist's studio" deployed the aura of art to justify nudity, like the Living Magazine Covers previously mentioned. In the "studio" the audience could peer over the artist's shoulder as he (of course) painted from a nude female model, only partly draped. Even more daring were those Covers, "beautiful girls in person," clad primarily in their pseudo-media presence and enframed in a mock magazine border. One of the types bore a close iconographic relation to Dalí's theme. This so-called "Venus of Venice" rose up on a fabric printed with shellfish (fig. 3.36). She was masked as if at a Carnival, yet bare-breasted, and enframed within an octagonal cutout beauty magazine "cover." Jack Sheridan's eight-minute show of these tableaux was prominently located near the giant National Cash Register, and adolescent boys sometimes wandered in and received an initiation remembered years later.[92] All these pretended to skirt a fine line between the naked and nude, essentially providing the former to the male gaze, rationalized with a veneer of the "artistic" license of the latter. Living Magazine Covers plainly expressed this duality on the exterior, with its panels of "artists models" strategically covered by canvases. The largest panel showed a palette on an easel and a canvas painted only with the words "Models Posing," an inadvertent popular art forerunner of 1960s word pictures.

Likewise Niles T. Granlund's Congress of Beauty, or what *Life* more frankly called "45 undressed show girls," performed in a condensed musical. In between shows the models could be seen "lying on the damp ground with practically nothing on." The *New Yorker* summarized it as "NTG's show of girls in a tent and girls in a garden, all fairly naked."

Next to these, Billy Rose's "slick, streamlined revue" was relatively egalitarian, with both Aquabelles and Aquabeaux, and considerably less prurient. There were identifiable headliners, male and female: 1932 Olympic backstroke champion (and Rose's fiancée) Eleanor Holm along with MGM *Tarzan* star Johnny Weissmuller. There were also dozens of synchronized swimmers and divers as well as singers and dancers, a cast of 350, in a 300-foot pool. Not only great location, and a 10,000-seat amphitheater, but

also gender egalitarianism perhaps contributed to the top gross of over $4.3 million in the two seasons of the Fair, while the other shows were projected to and mostly patronized by men only. Aquacade was widely reported as the hit revue to see, drawing attentions as diverse as the theatrically and musically knowledgeable Carl Van Vechten, who photographed it extensively, more than most of his subjects, and the 12-year-old Robert Rosenblum, who snuck into a distant seat and was mesmerized by its Busby Berkeley-like choreography.[93] These geometric patternings, as well as the changing costumes and backdrops, distinguished the Aquacade's style from the meandering, free-form "liquid ladies" of the more modest Dream of Venus.

3.36 Living Magazine Covers: "Venus of Venice,"
New York World's Fair, 1939. Smithsonian Institution.

While the Dream of Venus was frequently discussed in the popular press, almost all of the art magazines gave it a wide berth, focusing only on the official art exhibits on the main Fair grounds. Only the *Art Digest* covered it, and rather blithely, as a Freudian version of "what Broadway calls a 'girl show'." Yet among the non-art press its reception was notably good. Its true artistic core was perceived as unique, perhaps strange, yet distinct from the pseudo-artistic airs of its neighbors mentioned above. Though the *New Yorker* included Dream of Venus in the "Hoopla and Honky Tonk" section, it was distinguished in the listing on the strength of Dalí's vision. Many writers, jaded by the conventional appeals of the Crystal Palace or Congress of Beauty, rated Dream of Venus quite highly, if only for its novelty and originality.

There was a gap, however, between the critics' enthusiasm and "the people" that Dalí hoped to attract, though direct accounts of the latter are sparse. Fleur Cowles, probably an eyewitness, later reported incomprehension before the Columbus taxi. Likewise Clifford Orr was bemused at "the bewilderment of cash customers in Dalí's crazy girl show. They don't know whether to be angry, amused, or excited. They *do* know they're not bored."[94]

Similarly, there was little cognizance of Dalí among artists, many of whom were represented elsewhere at the Fair in large group expositions. The young Jimmy Ernst only recalled it as "the sad and sleezy Dali sideshow of bare breasted mermaids in a giant fish tank."[95] He perhaps parallels his father's abhorrence of Dalí's politics. Yet the realist Reginald Marsh proved to be a more sympathetic viewer, to judge from his watercolor of the same tank (fig. 3.37). It is packed with two mesh-covered divers and half a dozen spectators filing in front of the glass. Marsh suggests that the average spectator is the middle-aged male, just as in his numerous depictions of burlesque and strip shows. The one exception is the well-dressed young blonde woman who uniquely makes eye contact with the viewer. She seems to be of a similar age to the mermaids, and invites comparison between her station and theirs. Is she one of them off work? Or would she want to be? It remains ambiguous. Marsh is also interested in the rubber piano-mannequin and its contrast with the flesh-and-blood "Godivers." He depicts a fair amount of the detail of Dalí's painted undersea backdrop. He also cultivates a certain spatial ambiguity, with the active swimmer especially looming closer than we would expect. Despite having no

3.37 Reginald Marsh, *Dali's Dream of Venus,* tank, 1939. Pencil and watercolor.

sympathy for Surrealism, Marsh otherwise was an ideal viewer for Dream of Venus, given his longstanding interest in women, bathers, and swimmers, not to mention "Hoopla and Honky Tonk" shows. His interest is an index of the extent to which true Surrealism gives way to popular entertainment in the United States.

The Dream of Venus remains one of the rare examples of Surrealist architecture, although of a temporary nature and little more than a facade. Like most of the buildings, it was razed after the Fair closed at the end of 1940. Still it has always rated a mention in architectural surveys of the Fair, and of the period. One standard source appraised it as "the most architecturally arresting and certainly the most bizarre attraction in the amusement area." Yet the interior did not fare as well. "In spite of the sinister quality of Dali's obsessive pictorialization of eros and thanatos, the pavilion seemed oddly banal."[96]

Despite the conflicts attending its rushed construction and compromised realization, the pavilion in its first month was the premiere Surrealist environment in the United States. As such, it was an important beachhead for the experiments of the early 1940s, most notably Peggy Guggenheim's Art of This Century Surrealist gallery, as well as Marcel Duchamp's installation for *First Papers of Surrealism.*

Aftermath: Dalí in Hollywood (1941)

Dalí would return to the United States during World War II, but, unwelcome among the Surrealists in exile around New York, he opted for the west coast. He again courted the Hollywood community with portraits, film projects, and something new, a theatricalized benefit evening. His "Night in a Surrealist Forest" was held at the Del Monte Lodge Hotel, at exclusive Pebble Beach, on September 2, 1941, as a party for "refugee artists" with a costumed Dalí and Gala presiding. Many of the props he ordered suggest an expanded, outdoor version of the 1938 *Exposition Internationale*. As at the World's Fair, Dalí had no qualms about freely appropriating highlights of previous Surrealist installations. Most obviously, 24 mannequins and 5,000 burlap sacks were requisitioned, to top the previous numbers. The mannequins, with added animal heads recalling the first version of Dalí's 1938 mannequin, as well as the "Aphrodisiac Vampire" at *Dream of Venus*, stood interspersed at every fourth place at the dining table. The outdoor setting evoked a kind of *Midsummer Night's Dream*, of which in fact a film had recently been made. The film studio provided the animal props. Again it was a department store (I. Magnin) that loaned the mannequins. Rather amusingly, since coal sacks were not at all prevalent in sunny southern California, Spreckels Sugar of San Francisco came up with 5,000 empty hundred-pound sugar bags, which were stuffed with newspaper, thus outdoing Duchamp's 1,200. (Mrs. Spreckels soon became the sitter for one of Dalí's wartime society portraits.) They were supposed "to give a depressed feeling," but clearly did not.[97] Indeed, the shift from irritating coal dust to sweet sugar encapsulates the shift of mood from menacing or disconcerting to a saccharine spectacle of consumption.

Other elements are cobbled in, such as the nude "Sleeping Beauty" in an elongated bed with gardenias, a Hollywood rerun already premiered in Venus's dry tank at the World's Fair. The wrecked Chevrolet, photographed with a recumbent nude model inside and garlanded with ivy, amounts to a smashed-up *Rainy Taxi*. "In America people are always in automobile accidents," Dalí opined.[98] (He thus managed to anticipate Warhol's *Car Crash* paintings of 1962–1963.) With Gala in the banquet table/bed, there is a foretaste of Meret Oppenheim's concept for the banquet table at the 1959 *Eros* Surrealist exhibition, and its confluence of dining and oral eroticism.

Dalí's "Night" was a sensation, drawing over a thousand guests, including New York socialites and Hollywood stars such as Bob Hope, Bing Crosby, and Ginger Rogers. Nonetheless it lost money and, once expenses were paid, the only "refugee artist" aided was Dalí. In terms of exhibition history, it could be that Breton and Duchamp's subsequent plan for a benefit show was also a riposte to this more frivolous display of a Hollywoodized Surrealism.

Dalí, just then banished by Breton as "Avida Dollars,"[99] was for insiders hardly an unexpected exclusion from Breton and Duchamp's *First Papers* exhibition. It would, however, have been an unanticipated omission for the general American public, who equated him with Surrealism. Thus Dalí cast a shadow over the New York proceedings, in part because he had already organized this earlier benefit.

3.38 UPI photo, view of Dalí's "Surrealist Forest," Del Monte Lodge Hotel, Pebble Beach,
California, September 4, 1941. Corbis/Bettman-UPI.

The New World: First Papers of Surrealism (1942)

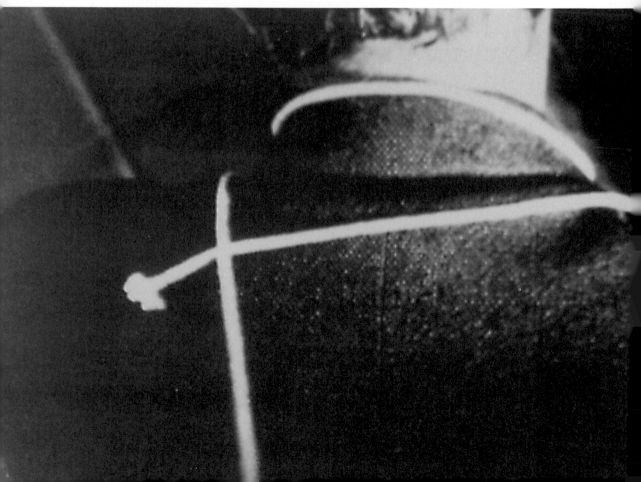

Whitlaw Reid Mansion:
The Architectural Context

Nine of the artists from the 1938 *Exposition Interna-tionale* found themselves in exile in and around New York after the German occupation of France. They formed the core group of the exhibition *First Papers of Surrealism* in 1942, named after the legal papers filed in a citizenship application. The artists thus underlined their émigré status, even as they opened the possibility of a sequel. Their show was staged at the premises of a war relief agency, the Coordinating Council of French Relief Societies, housed in the former Whitlaw Reid mansion at 451 Madison Avenue. Unlike the Galerie Beaux-Arts in 1938, the Reid mansion had been designed as a private home and not a space for exhibiting art. It was also something of a historic landmark, an early building produced by the offices of McKim, Mead and White. It was one of six houses commissioned by Henry Villard in April 1882 for a large lot on Madison Avenue between 50th and 51st streets. The Villard houses, built on Italianate models, were grouped around a central courtyard. The largest, the south wing of the group, was sold to Mrs. Mills Reid in November 1886 for $350,000. The Reids completed many of the interiors, commissioning John LaFarge, among others, for wall paintings. There were coffered ceilings, elaborate paneling, and gilding (the music room became known as the Gold Room). As befitted Whitlaw Reid's position as publisher of the New York *Tribune* and later ambassador to England, rooms were enlarged for the library and for entertaining. Following Mrs. Reid's death in 1931, the house was closed, and its furnishings were auctioned in 1935. By this time the residence was an anachronism in midtown Manhattan.[1]

When founded in 1941, the Coordinating Council of French Relief Societies united 15 different French aid societies and was headquartered at 4 West 58th Street. By the spring of 1942, it had arranged to move to the empty residence, thanks to the generosity of Mr. Ogden Reid. The music room on the first floor was "usually piled to the gold stucco ceiling with packing cases." The third floor had administrative and publicity offices. The second-floor drawing room was baptized the "Salle des Fêtes," and was used for lectures, concerts, and exhibitions. In May 1942 it was the site of weekly concerts conducted by Nadia Boulanger. From June 15 to September 15 it held Malvina Hoffman's sculpture exhibition *Men of the World*, which was quite popular. It drew 1,500 visitors in its first week, with a 25-cent admission charge and a percentage of the sales benefiting the Council. Her exhibit also involved an installation of sorts, fashioning "a garden setting in the high-ceiling rooms."[2] This was followed by Jean Pagès's war sketches made at the front, immediately preceding *First Papers*. The Surrealists were fol-

4.1 Whitlaw Reid Mansion, exterior, 451 Madison Avenue at 50th Street, New York.

Whitlaw Reid Mansion: The Architectural Context

lowed by an exhibition of Chinese art. Thus the space had a very
varied and pragmatic use. Elsewhere in the mansion one found
French cooking classes and a monthly series of luncheon lectures,
often by recent returnees reporting on the situation in France.
Speakers were quite well known and included Kay Boyle, Antoine
de Saint-Exupéry, and Janet Flanner. During the Surrealist show, in
November, a bookshop opened with 400 volumes. One wonders
whether Breton had any hand in instigating this, or at least whether
any Surrealist titles were stocked. From the pages of the Council's
Bulletin it is clear that, along with commendable relief efforts, the
organization also played a purely social role in the French exile
community.[3]

An esteemed critic, Henry McBride, imagined the Reid family rolling
in their graves at the Surrealist exhibition, while their guest, the late Duke
of Connaught, voiced the objections of the "other outraged shades."
McBride was both engaged and distracted by the show's surroundings.
"This installation and the strangeness of the house itself, packed as it is with
war material, far outrun the pictures of surrealism. The mansion, one of few
remaining palaces of the capitalistic period, should be preserved in its en-
tirety for a posterity which certainly would not believe it from a mere description."[4] Here he voiced what many others only intuited from the
juxtaposition of Surrealism and its incongruously ornate setting, along the
same lines as at Galerie Beaux-Arts yet even more so.

As a space Breton termed it not very desirable. Yet as a location it was
quite convenient, on Madison at the corner of 50th Street, near the Museum
of Modern Art and that of Non-Objective Painting as well as the galleries of
57th Street. It was also not far from where Breton did his radio work, and
from where he would take an apartment on West 56th Street following his
separation from Jacqueline that October.[5]

The second-floor *salle* of the exhibition is not overly large, a continuous
rectangular space twice as long as wide, about 25 by 50 feet. (The widely
published John Schiff installation photos are taken from the center, facing
north and south, and exaggerate the apparent length.) The end walls had
two windows each, which were covered, as were the three on the west side
(overlooking Madison Avenue). A chandelier hung at either end, and there
was extensive wood paneling. Most of the ceiling was covered by a large, Ro-
coco-style painting that Breton identified as scenes of love.

4.2 Max Ernst, *Surrealism* (1942), painted announcement for *First Papers of Surrealism.*
Courtesy Sotheby's, New York.

Two smaller rooms to the east abutted the ends of the drawing room (the entry from the hall being in the center). These small rooms seem to have been part of the exhibition also, as Edward Alden Jewell spoke of it as installed in "Reid's drawing room and in adjacent rooms of his Florentine palazzo."[6] These rooms were apparently not strung with twine in Duchamp's installation; thus Schiff did not make documentary photos of them, nor have any others come to light. One critic clearly distinguished between "string woven all through one exhibition room" whereas "in the next room hung early canvases by deChirico."[7]

To an extent not yet recognized, the Surrealists participated in both the social and relief efforts of the Coordinating Council. They sent out red-and-blue-lined tricolor postcards, announcing a $1.10 admission charge for the preview Wednesday evening, October 14, and a 50-cent fee during the following weeks, the money going to the Council. They prepared an innovative, illustrated catalogue to be sold. Max Ernst painted an imaginative announcement, including the dates (October 15–November 7) and the hours (Monday-Friday, 11–5:30, Saturday 2–5:30).[8] One source also mentions a benefit auction on opening night, though, if it took place, it was so small as to elude other accounts. More significantly, the Surrealists contributed drawings to the Council's 1943 fundraising calendar, *France in America*, which included about thirty pages from different types of writers and artists. Seligmann pulled a striking etching on yellow paper, and drawings by Dalí, Masson, and Tanguy were reproduced, along with others of more conservative artists. Surprisingly, even Duchamp weighed in with a bachelor drawing of 1913. The ad section included one for Schiaparelli's perfume line. The contributions for this calendar were solicited around July and August of 1942, in other words just around the time the exhibition planning was under way. Wisely the Surrealists ingratiated themselves with the Council. A final token of collaboration came at the inauguration of *First Papers*. There, Breton inscribed the Council's special "Golden Book for France." Its large parchment pages were also "illuminated" by Matta.[9]

Thus on several fronts the Surrealists cooperated with their hosts, for the benefit of French prisoners and children, presumably as a quid pro quo for the use of the site. Yet in some quarters this well-meaning effort was taken as suspect collaboration with the puppet Vichy government.

The Coordinating Council of French Relief Societies's humanitarian purpose was to raise money and supplies for French prisoners and for the adoption of French children. It also proclaimed itself a "center for all that French culture has contributed to our civilization."[10] After moving from 4 West 58th Street to the Reid mansion in early 1942, the organization had more space for events, and formed a committee for programming. The Surrealists' group exhibition proposal was brokered by the couturier Elsa Schiaparelli, already well known to them from their fashion connection of the 1930s, especially as a collaborator with Dalí. Schiaparelli did not have any official position within the agency, but met with the chair of its Prisoners committee, Anne Morgan, and hatched a plan to use the empty rooms "to centralize French culture and art as represented in America."[11] The previous solo shows of Jean Pagès and Malvina Hoffman were figurative and non-Surrealist. Thus the Surrealists, as at the Galerie Beaux-Arts, were invading a gilded interior not associated with them. In this case it was not even an art space but one pressed into service for a war relief agency.

The Coordinating Council projected itself as a charitable organization and avoided any overt political stance, as opposed to the France Forever organization. The latter was openly Gaullist and pro-resistance in its publications. As was common at the time, France Forever also organized benefit exhibitions, opening a Cézanne show that same fall, on November 18. It was held at the Paul Rosenberg Gallery, mustering an impressive roster of political sponsors beginning with Eleanor Roosevelt and including the governor and the mayor. Proceeds from the 50-cent admission were split between the organization and the "Fighting French Relief Committee." By contrast, the Coordinating Council's Anne Morgan was known as strongly pro-Pétain, as Schiaparelli recalled. The couturier herself was not above suspicion, with her Place Vendôme shop whispered to be catering to German officers.

Peggy Guggenheim recalled that "Schiap" approached her about organizing a benefit show. Jimmy Ernst remembered her coming to their house "to ask for Peggy's support in organizing a charity exhibition."[12] The latter, busy with her own plans for opening a gallery, connected Schiaparelli with Breton, whom she was supporting with a monthly stipend.[13] Breton had formerly opposed Surrealism's alliance with fashion, but in exile he had to compromise his anti-commercialism, perhaps in relation to his stipend. And perhaps he saw this as an opportunity to rebond the scattered group.

Yet the group was no longer as it had been. Former poet-collaborators Eluard and Hugnet, now estranged from Breton, had both remained in occupied France, as well as some of the artists who sided with Eluard. It was not until after the delayed landing of Marcel Duchamp in New York, the last of the Parisian artists to arrive in exile here, that the collaboration of 1938 could to a degree be revived in a new Surrealist manifestation. After delays in obtaining a visa, and his own apparent hesitations, Duchamp's arrival in June 1942 would soon lead to the realization of his earlier call for Breton to find him "an artistic mission in New York."[14] Indeed, Schiaparelli recalled that it was Duchamp (and not Breton) whom she approached in the first place to organize a show "completely modern and *d'avant garde*."[15] Contacts from his previous years in Manhattan certainly played a major role in getting this project off the ground, as signaled by the listing of his old supporters like Arensberg and Dreier in the catalogue with Schiaparelli and others among the eighteen sponsoring patrons. Duchamp's first hosts upon his arrival, Mr. and Mrs. Robert Allerton Parker, are also among them. Perhaps both the Guggenheim and Schiaparelli recollections are accurate; Duchamp did not expand on its origins, writing only "I was busy with a surrealist show with Schiaparelli and Breton."[16]

"Breton was very happy to see me," Duchamp recalled, "and so we started no later than August [on] a Surrealist show for charity."[17] His arrival was also widely noted in the press. Duchamp gave interviews to *Time* and the *New Yorker* in which he adopted a rather cavalier attitude, considering that the door of emigration from Vichy closed just after his departure. The *New Yorker* reported, "He has been living here in town for the past four months, after a highly uneventful escape from Occupied France, and has just helped to stage the surrealist show in the former Whitelaw Reid house." He elaborated to the *Time* reporter: "Last May he crossed in a Portuguese refugee ship. . . . 'The best crossing I ever had,' he told us. 'It was like a cruise.'"[18] Upon reading such breezy accounts, Walter Arensberg, who had labored to arrange and had paid for Duchamp's visa, took offense.

Apart from Duchamp disembarking on the 25th, June 1942 was also noteworthy for the publication of the first issue of the Surrealist magazine *VVV,* including Breton's "Prolegomena to a Third Manifesto of Surrealism, or else." On the eve of publication, Matta pronounced it "André at full strength."[19] After a long winter of planning and disputing, its appearance must have seemed an achievement. Although David Hare was listed as the editor, he acknowledged his role as a "front," being a U.S. citizen, while Breton decided on most of the contents. Hare felt that Breton's motivation included his own sense of history.[20] Surrealism usually had had its house organ, thus "Breton knew from long experience the important role a publication could play in holding together a group and attracting new adherents."[21] He announced as early as January that he was taking the review in hand and that, remarkably, it would not be exclusively Surrealist but open to committed intellectuals, including Americans such as Kiesler, Meyer Shapiro, and Sidney Janis.[22] In this aspect the review prefigured the wider net that would be cast for American artists to be included in *First Papers.*

According to one eyewitness, the publication of *VVV* "galvanized their energies," attracted new adherents, and resolved them to "demonstrate their powers" in a group exhibition.[23] Another condition was clearly the presence of enough Surrealists in America for a sufficient period of time to have created new works, together with the absence of any imminent prospect of returning to Paris. While

First Papers of Surrealism

most of the Surrealists emigrated in 1941, Duchamp's arrival was the needed catalyst. The prospect of his being the judicious co-organizer must have allayed the reservations of many who felt ambivalent about the iron-willed Breton, as well as stimulated the hope for another dramatic mise-en-scène as in 1938. This is the thrust of Masson's words, "unanimously we called on Marcel Duchamp."[24] Breton for his part was willing to overlook Duchamp's (and Ernst's) earlier gravitation toward Hugnet and the *Usage de la Parole* group, plus their support of the banished Eluard.[25] Or perhaps not completely. For upon their first meeting in New York, Breton interjected his criticism of Eluard, whereupon Ernst angrily argued with him.[26] With Duchamp that summer, however, Breton could not contain his possessive glee: "Duchamp is in New York. That is the most beautiful acquisition we have had."[27]

During the summer of 1942, Joseph Cornell phoned Peggy Guggenheim but found it "delightful and strange" that Marcel Duchamp unexpectedly answered the telephone. As a result of their "chance" encounter, Cornell noted, "he is coming out Friday which should give a much needed inspiration to get some of the objects completed."[28] Did Duchamp make the studio visit with the exhibition in mind? We can't tell for sure, though Cornell was ultimately included. It is clear that Duchamp even as a house guest managed to (re)insert himself into the middle of a key subculture of the New York art world. This was quite like John Cage, a Guggenheim townhouse resident at the same extraordinary time, and is at the origin of their own long-standing friendship.

The earliest specific trace of the *First Papers* project comes in two letters from Breton written on the same day, August 27. One, to Benjamin Péret in Mexico, solicits the participation of the group there. He speaks of "a Surrealist exhibition" to open on October 15, to be accompanied by a novel catalogue, and he asks for three paintings of Victor Brauner and two of Remedios Varo (Péret's wife) to be rolled up and shipped. At the same time he indicates his own depression, linked to troubles with Jacqueline.[29] The next letter to Péret begins with the news of Breton's separation from Jacqueline, who had become romantically involved with David Hare that summer at Wellfleet on Cape Cod.[30] Thus the organization of *First Papers* occurred during a time of great personal crisis for Breton. He also announced to Péret that he had moved uptown, living alone at 45 West 56th Street, nonetheless within walking distance of the Reid mansion and Peggy's soon to be opened gallery.

The second letter, to Gordon Onslow-Ford, also in Mexico, likewise announces "a Surrealist exhibition for October 15." Breton also emphasizes his work on the catalogue as "something new."[31] This apparently was the extent of out-of-town participation, as shipments from war-torn Europe were out of the question. The California contingent, Dalí and Man Ray, are noteworthy for the absence of invitation.

Shortly thereafter, in early September, a number of American artists received identical carbon copies of a typed letter of invitation in French from André Breton, "at the behest of Madame Schiaparelli."[32] By this time the selection seems to have been finalized, as the letter lists the names of 41 artists in four columns. Breton indicates that works by psychic mediums and American "primitives" (Indian objects) will also be shown. And he makes a special plea for "Surrealist objects," though in the end few appeared. Artists were to submit a list of works they would like to exhibit, including a photo of one that is unpublished, by September 15. This implies that the artists themselves chose which pieces to show. The exhibition of approximately 105 works would open merely a month later, on October 14.

Extending themselves to their hosts, the Parisians incorporated many more American artists than they had in 1938. Several of the young American artists included in the show were known in the Peggy Guggenheim circle and would soon participate in exhibitions at her gallery. Yet in Jimmy Ernst's opinion, "the gesture toward Surrealist protagonists working in America was meager and justified, in terms of quality, only by the inclusion of works by David Hare and William Baziotes. Fine painters like Kamrowski, Gorky, Tanning, Margo, Stamos, Kelly or any of the known artists from the California group were absent. . . . They still would have added a missing element and certainly would have outshone some selected syncophants who were barely beyond their tenth painting or recipients of nepotism, like me."[33] For the former, Ernst is probably alluding to Motherwell, who had not been painting for very long, and in fact had his exhibiting premiere at *First Papers*. "Nepotism" probably also accounts for John Goodwin, half-brother of Hare and son of the architect Phillip Goodwin, trustee and builder of the Museum of Modern Art.[34] Among others who may fall under the younger Ernst's accusation were Barbara Reis,

First Papers of Surrealism

daughter of frequent hosts of the Surrealists and backers of *VVV*;
Kay Sage, wife of Tanguy yet surely an accomplished painter in her
own right; and Laurence Vail, ex-husband of Peggy Guggenheim.
Another relative unknown difficult to account for is Ralph Nelson,
born in 1914, who lived only to the age of 39. He had studied with
Hofmann and passed through a Surrealist phase before turning to
abstraction.[35] A more prescient choice was Hedda Sterne, who recalls showing some of her collages. She would be included in group

4.3   John Schiff, Duchamp's *Mile of String* at *First Papers of Surrealism*, October 14–
November 7, 1942. From left, Klee (below), Ernst sculpture (on piano), Chagall,
Calder sculpture, Picasso collage, Motherwell. Philadelphia Museum of Art,
Marcel Duchamp Archive.

shows at Peggy Guggenheim's gallery the following year. With Kay Sage, she was one of few women artists in *First Papers*, presaging her role as the only female in the famous group photograph of the Abstract Expressionist "Irascibles."

Connections also played a role in the European selection. The appearance of Marc Chagall's early painting *To Russia*, prominently placed at one end of the center aisle (fig. 4.3), can only partly be seen as a gesture to his proto-Surrealist fantasies as a historical forerunner. Chagall had been included in Pierre Matisse's *Artists in Exile* exhibition, alongside some of the Surrealists who were also represented by this gallery. Pierre Matisse is listed as one of the sponsors of *First Papers*, and Breton and others wanted to placate him. Matisse's gallery staged a simultaneous Chagall show, which was reviewed together with *First Papers* in a few cases, though the artist always dissociated himself from the Surrealists.

Similarly, the inclusion of Morris Hirshfield would have been welcomed by Sidney Janis, who was promoting this self-taught artist. Peggy Guggenheim owned one of his nudes, *Woman at a Window*, which became a protagonist in a playful staged tableau of Ernst, Breton, Leonora Carrington, and Duchamp, photographed by Matta in her apartment (fig. 4.4). Or, rather, one could say "Rose Sélavy," since Duchamp artfully aligns his head with Hirshfield's painted female body, as if to identify with it. Likewise Ernst's head becomes that of the "bird-man" in his own *Surrealism and Painting* behind him, which would be his signature canvas in *First Papers*. Next to Breton there is a headless mannequin sporting one of Peggy's colorful boas.

Janis is listed as one of the sponsors, and he even contributed a brief introductory essay to the *First Papers* catalogue. In it, he speaks in rather general terms, and like Barr suggests Surrealism's historical pedigree. He also sounds a theme familiar from 1938, but now in the midst of full-scale world war, that Surrealism is "a manifestation of the personality of our time, of its nervous system and its mentality." Furthermore Janis loaned his two young sons as Duchamp-assigned "players" at the opening, all suggesting that he was quite involved with the project.

A most significant noninclusion was Jackson Pollock. Motherwell later said that he invited Pollock, but that the latter did not want to be part of a group. Recent biographers have questioned this rationale, as Pollock had participated in John Graham's McMillen

4.4   Photo by Matta of Breton, Duchamp with Morris Hirshfield's painting *Nude at the Window* (1941), Ernst, and Leonora Carrington at Peggy Guggenheim's townhouse, 440 East 51st Street, New York, c. 1942. Courtesy Ann Alpert papers, Young-Mallin Archives.

Gallery show earlier in the year, a group show including Americans and Europeans.[36] Furthermore it appears very unlikely that Motherwell would have been deputized to bring in Pollock, as Breton sent formal letters to the other Americans, as we have seen. It would be left to the "Spring Salons" and other exhibits of new talent at Art of This Century from 1943 to more tellingly assay the emergent young Americans, as Guggenheim moved away from the sway of Breton, her decamped husband Max Ernst, and the French Surrealists.

If Jimmy Ernst, as an insider, criticized the local inclusions as "meager," others were energized and galvanized by their promise. One recalled: "The show at the Reid Mansion was a focal point for young artists who were meeting the European Surrealists. This was a great period for us in the New York art community. . . . I began meeting people like Matta, Gordon Onslow-Ford, Motherwell."[37] Motherwell felt that the young Americans were prominently displayed within the installation. "Picasso got the worst place, and myself and Baziotes got the best place."[38] As an outgrowth of *First Papers*, a group of young Americans gathered at Matta's studio, hoping to create works that would warrant a showing at Peggy Guggenheim's. Matta himself later linked his rising star among the only slightly junior Americans to his appearance in *First Papers*, where his "scintillating" large painting *Earth Is a Man* attracted wide praise.[39] "There was a big Surrealist show—it was organized by a French refugee committee of liberation. Then I think it was that all of you realized that you had in me someone who knew something about all of this. This show awoke a lot of things in you."[40]

Breton's and Duchamp's thoughts must have gone back to the *succès de scandale* of four years earlier, prompting a desire to create again an overarching Surrealist space, necessarily on a more limited budget. Although "to camouflage" had taken on a different meaning with war under way in 1942, this premise remained as it had been in 1938. Again the given space was historical in style, for the Reid mansion had the gilded moldings of Renaissance revival, based on the Palazzo della Cancelleria in Rome—in the estimation of Peggy Guggenheim, "an ugly, old-fashioned building."[41] In this instance it was not so much covered as distracted or partially obscured, as were many of the paintings mounted on parallel rows of movable partitions. As Schiaparelli described it, "lofty rooms were divided by screens for hanging purposes, and between them ropes were stretched to form a labyrinth directing visitors to this and that painting with a definite sense of contrast."[42] However, she was alone in the impression that the stringing was meant to direct the viewers. The Schiff photos do show that the stringing varied in density, with some partitions completely blocked and others more open (figs. 4.3, 4.5), but no other witness reported this as systematic or purposeful.

The total amount of string used was undoubtedly not measured exactly, and various figures have been given. "Sixteen miles"

4.5   John Schiff, Duchamp's *Mile of String* at *First Papers of Surrealism*, October 14–
      November 7, 1942. From left: Picasso collage, Tanguy (center), Magritte (top),
      De Chirico, Arp. Philadelphia Museum of Art, Marcel Duchamp Archive.

4.6   Man Ray, *Enough Rope* with inscription, from *Objects of My Affection*, manuscript,
      1944. Courtesy Galerie Aronowitsch, Stockholm.

was the early favorite, as announced in the press release for the show. It refers to the total amount Duchamp purchased, though in the end he only deployed a fraction of that. And then there is the story forwarded by Duchamp himself, that the first winding caught fire in the hot lights and burned, without damage to the pictures. This has apparently led to estimates like "two or three miles," assuming that the entire first mile was ignited, which is very unlikely. Harriet and Sidney Janis early on stated three miles. There has even been the inexplicable estimate of "five," all of which unduly confuse the issue.[43] *Mile of String* seems most accurate for what actually was installed.

Along with Dalí, another more puzzling absence, although he was accessible, was the former "master of lighting" Man Ray. His old friend Duchamp barely mentioned to him "a Surrealist show which has nothing in common with that of Paris."[44] He definitively cast his lot with the alternative *View* magazine group soon after being overlooked, publishing essays and photographs of the editor's sister, Ruth Ford. A delayed response, perhaps after seeing the Schiff photos, was his own solarized close-up of crisscrossing strings (fig. 4.6). Titled *Enough Rope*, it effectively puns on the common phrase beginning "Give them . . .". Thus his implicit satiric commentary that the Surrealists "hung themselves," in both senses, amidst the strings at the Reid mansion.

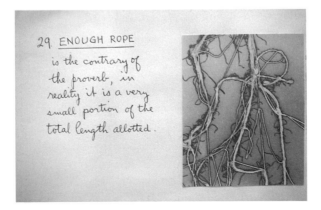

29. ENOUGH ROPE
is the contrary of the proverb, in reality it is a very small portion of the total length allotted.

The basic material used in the *First Papers* installation has been partly ascribed to the limited funds available. Duchamp recalled that there was no money from Schiaparelli, and that he obtained the string as a commercial exchange from a business contact. "I had a friend, even almost a relative, in Boston who is an accountant in a cordage place for Boston Harbor. And he sold me that 16 miles of string—it was a regular business." When pressed, Duchamp denied any larger intent: "It was just the cheapest form of attracting the attention of the public to Surrealistic surroundings. See that is all I wanted to do, nothing special."[45] While it is true that the production values were considerably less than in the 1938 *Exposition*, Duchamp's installation was not exactly threadbare. It responds specifically to the heavy moldings and ornate decor of the Reid mansion with a lightness of touch and simplicity that are highly effective. Breton speaks of it countering the gilding and love scene on the ceiling in the reception room. This simplicity generated multiple metaphors on the part of other artist-participants and contemporary critics. Typically with Duchamp, a seemingly simple gesture unfolds into complex associations as well as thorny issues. Not the least of these is a resistance to perambulation, a specific frustration of the spectator, the creation of an exhibition space that seems to nullify its basic function of exposing.

Yet the string does not negate the function of the eye: to see. Even in the densest webbings bridging the partitions, one could clearly still peer through to view the pictures in that aisle. It is as if Duchamp wished to split the bodily experience of the spectator from the optical one. He underlined such a distinction in a 1953 interview, saying of the string: "It was nothing. You can always see through a window, through a curtain, thick or not thick, you can see always [all the way?] through if you want to, same thing there."[46] Therefore on one level the string is a careful choice, one of the few materials (like Duchamp's glass) that block the viewer physically yet allow optical penetration. In this way Duchamp literally disembodies the Surrealist preoccupation with the corporeal.

There are also interesting implications to Duchamp giving up total control of the stringing. By freely collaborating with others, he undermined traditional notions of unique authorship. He recalled Breton, Jacqueline Lamba, David Hare, and Ernst as being on the scene and participating. Hare's then-wife, Susanna, recently remembered "being one of several stringers of twine working under Duchamp's direction without benefit of explanation."[47] This is important, for until recently the Duchamp literature has not acknowledged anything other than his solo creation. It is clear now, however, that there has to be allowance for what Amelia Jones rightly termed "slippages of the authorial *I*."[48] (A biographical curiosity: the twining was done by two couples who were in the process of splitting up, with the new relationship between Jacqueline and David Hare becoming public just at this time. So that within the group a hidden association of *unraveling*, and perhaps *intertwining*, accrues to the material chosen.)

This abandonment of exclusive control, perhaps merely for expedience, nonetheless implies that the precise resulting form was not a vital concern. Indeed, Duchamp even apparently solicited Alexander Calder's participation, with one or two cubic meters of square, torsioned papers being affixed to the strings, presumably to further obscure the spectator's view. It did the latter too effectively; Breton objected to this "pleasantry," and the "papillotes" were removed. But not before they were previewed by a critic who reported that "queer little bird-like forms made of paper descend here and there."[49] Another even mistakenly gave Duchamp and Calder equal billing as installers.[50] Calder is said to have used paper as a material pun on the naturalization process of the exhibition title.[51] Masson was present and recalled that Breton did not appreciate the humor of the gesture. So the installation did not incorporate potential "figures," instead it remained a nonobjective linear division of the room's space. This proved to be important, for it would be influential as a nonfigurative installation, yet one that was also "biomorphic," not geometric. The latter would have signaled the older European tradition of Constructivism and neo-Plastic art, such as the taut, suspended string in the abstract gallery of Art of This Century.

The ceilings were rather high, which presented some difficulty, especially as Duchamp wanted to obscure them as he had done at the Galerie Beaux-Arts. He was aware that "that mansion was full of marvelous ceilings, famous ceilings . . . and chandeliers." These were frescos and inlaid panels commissioned by the Reids in the late nineteenth century, by artists as notable as John LaFarge. Breton mentioned to one correspondent "le plafond d'amours." To the heaviness and ornateness characteristic of these Victorian interiors, Duchamp poses the whiteness and lightness of thin cotton string. Horizontal stringing across the ceiling had to be anchored to the chandeliers, which led to another problem: heat causing the spontaneous combustion of the twine. "I was just standing there," Duchamp said, "when the black spots appeared and in another second glowed and burst into flame."[52] Afterward, the stringers avoided the lights but still partly used the hanging part of the chandeliers as necessary anchors to span the ceiling.

String is fairly novel as an art material, though one could cite Jean Arp's series of string collages, or Gabo's threaded plastics. Beyond its connections to the readymade concept, the choice of string deeply resonates within Duchamp's oeuvre. As is typical with this artist, themes are conserved and cross-referenced, so a gesture is rarely as new or dissonant as it seems.[53] Thus string as a material has its precedents, as well as afterlife, in Duchamp's oeuvre. It is present at the very turning point from Cubism to the object, the *Chocolate Grinder No. 2* (February 1914), where carefully sewn thread reinforces perspectival and three-dimensional illusionism. Closer in form yet still wound up, it is part of the enclosing volume in *With Hidden Noise* (1916).[54] Thus in both these cases string—suggestively close to the artist's line and thus two-dimensionality, as in the template of *Three Standard Stop-pages*—is used paradoxically to reinforce volume, or three-dimensionality. Closer still, at least in concept, is one of the notes in *The Green Box*. This states a "recipe" of materials that would make a very poor meal (à la the shoe that Chaplin aims to consume in *The Gold Rush*) but a very interesting and novel object sculpture. "Recipe" proposes a *length* of string, five meters in this case, but implicitly extendable.

And, as we might expect with Duchamp, there may be linguistic levels of interpretation involved. The term *fil de la Vierge* (gossamer), or maiden's string, links to the thematic of virgin/bride in Duchamp's oeuvre. One "web," then, is the metaphorical one of connection and cross-reference within Duchamp's work, spinning and doubling back on itself.

As for the amount of string ultimately used, as O'Doherty notes, "the unverifiable quantification gives a conceptual neatness to the epigram."[55] Sixteen miles of string were announced in press releases, and in the official organ of the Council: "The labyrinth woven from sixteen miles of ordinary white string which Marcel Duchamp invented as a setting to contrast with the gilded panels and crystal chandeliers of the former drawing room in which the exhibition was held, aroused much interest as the show itself."[56] This important account testifies to the impact of Duchamp's work among non-art professionals at the time, and mentions the basis for their appreciation: *invention*. (This traditional criterion was later echoed by Breton.)

Far less than sixteen miles was sufficient to create the desired effect. Duchamp admitted to "complete miscalculation" of the amount needed. With so much left, the upshot was that "I gave it away. It made someone very happy—a kind of insurance, string enough to last him the rest of his life," as the amusing story goes.[57] Could this unnamed man have been Joseph Cornell? And the string used in the mansion was not especially preserved after the show, implying that it had no existence as an "art object" beyond its specific context, thus foreshadowing site-specific installations of our own day. Yet the idea of string soon appeared as a set installation by Maya Deren for her film *Witch's Cradle* of 1943. Deren's choice of string clearly follows Duchamp, though she freights it with metaphorical import, discussed below, that brings out his nonmetaphorical presentation by contrast.

Given: His Twine

In its nonfigurative form the string participated in the new wing of "abstract Surrealism" as recently described (and sanctioned) by Breton and best embodied by Matta. Indeed some scholars have detected Duchamp's influence on the spatial white lines that appear in Matta's paintings. One very knowledgeable contemporary observed that toward the end of 1942, Matta's works had "new white lines which floated like threads on the swimming space beneath. It would be interesting to know whether this new style was partly inspired by the installation designed by Marcel Duchamp."[58] Given Matta's general admiration for Duchamp, this seems likely.

There is also a strong dialogue with "a huge new Freudian nightmare by Surrealist Ernst. Painted specially for the exhibition, *Surrealism & Painting* depicted a nest of multicolored bosomy birds, from whose naked, writhing limbs a semihuman arm emerged to paint its creator's conception of the disorderly universe."[59] This picture within Ernst's picture is a nonobjective linear configuration, looping and arcing within the given space, as does Duchamp's environmental string. It was generated by, or imitates, the new technique of "oscillation" that Ernst had begun to experiment with the previous summer, in which a punctured paint can swung over the canvas dripped linear patterns. Duchamp, who lived at the Ernst and Peggy

4.7   Max Ernst, *Surrealism and Painting*, behind strings, at *First Papers of Surrealism*; exhibition review in *Newsweek*, October 26, 1942.

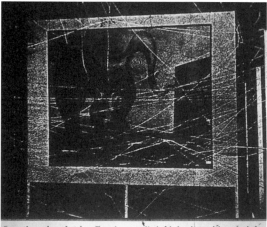

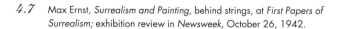
Seen through real string, Ernst's surrealistic bird paints with a man's han

Guggenheim triplex shortly after his arrival in the United States, most likely saw these paintings early on. Indeed, in the amusing photo of Duchamp, Ernst, Carrington, and Breton at Peggy Guggenheim's, *Surrealism and Painting* is prominent behind them. Another critic cited the Ernst as "the central canvas," and heightened the connection by reproducing it in situ, "seen through real string" (fig. 4.7).[60] In this view, documenting the spectator's experience, the strings seem to come from the brush of Ernst's Loplop-like alter ego. Ernst, by his title, preparation, and reproduction of the work in the catalogue, indicates the intention to unveil a summary program picture, attuned to the material of Duchamp's installation.

Installation, unlike painting, is a temporally bound form, ceasing to exist once the exhibition is over; and the impulse to preserve any "relic" was not yet felt. The Surrealist displays do have a two-dimensional afterlife in photodocumentation, of a type now familiar after three decades of site-specific and installation sculpture. Duchamp did take the trouble to commission John Schiff, who had photographed his works at Katherine Dreier's, to shoot the two documentary photos that are now our fullest record of the strings (fig. 4.3, 4.5). Dreier seems to have suggested it, to judge from Duchamp's written response, musing "Yes, very good idea, to have the strings photographed."[61] He soon reported that Schiff had done so.[62] The photos are as straightforward as possible, taken from the middle of the room, pointing directly north and south. Schiff apparently did not photograph the two small side rooms *sans* strings, so we can infer that the *Mile of String* itself was his prime subject rather than the exhibition.

One other photographer made his way to the Reid mansion. In Arnold Newman's photographic portrait, Duchamp himself appears behind a small portion of the strings. In this case the portrait was undoubtedly done at the photographer's request, number 38 of his ongoing series of artists which would reach 87 when exhibited in 1945–1946. The setting was more likely Duchamp's idea, though Newman did favor evocative or telling backgrounds in others of the series. Duchamp's pipe is a nice touch, removing him from the realm of the artisan to that of the thinker. It was cropped out in the published version of Newman's portrait exhibited in later years, which focused on the eyes. Another apparently rejected version of the artist behind the strings was published only recently. In it Duchamp appears in profile, pipe still in hand, facing toward a partly visible corner of his early painting *Network of Stoppages* (1914).[63] That painting is hung on the wall between the perpendicular freestanding partitions. If asked, Duchamp would have discouraged his association with painting, which may suggest why the photograph was not published at the time. There is no trace of other photographic response to *First Papers*. Altogether, the degree of reaction is notably meager compared to the many who photographed the 1938 show. *First Papers* is thus more poorly documented as to its precise contents and display, apart from the *Mile of String*.

Are there other indices for how the strings were regarded at the time? Breton for one was an early enthusiast. Although aware of the collaboration, he even insisting on old-fashioned individual authorship for the *Mile of String*. How else to regard his claim for the "imaginative compass" "affirmed, *quite detachedly from the consecrated forms of expression,* by the appearance of his signature appended to Twine Rigging at the International Surrealist Exhibition"?[64] Breton's emphasis on signature (and thus unique authorship) is not based on any mark made on or attached to the string it-

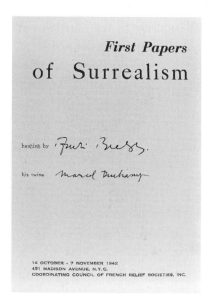

4.8 *First Papers of Surrealism* catalogue title page, 1942.

self, but rather on Duchamp's handwritten signature on the title page of the catalogue (fig. 4.8). It follows the somewhat ambiguous words "his twine," which could refer to Breton as "twin." There is no small irony in the fact that this apparently handwritten autograph is in fact not unique but rather printed and mass-produced.

Like Ernst, Breton seems to have created an object for the show which referred internally to the "Twine Rigging." His *A Torn Stocking* included spools and strands of thread among its found objects, implicit "generators" (or offspring) of the string.

Photodocumentation of the "Twine Rigging" was first reproduced (upside-down!) in *VVV* in March 1943 (fig. 5.4), then in the 1945 Duchamp issue of *View*, along with the above-quoted praise by Breton. In the former the ceiling effectively becomes floor, thus accomplishing the interrelating of these zones that the coal sacks and their consuming brazier had in 1938. In the *View* special issue Harriet and Sidney Janis go further than Breton in clearly claiming not only authorship, but also the "veritable maze of cobwebs" specifically as a "work of art." "Despite the prevailing idea that Duchamp has abandoned art," they wrote, anticipating Jones, "the high spiritual plane on which all his activity is conducted converts his dada installation at a surrealist exhibit into a work of art."[65] On the one hand this is disappointingly didactic in its insistence on "isms," refusing to release Duchamp from the tag "dada." On the other the Janises' statement, with its claim for *all* his activity, opens the door to the conceptualist proposition of "life as art."

Likewise the *Newsweek* writer, while stressing that "Duchamp hasn't painted in twenty years," recognized the "fantastic labyrinth" as "the show's chef d'oeuvre." This oeuvre even had a verifiable purpose, "intended to 'combat the background,' which it does effectively."[66] Thus at least for these critics it was received as a work, and could be appraised as such and compared to other more traditional works.

Reception begins with the coexhibitors. "Why did the other artists stand for it not once but twice?" O'Doherty wonders, and concludes, "in delegating him to provide [attention], the artists were playing little Fausts to an amiable demon." Protest is thus "preempted, for the harassment of their work is disguised as harassment of the spectators, who have to high-step like hens around it."[67] Still, Duchamp recalled a minor insurrection. "Some painters were actually disgusted with the idea of having their paintings back

of lines like that, thought nobody would see their paintings."[68] He
had to "fight" against this reaction, and prevailed in the end. So we
get a sense again, as in the darkness at Beaux-Arts, of other artists
being uncomfortably aware that the mise-en-scène was upstaging
their individual works. And we know that Duchamp at this point
was not invested in painting per se, so that the installation could be
taken as a gesture against this traditional medium, or at least was
perceived as such by some of the participants. Thus Breton's pre-
emptive report to Remedios Varo, assuring her that her paintings
were still beautiful, "even across the white strings."[69]

The critics often spoke of the strings as barriers. Most gleefully
one chortled: "While we were in the exhibition a lady and her umbrella successfully tangled with some of those sixteen miles of string."[70] Henry McBride
noticed that an old painting by Duchamp "nestles behind a particularly thick
wad of cobwebs,"[71] so even his own canvases were not spared.

Two of those closest to Duchamp echoed McBride's representational
metaphor of spider webs. Masson, who had witnessed Calder's folded papers during the installation, spoke of *toile d'araignées fort joliment disposées*,
which in French also incorporates the word for canvas (*toile*). Secondly,
Calder himself prominently exhibited a large black standing mobile *Spider*
of 1940, on the raised platform at the end of the room, obviously providing
the putative spinner of these webs (fig. 4.3). One might wonder whether, in
view of various deteriorating couple relationships, this is specifically the
black widow? This type of reading is effectively sanctioned by Duchamp in
his transparent spiderweb frontispiece to the deluxe edition of Lebel's 1959
monograph on his work. With the page down, the spiderweb overlaps Man
Ray's photo of an alluring nude woman, such that the dense center of the
web marks her pubis as bull's eye. Thus the spider web is the most multiply
apt of the anthropomorphic metaphoric responses.

Although not present in New York, Man Ray plausibly associated the
material chosen with Duchamp's door for the Gradiva Gallery: "String and
glass . . . may have been an effort to obtain transparency-invisibility."[72]
Whereas a potential eyewitness, the painter Peter Busa, related it to the
New York art world context, in terms of opposition: "Duchamp's touch was
evident in miles of string he used to give the exhibition an outcast quality, to
show that this was genuinely outside the official gallery scene."[73] Here is a

hint of the protest tenor of installations of the 1960s, and their use of "impoverished" materials.

Simplicity in itself seems to generate an opposite critical reaction of overinterpretation, or at least establishes a critical space allowing the free play of associations. *Art Digest* thought of the installation as a connecting thread that brought some overall binding to uncomfortably disparate works: "A geometric semi-cocoon [sic] which provided the proper labyrinthine atmosphere and served both to unify the exhibition and to awe the visitor."[74] The naive painters like Hirshfield and American Indian art were particularly disturbing to this reviewer's sense of coherence; thus the string was a welcome "binder." The *Times* similarly called it "quasi-geometrical string mesh," probably referring to the fact that the main planes established were fairly cubelike, echoing the partitions and the room itself.

Robert Coates ambitiously took the twine as a trope for Surrealism as a whole. He viewed it as an index of the work done and imagined the actual process of the stringing as fresh at the outset, tiresome by the end. This becomes his metaphor for the life cycle of the whole movement, which he felt "has grown tired and tedious and a little repetitive."[75] This was a clever way to express a fairly common sentiment, already voiced in 1938, that the movement was no longer *le dernier cri*.

Similarly clever was *Time*'s image: "a striking installation: a cat's cradle,"[76] referring to the children's hand game played with formations of string. This suggestion was taken up by Maya Deren with the rather Jungian use of string in her film *Witch's Cradle*, shot late the next summer before Art of This Century opened for the fall 1943 season. The title may refer to a phase in the game cat's cradle and/or to a magical spell device.[77] Along with the Surrealist works in Peggy Guggenheim's gallery, the film's main prop was lengths of string; indeed Deren subtitles one section "string travel." It utilized a web of string placed in one part of Art of This Century in direct emulation of Duchamp's installation. Beyond this material coincidence, Deren even "asked Duchamp to help her prepare the scene by stringing some strings."[78]

The film's two actors were, somewhat surprisingly, Duchamp himself and Matta's young wife Ann. Deren had approached Duchamp for advice on filming Surrealist objects; then he took on a role. The film begins with them sitting in a cafe, the man "play-

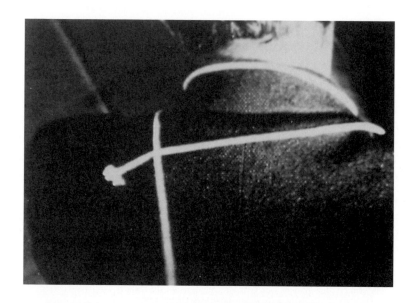

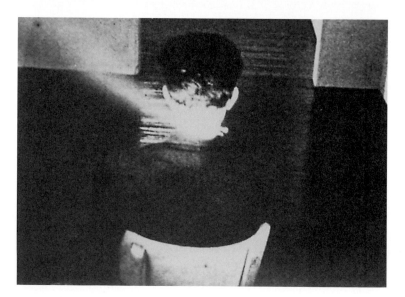

4.9　Maya Deren, Duchamp with string stills, *Witch's Cradle,* unfinished film, summer 1943.

ing string game with his hands," recalling cat's cradle. Soon Duchamp is caught in "alive string" that circles his neck; thus he is trapped in the witch's cradle. Then in the "string travel" section the camera moves along the cord, encountering various artworks, beginning with Max Ernst's. Sequence 12 is described as "camera rights itself to one side of string, taking in lined Ernst."[79] Deren thus (re)enacts a connection between Duchamp's string and the linear configurations in canvases like Ernst's *Surrealism and Painting*, one that I have posited above as already intended by the two artists. In the later part of the film, the woman character is ascendant. She grasps the string as a kind of rein that she follows into the subconscious. String becomes a multiple metaphoric connector, both the social fabric of interhuman relations as well as intrahuman circulatory systems and the mind. Here Deren's heavy, deliberate symbolism elaborates her interest more than Duchamp's.

A single clip of sequence 10 with the camera revolving around Duchamp's head was published in the 1945 Duchamp issue of *View*, and a rough cut had been screened to a select audience in Kiesler's studio.[80] So one could add *actor* to Duchamp's expanded definition of the artist's field, though this experimental film remained in obscurity. It was never finished to Deren's satisfaction, and the print was unlocated until recent years, when it was released on videotape. Nonetheless, given Duchamp's close involvement, the film script can be seen as meditation on and a symbolic reworking of "his twine."

More recently, a Masson scholar linked "his twine" to "an Ariadne's thread," a metaphor prevalent in Masson's works of the late thirties, which elaborate on the labyrinth and the Minotaur as well.[81] But Ariadne's thread was laid along the floor of the labyrinth, not in the air, and represented a path to retrace, not an obstruction. The mythic level of this metaphor, while popular with other Surrealists, does not ring true for Duchamp's interests. It is more apposite to Kiesler's thread at the 1947 Maeght exhibition. Duchamp's is everywhere *but* on the ground, does not lead anywhere or locate direction, rather confuses direction. It is worth noting that in their interview, Cabanne proposed the word *labyrinths*, which Duchamp quickly corrected to *strings*,[82] thus effectively foreclosing this mythic interpretation. If needed, a more appropriate parallel in classical myth would be to Arachne, with the spinning of thread associated with the length of life, as well as the origin of arachnids.

Given: His Twine

Another questionable metaphor comes from Masson himself, who speaks of the pictures imprisoned "as if in a concentration camp."[83] The analogy comes out of a postwar context, and even then the strings can hardly be understood as being as menacing, or as ordered, as barbed wire. Although Masson's metaphor says more about his own experience in internment camps than about Duchamp's intent, it does remind us how the actuality of the war loomed over the participants.

The Janises stretched the string to cover the complexity of modern art as a whole. This was the projection of a topic Sidney Janis had dealt with in a book. Marcel Jean's association was with cobwebs on old wine bottles, an epicurean choice, and one happily implying that Surrealism was better with age. Yet Jean was not present in New York, and most likely conflates this installation with Duchamp's wine bottle cover for *View*. Even as one rejects these readings, they vividly reinforce the effective, open-ended simplicity of the stringing which ignited this delirium of overinterpretation.

On the other hand quite a few minds were not yet prepared for installation display as artwork. Aside from the lady with the umbrella, some critics completely opposed the string, such as the archconservative Royal Cortissoz: "Least of all are [Surrealism's] obscurities clarified by the placing of some of the paintings assembled . . . behind a web of white string. A device of that sort is merely absurd."[84] Similarly, *Art News* growled, "Great pictures don't have to be snarled up in publicity and sixteen miles of string to get themselves looked at." This created part of the aura of "inexcusable *chichi* for a warring world," the same uncomprehending charge of blithe irrelevance that the Surrealists had heard just before the conflict.[85] Finally, critic Emily Genauer focused on her own discomfort: "It's all odd as can be, irritating at first, silly afterward."[86] Yet even the outraged reactions nicely demonstrate that what Dore Ashton suggestively termed Duchamp's "lure to the press" was effective.[87]

"Vernissage Consacré aux Enfants Jouant, à l'Odeur du Cèdre"

Compared to the elaborate, even magical events promised at Galerie Beaux-Arts, the *First Papers* opening on Wednesday evening, October 14, 1942, was fairly simple. The promised "cedar odor" was clearly derived from Péret's earlier roasting coffee smell, "odors of Brazil." None of the reviews mention scents, however. The earlier emphasis on the multisensory was played down or not carried out. Tricoleur announcements were sent out, white cards bordered with red and blue lines, indicating that a higher admission ($1 plus 10 cents tax) was charged for the benefit preview. This began at 8 p.m., earlier than the Paris event. The imagery of the flag, combined with noble purpose, is quite a remove from the Beaux-Arts card with its strange automaton-monster.

"Children playing" replaced the dances of Vanel as the major opening "performance." As one scholar has noted, Duchamp's idea of inviting children was conceived far enough ahead of the opening that it could be printed in the front of the *First Papers* catalogue.[88] Duchamp carefully instructed Carroll Janis, eleven-year-old son of the collector and sponsor Sidney, to gather some friends, play ball, and not to cease if confronted by grownups.

The exact form of that play seems to have been left to the kids. Carroll Janis recalled arriving with six friends, dressed for the occasion in "baseball and basketball and football uniforms and spikes." There were also "a like number of girls in little groups, skipping rope, playing jacks and hopscotch."[89] Duchamp fully anticipated that a certain awkwardness would arise between children and the black-tie adults. March Avery, daughter of the painter Milton, was one of the children: "We were encouraged to run about and I remember feeling somewhat uncomfortable both because I didn't think it was proper behavior and also because I sensed that some of the guests were of the same opinion."[90] If asked, they were to indicate they were playing at the behest of Duchamp. Duchamp proudly reported to Dreier that he did not attend the opening. Thus the basic obstruction was set in motion without any mechanism for it to stop, as Duchamp was not present to revise his orders. Apparently play went on all evening, from the youths' early arrival, "when we had all the huge rooms to ourselves and we started throwing balls. Just kept on through the whole evening and it got so crowded and we kept playing. Our instructions were to ignore everybody and just play to our heart's content. We just loved it." By one account eventually quite a few of the adult guests joined in the play.[91]

Duchamp wrote Dreier, "The opening of the Surrealist show took place last night and seems to be quite a success. I was not there (This is one of my habits). But reports indicate that the children played with great gusto. When you come to town we will go together."[92] Thus the childlike replaced the sexualized "hysteria" of the partly clad Hélène Vanel.

The game of nationalism was also played out, as the invitation card hints. One "shocking" tale in Schiaparelli's biography is her description of the Council's president as a Vichy sympathizer,[93] which accounts for the presence of a bust of figurehead Maréchal Pétain at the entry to the exhibition. Jimmy Ernst reported that this sparked a very different incident at the opening: "Some of us, the younger people, led by Matta, protested and asked for our elders' influence in having the offending bust removed. We were told not to rock the boat."[94]

Others were apparently aware that fundraising for Vichy France was a partly compromised gesture. Charles Henri Ford, rival editor of *View*, was quick to gossip, "Breton seems to have completely disintegrated and he's just had the bad taste to organize a Surrealist show sponsored by a French relief business that is pro-Vichy and anti-British!"[95]

The participants emphasized that the money raised from the show would go to French prisoners. Such benefits were a commonplace. The proceeds from Peggy Guggenheim's gallery opening the following week were likewise to benefit the American Red Cross, an unimpeachable cause.

The *Times* critic went so far as to assure his readers that they were supporting "Surrealism's all-out against the Axis."[96] All these, like the door to the exhibition covered in American flags, were, as Breton noted, a sign of the nationalistic times.

5

The Disembodiment of Surrealist Exhibition Space and Its Dissemination

eggy Guggenheim's summer of 1942 at Wellfleet, Massachusetts, was cut short when her husband, German-born Max Ernst, came under police investigation as an enemy alien. The couple returned sooner than planned to their New York triplex, where Duchamp had been a guest since shortly after his arrival on June 25 (having stayed first at Robert Parker's). Peggy later wrote that she made passes at Marcel to incite Max's jealousy. Whatever the reason, Duchamp soon moved again to a private room at Frederick Kiesler's Greenwich Village apartment. On October 2 Stefi Kiesler notated that she "cleaned Marcel's room."[1]

Indeed, Frederick Kiesler is listed as a participant in *First Papers of Surrealism* in Breton's invitational letter of early September. Since March he had been busy with the commission for the design of the rooms of Peggy Guggenheim's Art of This Century gallery, and in contact with Breton and the Surrealists. The gallery was projected to open well before *First Papers*, though it was delayed and ultimately followed by a week. For the grand opening, Guggenheim deliberately wore mismatched earrings. One abstract, one Surrealist, and likewise one American, one European, the earrings signified her impartiality with respect to the art movements.[2]

Similarly, the competing ideologies of exhibition space, abstract versus Surrealist, were each given their characteristic separate but equal areas within Art of This Century. The abstract gallery effectively demonstrates that string (or rope) could be used to define linear and geometricized supports. The Surrealist gallery, as at the Galerie Beaux-Arts in 1938, was closed off from the outside world and utilized darkness, in this case punctured by dramatic spotlighting. As Kiesler's lights were programmed to go on or off randomly, visibility itself was again put in doubt. Another parallel was in the use of (distracting) sound in the gallery, in Kiesler's case subway train noises, which were soon discontinued. Yet for a time they metaphorically transformed the tunnellike space to one underground, evoking danger. Though Kiesler, residing in New York, would not have seen the Galerie Beaux-Arts exhibition himself, photodocumentation was widely available. And his patron Peggy Guggenheim had closely witnessed its installation process, with Duchamp as her guide. "I went there everyday with Marcel," she recalled. "He was putting the exhibition together."[3] More original were the unframed paintings (at Guggenheim's insistence) projected from the concave side walls, mounted on sawed-off baseball bats with joints that allowed the pictures to be tilted. Innovative, too, were Kiesler's multifunctional, biomorphic chair-bases, although developing from the concept of the Seligmann stool and other Surrealist art-furniture at the Galerie Beaux-Arts.

A third, less-known space at Art of This Century, the "kinetic gallery," introduced controlled viewing devices for the reproductions from Duchamp's *Valise*, small works by Klee, and Breton's object-poem *Portrait of the Actor A.B.* To activate the Duchamp viewer, one had to turn a large wooden spiral, which would move a belt with the reproductions into view of the peephole. As a small-scale multiple, the *Valise* might easily have been examined by hand. Thus the elaborate viewing device eliminates the manual pleasure for a sheerly optical one. To view the *Portrait*, a lever pulled down would open a shutter through which Breton's self-referential construction became visible. It was this area of the gallery that critics dubbed "a kind of artistic Coney island," or "a penny-arcade peep show without the pennies."[4] As such it recalls Julien Levy's original plan for a Surrealist nickelodeon arcade for the World's Fair. As in the popular culture peep show, there is only one fixed point of view and the spectator's experience is entirely regimented. Such mechanistic,

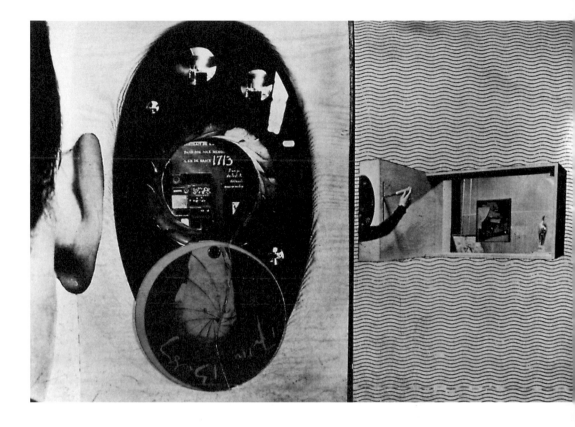

experimental viewing devices are not especially Surrealist in themselves. They represent a new kind of controlled, limited exhibition
mode oriented toward the individual and the personal. Such regimented viewing would be the basis for Duchamp's last work, the
peephole *Etant donnés*—a delayed realization of Levy's concept of
a Surrealist nickelodeon, crossed with the pornographic peep show.
Given the incorporation of the *Valise* in the "kinetic gallery," and
the fact that Duchamp was subletting a room from Kiesler, there
was a good opportunity for interaction between them before the
opening of Art of This Century. There is not enough evidence to
specify, however, whether either influenced the installation ideas of
the other. Presumably Duchamp would have been more of an idea
man, while Kiesler was more knowledgeable about construction
and technical possibilities.

Since Art of This Century was open from October 1942 through May
1947, its curved-wall gallery has been the best-known Surrealist space of the
period. It was often photographed and published and tends to overshadow
memories of the transient *First Papers*. One aim of the present study is to
make clear its forerunners and period context. Kiesler was not a formal
member of the Surrealist group; the Surrealist mode represented for him an
appropriate design choice for that part of Guggenheim's collection. While
it was clearly highly effective, it was already on the menu of such choices by
1942, as Peggy realized.

Even as Art of This Century was about to close, Kiesler, now recognized for Surrealist spaces, received two additional opportunities to create
exhibition installations. The first, for the exhibition *Blood Flames*, was
largely accomplished with bands of paint uniting the different rooms of the
Hugo Gallery. The second, in the summer of 1947, was his extensive work
on the Surrealist exhibition at the Galerie Maeght, Paris, particularly in carrying out the "Salle de Superstition."[5] There he united the different rooms
by running a string through them, echoing the material Duchamp used in
First Papers.[6] In this case the string clearly evoked the means of finding passage through the Minotaur's labyrinth (perhaps another prompt for this
myth being misleadingly associated with *Mile of String*).

The Galerie Maeght exhibition was the next official Surrealist manifestation after *First Papers*, and was based on the continuing collaboration of
Duchamp and Breton. The latter developed an extensive iconographic pro-

5.3   Robert Rauschenberg, *Bed,* 1959 *Eros* installation, Galerie Cordier, Paris.

gram focusing on myth. The viewer ascended 21 steps labeled with book titles, then entered the "Hall of Superstitions." A labyrinth contained twelve niches whose "altars," created by artists, corresponded to signs of the zodiac. The overall results, it is generally conceded, are arcane and disappointing. Even Breton wrote Enrico Donati that the show was neither a critical nor a financial success.[7] In terms of installation practice, its overly literary and programmatic character represents a retreat from an abstract environment, confirming a certain ossification or waning of the movement in the postwar years.

Twelve years later the next international Surrealist exhibition, opening in December 1959 at Galerie Cordier, Paris, signaled two aspects of the future of installation. One was the inclusion of Jasper Johns and Robert Rauschenberg, an important yet little-remarked direct connection between Surrealism and the younger generation of image-makers. Rauschenberg's *Bed*, a controversial combine painting, includes an actual pillow and cover as part of the painted and drawn vertical surface. Rauschenberg's participation in the Cordier show, which was devoted to the theme of Eros, would support reading *Bed* as a site of erotic encounter. (Likewise for Johns's *Target with Plaster Casts*.) Another connection would be Meret Oppenheim's ritualistic *Feast* at the opening, concurrent with similar performative experiments in the incipient Happenings and Fluxus groups. Before they were proto-Pop, Johns and Rauschenberg were neo-Dada or Surreal, had met Duchamp and admired his work. Even at the time, Calvin Tomkins defined environments and happenings as "a form of spectator involvement that Duchamp practiced—less earnestly and somewhat more wittily—in the installation of several Surrealist exhibitions."[8] A number of critics have thus recognized Duchamp as a bridge to the younger generations of contemporary installation artists.

 The *Mile of String* by Duchamp and friends set a theme that was carried out in the works of several exhibitors. It served as the setting and barrier for Arnold Newman's photographic portrait of Marcel. And, as we have seen, it inspired responses on the part of Maya Deren and, less directly, Matta. The installation also impressed *Vogue* editor Alexander Liberman, who was moved to commission Duchamp to design a cover on the theme of "Americana."[9]

An unintended, "chance" dissemination becomes possible once the *Mile of String* is reproduced upside down in *VVV* (March 1943) and the ceiling portion effectively becomes "floor" (fig. 5.4).[10] This strikes one retroactively as suggestive of Jackson Pollock's mature "pour" paintings, from 1947 on, created on a canvas spread on the floor. In fact Pollock even made a few automatist poured canvases in 1943. Among aspects that argue against a too facile analogy are the energies of Pollock's skeins, as opposed to the more meandering pace of Duchamp's string. But there are material and procedural correspondences, such as the question of finish. In both cases there is a visualization of the goal, but the question of precisely when the artist stops is undetermined and only emerges in the process of "throwing" the lines. In

SOUVENIR DE L'EXPOSITION SURREALISTE 1942   (*Ficelles de Marcel Duchamp*)

5.4   Duchamp's *Mile of String* reproduced upside down, *VVV*, March 1943.

5.5   Man Ray, *Les mannequins* (Paris: Petithory, 1966), cover.
(Opposite)

both, too, line is no longer a contour. It does not bound, rather it is a unit in the filling of a given container.

If one thinks of the *Mile* not as linear but as an environment, it has a distant echo in the surrounding quality of Pollock's late 1950 exhibition at Betty Parson's gallery. There three monumental canvases covered the walls of one room, creating a kinesthetic spatial whole. At least this is how some viewers saw it, including Allan Kaprow, who wrote, "Mural scale paintings ceased to become paintings and became *environments.*" For Kaprow this was a bridge that led to action in actual space. "Pollock left us at the point where we must become preoccupied with and even dazzled by the space and objects of our everyday life, either our bodies, clothes, rooms, or, if need be, the vastness of Forty-second street."[11] By this string of association, Duchamp and friends' *Mile* becomes an ancestor of the environments and happenings of the 1960s. Both would acknowledge the necessity of the tolerant spectator, who might well be subject to distraction and disorientation.

During the 1960s the burgeoning interest in Dada and Surrealism led to various recreations and reeditions, driven by art market demand. Even

5.6 Eva Hesse, *Untitled* (1970), detail, the artist seen through string.

Surrealist exhibition space, although intrinsically resistant to commodification, was revisited in various guises. In 1966 Man Ray undertook the first publication of his self-styled "resurrected" mannequin photographs, referring to the fact that they had been stored and feared lost during the German occupation. *Les mannequins* documented fifteen of those from the 1938 exhibition "street," omitting only Arp's covered mannequin. The photos were published in a deluxe limited edition of 37, by Jean Petithory. The gold foil cover features a divided head shot of Ray's own "bubble pipe" mannequin. These have subsequently become the best-known documentation of the mannequins, overshadowing other photographers, and have been widely reproduced in publications and exhibitions.[12]

The mannequins themselves were partly re-presented in a 1981 exhibition as the starting point for postwar art in Paris. Curators at the Centre Georges Pompidou chose to begin the *Paris-Paris* exhibition with an updated staging of part of the street of 1938. Instead of clippings on the wall behind, however, the recreated mannequins were placed before mirrors. In this way the spectator's gaze is reflected and returned, a rather postmodern confrontation that drew mixed reactions.

Likewise Salvador Dalí, having become a parody of self-appropriation, re-recreated the *Rainy Taxi* for William Rubin's large Dada and Surrealism exhibition at the Museum of Modern Art in the riotous spring of 1968. Made from a dated British taxi, an antique 1936 Austin, it echoed the year of the London Surrealist exhibition. As in its first incarnation, it stood outdoors, this time in the Museum's sculpture garden. Dalí said he "assembled it by telephone," although he did appear to add a "necklace of live leeches" to the snails he obtained from a French restaurant.[13] This third version ultimately parked at the Dalí Museum in Figueras. A successor to *Rainy Taxi* is Edward Kienholz's *Back Seat Dodge, '38* (1964). It likewise sets two mannequins into a vehicle, yet in an overt sexual encounter. Though Dalí's *Taxi* is not as literal in its sexuality, there are many points of similarity.[14] Subsequently a number of artists, from Rauschenberg to Warhol, have customized cars as sculptural "artwork." For example Sylvie Fleury's *East of Eden* (1994) is a luxury car decked out with roses and other foliage, though not quite as densely as Dalí's cab.

Dalí's Dream of Venus pavilion had less direct impact in the art realm, but it was echoed in 1940s film. Maya Deren's *At Land* dealt with the theme of Venus Anadyomène, born out of the sea. Much of its enigmatic action takes place along a beach, recalling the "Beach of Gala Salvador." Likewise Ian Hugo's *Bells of Atlantis* treats a dreamy, undersea world. Perhaps the best realization of Dalí's wet-tank ideal is in a recent video of Swiss artist Pipilotti Rist. Her *Sip My Ocean* is an enchanting view of a female swimmer that uses close-ups to convey erotics, yet it is also a playful exploration of the underwater world.

Like Kaprow, Eva Hesse is an important artist who, in formulating a response to Pollock, approached Duchamp as ancestor, via the art historical "grandfather principle." Her late works *Right After* (1969) and *Untitled* (1970) levitate linear "rigging" in the space of a room. In the former a regular network of fiberglass cord covered with resin is visually quite close to the looping parts of the *Mile of String*. The later piece, with latex-coated string and rope of differing thickness, is more variegated in material yet still reminiscent of the more dense sections of the *Mile*. Hesse was photographed in her studio peering through *Untitled* (1970; fig. 5.6), thus echoing Duchamp's pose in Arnold Newman's photograph at the Reid mansion. And like Duchamp's, both Hesse pieces manage to banish any figurative allusion for a strictly abstract network whose precise form is determined by the size of the room container. As such, these works by Hesse have been analogized to Jackson Pollock's webs, "projecting Abstract Expressionist 'all-over' into actual space, a cosmos."[15] But clearly the *Mile of String* is a more telling precedent, one already cast in a literally environmental mode.

As a critic, with his essays on the gallery cube published in 1976, Brian O'Doherty was instrumental in raising the consciousness of a new generation of contemporary artists about the history of exhibition space, including Duchamp's installations. As the artist Patrick Ireland, he himself extensively explored the use of string or rope in room installations, beginning in 1973. These tend, however, to be more orderly than *Mile of String*, situated in relation to the space of the room, a point he overstresses in his essay on Duchamp's piece.[16] His works recall more the geometrism of the ropes in the abstract gallery of Art of This Century.

Her Twine

Beyond the example of Hesse, string has been a viable material in the hands of a number of contemporary women artists, who have reclaimed the material for their gender. This was seen in the early days of feminist art, when "the subversive stitch" and other traditionally female-gendered methods demanded attention on a serious level.[17]

Faith Wilding created a *Crocheted Environment* (also called *Womb Room*) at the Womanhouse at Berkeley in 1972. By utilizing crochet—typically viewed as a woman's domestic skill—as a fine art medium, she undermined traditional categories and expectations. Her "subversive stitch" in its immediate context may have been more directly aimed at Minimalism, but it ends up taking on *Mile of String* as well.

Mona Hatoum's *Recollection* (1995) challenges visibility, but with ethereality rather than darkness as the Surrealists had done. As viewers approach what appear to be balls of thread on a table, they feel slight sensations on the skin. They eventually realize that clear threads hang from the ceiling. With the utmost delicacy, Hatoum produces a kinesthetic response to the threads, as *Mile* does. She also evokes a connection with our own bodies when we learn that she has used her own hair to weave these threads.[18] The "hairspace" is hung vertically with five inches between strands. Here ones also recalls Duchamp's dropped threads, the *Stoppages*, a chance unit of measure.

For a performance on November 7, 1973, Mierle Ukeles enacted a connection to Duchamp by utilizing cord. She began at the Philadelphia Museum by holding a small fan to air the *Large Glass* in the collection. Then immediately outside the Museum she attached the end of a large ball of twine to the fountain visible from the window behind the *Large Glass*. She "unreeled, dropped, extruded the string" down the Museum stairway, a considerable distance along the Benjamin Franklin Parkway, to Moore College of Art. (In the Moore gallery examples of her maintenance art had been in a group show.) Having enacted her own "Mile of String" as a linear connection rather than an obstruction, Ukeles acknowledges Duchamp as an influential forebear. After phoning the Museum to announce completion, she cut the cord, thereby also creating her own independence from such paternity. She reminds us that even simple materials can have narrative as well as gender implications. Her choice of string was in part motivated by the double meaning *fil/fille:* thread/daughter, as well as a brief conversation she had with Duchamp at his New York show in 1963. The question she put at the time prompts the title of the action *Now That You Have Heirs/Airs Marcel Duchamp*.

There are innumerable other examples that could be cited, as room installations have become a dominant mode of sculptural production in the past decade. Installation has even spread to mass culture, as in "rain forest" environmental theme restaurants. It is noteworthy that so many women artists have been the ones to extend Duchamp's experiments, though no doubt these are often mediated by other sources.

From our perspective, some of the debates around Surrealism have long since cooled, such as those over political alignments of the period. Other issues, once overlooked, now elicit growing attention, such as the role of the body, and gender and sexuality in art—reviving interest, in turn, in the formerly marginalized photographs of Hans Bellmer and Claude Cahun. The spectator's body in the exhibition environment can be seen as the ultimate extension of this issue. Thus the exhibition displays of Surrealism are clearly one aspect of the movement most relevant for installation artists today.

5.7   Mierle Ukeles, *Now That You Have Heirs/Airs,*
Marcel Duchamp, Philadelphia, 1973, photograph.
Courtesy Ronald Feldman Fine Arts, New York.

Conclusion

Surrealist exhibition installations remain complex in origins, intent, and meaning. In retrospect there is an internal logic in increasingly activating the viewer's kinesthetic response that propelled the Surrealists' step-by-step expansion to the concern with the object, then with architecture, and finally with installation space. There is also an internal appropriateness to what I would term late Surrealism's increasing theatricalization of presentation in the public sphere. The installation afforded the opportunity to extend the "poetics of the marvelous" into actual space, thereby transforming a mundane setting into a Surrealist one. Yet these factors are hardly deterministic, and do not account for the arenas nor the specific form of the installation.

Nonetheless, Surrealism's concern with real space tends to reinforce its position as a branch of realist art. Apologists for Surrealism have often tried to shoehorn the movement into modernist practice, a view that has emphasized the Miróesque and automatist factions while disowning Dalí and his commercialization. This view is embarrassed by the profoundly *anti*-modernist features of Surrealism. Nonetheless, it makes most sense to see Surrealism's public exhibition spheres as actualizations of the spaces within the "painted dream," Dalí-Magritte wing of the group. So, too, late Surrealism's sorties into the gallery sphere bear an uncomfortable relation to Dalí's self-marketing. Dalí's "transgression" perhaps was not so much commercialization per se, but his overblown and insufficiently ironic embrace of it. As one contemporary of the period remembered, "They were all Avida Dollars."[1]

The resistance to this logic is in itself an episode in postwar critical thinking. Clement Greenberg viewed Surrealist painting as revivalist, "suffering from being literary and antiquarian." He singled out Dalí for "promoting the rehabilitation of academic art under a new literary disguise," while exempting Miró and Picasso.[2] This criticism deepened when Michael Fried cast an undue taint on the "theatrical" in his influential 1967 essay "Art and Objecthood."[3] Shortly thereafter, in his landmark catalogue, William Rubin made apologies for Surrealism's "poetic content." He posited that the American abstractionists necessarily "expunged the quasi-literary imagery that had earlier related their paintings to Surrealism."[4] In this influential view, aspects of Surrealism had to be deleted, to be gotten over, for modernist art to progress.

As Hal Foster has noted, there has been a second wave in the devaluing of Surrealism. The neo-avantgarde of the 1960s and 1970s revived Dada and Constructivism. Duchamp's star soared, based on his early, Dada period, while his Surrealist collaboration remained little known or commented. Finally, by the early-1990s, Surrealism's "counter-modernist status" became one of its claims to current critical attention.[5]

Yet the previous practice of separating Duchamp and Surrealism is no longer justifiable with regard to the 1930s. Exhibiting his readymades as Surrealist objects, collaborating with Breton on *Au lavoir noir*, serving on the editorial board of *Minotaure*, designing a glass door for the Gradiva gallery, and carrying out large-scale exhibition installations, Duchamp is clearly in the thick of Surrealist activity. He participates in the internal politics of shaping its shows, and even in aligning with Hugnet's dissident group for a passing moment in 1939. Thus it is worth contemplating how Duchamp's input inflected the development of the movement. Certainly the installations are one of the new features and main achievements of late Surrealism. More generally, Duchamp stretched Surrealism in an ecumenical direction, thereby contributing to the critical space for offshoots. The most notable was the abstract branch, which proved to be the most telling in its impact on the New York School.

Conclusion

On a fundamental level, to exhibit is to put one's works into the marketplace, a practice that was institutionalized only in the nineteenth century. As artists from at least the Futurists onward soon discovered, an installation spectacle is one method to elicit public attention. In a Warholian view, the widespread commentary on the 1938 *Exposition Internationale* would comprise the enterprise's success, regardless of whether such commentary was favorable to it. Dalí's World's Fair pavilion was also quite widely commented upon, especially in the popular press. His masked ball of 1941 made news on the west coast and drew the attention of the Hollywood community. Only *First Papers* (1942) seemingly failed to distract a wider public from its preoccupation with the war in Europe. Further, the display did not engage the wide range of photographers that had responded in 1938. Thus within art history it was less documented and largely eclipsed by Kiesler's designs for the Surrealist gallery of Art of This Century. Unlike Peggy Guggenheim's collection, the works in *First Papers* were for sale, though few found buyers. After these disappointing results, the Surrealists did not stage a second American exhibition, but rather waited until after the war to regroup and test the marketplace with their 1947 Paris show.

It would be too simplistic to attribute the development of the installation spectacle merely to the commercialization of Surrealism. While they eagerly accepted the invitation extended by the Galerie Beaux-Arts, the Surrealists clearly resisted accepting a conventional apotheosis, and disturbed the usual givens of exhibition viewing. Their plans for a mise-en-scène cost the gallery time, money, and no small annoyance, as is still lodged in the memory of the Wildenstein family. They also both courted yet disturbed the opening-night crowds. The invitees could hardly see, could not promenade easily through the obstacles to normal passage, and emerged with Duchamp's coal dust on their designer clothes. But the chic and fashionable had received unique, striking invitations that lured them to turn up for the event, promising various forms of sophisticated diversion, which they certainly found. At the vernissage an important chapter in the intertwining histories of art and fashion was written. *Vogue* and other fashion magazines gave the exhibition considerable coverage, breathlessly listing in attendance a who's who of the world of *mode:* Nathalie Paley, Bettina Bergery, "Schiaparelli in paillettes, Madame Ralli," all the while wondering "What fashion points will be inspired by this exhibition?"[6] In this, too, late

Surrealism followed Dalí's lead: that of his earlier design collaborations with Schiaparelli and his circulation in the couture houses.

Duchamp's correspondence with Katherine Dreier details his participation in a 1935 Parisian inventors' show, in an attempt to find financial backing for marketing an edition of his optical discs, the *Rotoreliefs.* The commercialism of such enterprises (like Breton's Gradiva Gallery soon after), long passed over in the literature, provides an appropriate perspective to consider the subsequent exhibition installations. The latter's increased spectacular aspects seem calculated to garner public attention, not to mention *haut monde* chic. While Duchamp amusingly presented himself at the time as "retired" from art-making, it is now clear that this pose was disingenuous. Some of his art world activities, such as the publishing of multiple editions (especially the *Valise* project), or his role as an art consultant to prominent collectors and dealers, were frankly commercial. Others, notably his installations, although obviously involving market and art world power and politics, also pioneered new paradigms of what being an artist involves, and expanded the field of what creating a "work" could be.

For Duchamp, exhibiting with the Surrealists was a significant step in his reemergence in the art world, even as he was carefully singled out as an impartial "outsider" to the core group. Its precondition was Breton's creating a critical space for the *Large Glass* and for the readymades within the widened domains of late Surrealism. Considering the personnel involved in this subculture, the long-standing Breton-Duchamp alliance stands out as remarkable. As one observer of *First Papers* noted, Duchamp was the buffer who made dealing with Breton more palatable: "It took Duchamp to know what to do about Breton. He had real authority."[7] Perhaps this Faustian bargain begins to answer O'Doherty's pointed question: why did the artists put up with Duchamp's overarching (and attention-grabbing) installations?

This topic also raises the broader question of when in the history of modernism exhibition space itself becomes ideological, or viewable as a "work." There are enough examples from the beginning of the 1920s to conclude that Surrealism did not pioneer in this area, but was rather adopting a mode of avant-gardism in installation practice. The question is more whether such gestures were already part of the avant-garde "apache dance," a token of (bankable) resistance before the seemingly inevitable coopting.

Conclusion

1 Ideological Exhibition Spaces and Surrealist Exhibitions

1. See *The New Painting: Impressionism 1874–1886*, exh. cat. (San Francisco: Fine Arts Museums of San Francisco, 1986), for a detailed account of these exhibitions.

2. The show is extensively documented by Helen Adkins, "Erste Internationale Dada-Messe," in *Stationen der Moderne* (Berlin: Berlinsche Galerie, 1988), pp. 157–169.

3. See Bruce Altschuler, *The Avant-Garde in Exhibition: New Art in the 20th Century* (New York: Abrams, 1994), chapter 5.

4. See Nancy J. Troy, *The De Stijl Environment* (Cambridge: MIT Press, 1983), pp. 122–132.

5. Discussed in depth in Mary Anne Staniszewski, *The Power of Display: A History of Exhibition Installation at the Museum of Modern Art* (Cambridge: MIT Press, 1998), pp. 61–83. See also chapter 1, where Kiesler and Lissitzky are illustrated and analyzed, pp. 13–21.

6. Much of this dialogue, still ongoing, is suggestively surveyed in Richard Martin's collagelike *Fashion and Surrealism* (New York: Rizzoli, 1987).

7. André Breton, *What Is Surrealism? Selected Writings*, ed. Franklin Rosemont (New York: Monad, 1978), p. 141.

8. Altschuler, *The Avant-Garde in Exhibition*, p. 133.

9. Roland Penrose, *Scrap Book 1900–1981* (New York: Rizzoli, 1981), p. 60.

10. Ibid., p. 62. Costs were also low, as insurance was only slightly over 20 pounds.

11. Ian Dunlop, *The Shock of the New* (New York: McGraw-Hill, 1972), pp. 203–204, based on the recollections of Roland Penrose. Penrose, *Scrap Book*, pp. 63–67, publishes seven installation photos. The Getty Research Institute has a complete documentation in 18 installation photos (92.R.76*).

12. Alfred Barr to Paul Eluard, telegram of March 12, 1936, in "Fantastic Art, Dada, Surrealism" exhibition archives, Registrar, Museum of Modern Art. Eluard's telegram response the next day was favorable: "New York possible November."

13. Museum of Modern Art press release of May 23, 1936, in Alfred Barr papers, Archives of American Art, roll 2166: 99. At that point the show was scheduled to open November 11, and Barr was said to be "spending several months in Europe this summer collecting works."

14. Eileen Agar, *A Look at My Life* (London: Methuen, 1988), p. 117.

15. Barr to Duchamp, letter of May 8, 1936, predicting arrival in Paris on the 19th or 20th. Duchamp sailed on the 20th. Barr to Duchamp, letter of August 7, 1936, refers to "our brief meeting before you sailed." "Fantastic Art, Dada, Surrealism" exhibition archives, Registrar, Museum of Modern Art.

16. Margaret Scolari Barr, "'Our Campaigns': 1930–1944," *The New Criterion*, special issue (1987), p. 44.

17. Barr papers, Archives of American Art, roll 3261: 626–687, and Margaret Scolari Barr, "'Our Campaigns': 1930–1944," pp. 45–46. She describes in detail a visit to Leonor Fini. Mrs. Barr was an important participant in the developments, as she was Barr's French translator.

18. Barr papers, Archives of American Art, roll 3261: 590, 591.

19. Margaret Scolari Barr, "'Our Campaigns': 1930–1944," p. 44.

20. Eluard reported receiving two thousand francs, Breton twice that amount. Paul Eluard, *Letters to Gala* (New York: Paragon, 1989), no. 210 (late July/August 1935), pp. 208–209.

21. Eluard to Barr, letter of July 13, 1936; Barr to Eluard, letter of July 18, 1936; Barr to Breton, letter of July 18, 1936. As the latter is addressed to Breton's Paris home and he was in the country, it is unlikely that he received it right away. Barr did not get a reply until early August. "Fantastic Art, Dada, Surrealism" exhibition archives, Registrar, Museum of Modern Art.

22. Barr to Man Ray, letter of August 6, 1936, "Fantastic Art, Dada, Surrealism" exhibition archives, Registrar, Museum of Modern Art.

23. Barr to Arp, letter of August 7, 1936; Barr to Ernst, letter of August 7, 1936, "Fantastic Art, Dada, Surrealism" exhibition archives, Registrar, Museum of Modern Art.

24. Paalen to Barr, letter of August 23, 1936, "Fantastic Art, Dada, Surrealism" exhibition archives, Registrar, Museum of Modern Art.

25. Duchamp letter to Breton, mistakenly dated "22-8-36" (actually September), Bibliothèque Littéraire Jacques Doucet, Paris. Duchamp suggests that the three of them meet for lunch at brasserie Lipp on Thursday.

26. M. Barr, Paris, to Alfred Barr, Vermont, telegram of September 12, 1936, in "Fantastic Art, Dada, Surrealism" exhibition archives, Registrar, Museum of Modern Art.

27. Margaret Scolari Barr, "'Our Campaigns': 1930–1944," pp. 45–46.

28. Mesens to Barr, letter of October 4, 1936; Tzara to Barr, letter of October 6, 1936, "Fantastic Art, Dada, Surrealism" exhibition archives, Registrar, Museum of Modern Art. Barr managed to appease Tzara with an explanation of his position, including the news that Breton would not be writing for the catalogue (letter of November 7, 1936).

29. Dalí to Breton, letter of December 28, 1936, quoted in José Pierre, "Breton et Dalí," in *Salvador Dalí rétrospective 1920–1980*, exh. cat. (Paris: Centre Georges Pompidou, 1979), p. 137.

30. S. Kahn to Barr, letter of January 7, 1937, "Fantastic Art, Dada, Surrealism" exhibition archives, Registrar, Museum of Modern Art. Eluard, *Letters to Gala*, no. 226 (January 6, 1937), p. 223.

31. Marcel Jean, "The Relationship between Surrealist Artists and Writers," typescript of a talk given March 27, 1968, at Museum of Modern Art, pp. 15–16 (Museum of Modern Art archives). Barr's approach seems to have impacted Breton's later historiography, such as "On the Survival of Certain Myths" (1942).

32. Noailles to Barr, letter of January 22, 1937, "Fantastic Art, Dada, Surrealism" exhibition archives, Registrar, Museum of Modern Art.

33. "Fantastic Art, Dada, Surrealism" exhibition archives, Registrar, Museum of Modern Art.

34. Dunlop, *The Shock of the New*, p. 224. See his chapter on "Entartete Kunst," and Stephanie Baron, ed., *"Degenerate Art": The Fate of the Avant-Garde in Nazi Germany*, exh. cat. (Los Angeles: Los Angeles County Museum of Art, 1991).

35. Jimmy Ernst, *A Not-So-Still Life* (New York: St. Martin's, 1984), p. 94.

36. James D. Herbert, *Paris 1937: Worlds on Exhibition* (Ithaca: Cornell University Press, 1998), p. 37.

2 The Origin of Surrealist Exhibition Space: The 1938 Paris Exposition Internationale du Surréalisme

1. "Paris Joke: Art World Ponders Surrealist Show," *New York Times*, March 6, 1938, p. X9. Raymond Cogniat did issue a release for the gallery saying that the exhibition followed in the suite of the "étapes." This was widely quoted and excerpted in the press, including the house organ *Beaux La presse face au surréalisme de 1925 à 1938* (Paris: Centre National de la Recherche Scientifique, 1982), pp. 211–212, where it is misidentified as a preface to the *Dictionnaire abrégé du surréalisme*.

2. Max Morel and Jean Bazaine, translated and quoted in Martica Sawin, *Surrealism in Exile and the Beginning of the New York School* (Cambridge: MIT Press, 1995), p. 8.

3. Georges Hugnet, "L'exposition surréaliste internationale de 1938," *Preuves*, no. 91 (September 1958), reprinted in his *Pleines et déliés: souvenirs et témoignages, 1926–1972* (La Chapelle-sur-Loire: Guy Authier, 1972), p. 324. Sawin, *Surrealism in Exile*, p. 10, is in accord with this explanation; Daniel Wildenstein told me that Seligmann had nothing to do with it.

4. André Lhote, "Du naïf au pervers," *Ce Soir*, January 22, 1938, p. 2.

5. The show was in Tenerife, Canary Islands. Eluard referred the matter to Breton, who had to appeal back to Picasso, since the informally organized exhibit was uninsured. Breton letter to Picasso, June 30, 1936, with Wildenstein letter to Eluard of June 20 enclosed, Musée Picasso Archives, Paris. The damaged painting, *Métamorphose*, was valued at 30,000 francs.

6. Eluard letter to Alfred Barr, November 12, 1937, "Fantastic Art, Dada, Surrealism" exhibition archives, Museum of Modern Art. However, *Celebes* is not listed in the *Exposition* checklist. The Museum replied on December 22 that it was unable to purchase the painting and was returning it. Apparently it did not arrive in good condition, as the Museum paid 200 francs damages in April. It was soon acquired by Roland Penrose.

7. Raymond Cogniat, "L'exposition surréaliste," *Beaux Arts* 75 (January 14, 1938), p. 1. See also note 1.

8. "Le surréalisme à Beaux-Arts," *Beaux Arts* 75 (January 14, 1938), p. 1.

9. "Surréalisme," *Beaux Arts* 75 (February 4, 1938), p. 1. An exhibition of works by El Greco immediately preceded the Surrealists at the Galerie.

10. Breton letter to Picasso, March 15, 1937, Musée Picasso Archives, MP 3649. In a slightly earlier letter, Breton is searching for spaces on the Left Bank. For advice he consulted the dealer Pierre Loeb. Breton letter to Edmond Bomsel, February 4, 1937, exhibited in *Surrealism: Two Private Eyes* (New York: Solomon R. Guggenheim Museum, 1999), not catalogued.

11. *André Breton, la beauté convulsive* (Paris: Centre Georges Pompidou, 1991), pp. 235–236. After Gradiva failed, the door was destroyed at Duchamp's request.

12. Michel Leiris, *Journal: 1922–1989* (Paris: Gallimard, 1992), entry for October 2, 1966.

13. Hugnet, "L'exposition surréaliste," p. 323. He does not specify the participants, but seems to include himself among the "plenipotentiaries."

14. André Thirion, *Révolutionnaires sans révolution* (Paris: Laffont, 1972), p. 452.

15. Hugnet, "L'exposition surréaliste," pp. 327–328, 330.

16. Eluard to Mesens, undated letter, quoted in *Paul Eluard et ses amis peintres, 1895–1952* (Paris: Centre Georges Pompidou, 1982), p. 153.

17. Elsa Thoresen-Gouveia to José Vovelle, quoted in *Obliques*, no. 14–15 (1977), p. 55.

18. Henri Hérault, "Lettre de Paris: Surréalisme," *Marseille Libre*, February 6, 1938, clipping in Musée Picasso Archives.

19. "Surrealist Art: Strange Exhibits in Paris," London *Times*, January 21, 1938, p. 11. The same correspondent was the only one who noted that the taxi's headlights were left on in the daytime. Dalí's sculpture was *not* in the gallery's lobby, as is usually stated.

20. René Guetta, "L'expo du rêve," *Marianne*, no. 275 (January 26, 1938), p. 13. Guetta also spoke of a "torrential" rain, and a "chauffeur-crocodile." See also Pierre du Colombier, "Chez les surréalistes," *Candide*, February 3, 1938, clipping in the Musée Picasso Archives.

21. Bettina Wilson, "Surrealism in Paris," *Vogue* 91 (March 1, 1938), p. 144.

22. Jean Paul Fraysse identifies both Millet's *Angelus* and *The Gleaners* printed on the passenger's cretonne dress. The latter is visible in Ubac's photo (fig. 2.6). Fraysse, "Un art d'insolite grandeur," *Le Figaro Littéraire*, January 29, 1938, clipping in Seligmann archive.

23. Simone de Beauvoir, *The Prime of Life* (New York: World, 1962), p. 258.

24. B., "Ein Kunstsalon als Tollhaus," *Münchner Abendblatt*, January 24, 1938, p. 2. Also "Was ist 'Surrealismus'?," *Neue Freie Presse*, Vienna, January 26, 1938 (Arbeiterkammer für Wien Dokumentation, clipping 26357).

25. Louis Aragon, *Paris Peasant* (1926; Boston: Exact Change, 1994), pp. 40, 49.

26. "Dans une odeur de café grillé . . . ," *Paris-Midi*, January 18, 1938, clipping in the Seligmann Archives.

27. "Escargots surréalistes," *Beaux Arts*, no. 265 (January 28, 1938), p. 2.

28. I am grateful to Professor Kirsten Powell for this suggestion.

29. The text of Dalí's sign is quoted in Hugnet, "L'exposition surréaliste," p. 339, and reproduced in *La planète affollée: Surréalisme, dispersion et influences, 1938–1947* (Marseilles: Direction des Musées, 1986), p. 33. According to the manuscript for the placard on the car, there were to be 200 snails, though there seem to be visibly fewer.

30. James D. Herbert, *Paris 1937: Worlds on Exhibition* (Ithaca: Cornell University Press, 1998), p. 148. He also notes that the *Three Penny Opera* was revived in Paris in September 1937.

31. For instance, when the Dalís were in New York, Eluard urged them to arrange to supplement the four paintings he was lending to the London exhibition. Paul Eluard, *Letters to Gala* (New York: Paragon, 1989), no. 216 (April 1936), p. 215.

32. José Pierre, "Breton et Dalí," in *Salvador Dalí retrospective 1920–1980* (Paris: Centre Georges Pompidou, 1979), pp. 137–138. Breton soon started calling Dalí "Avida Dollars," the infamous anagram of commercialization.

33. Julien Levy, *Memoir of an Art Gallery* (New York: Putnam's, 1977), p. 205.

34. *Paris Soir*, illustrated in Sawin, *Surrealism in Exile*, p. 5. Two of Denise Bellon's photos appeared at the time in *Paris Magazine*, no. 80 (April 1938), along with nude models.

35. "Surrealism in Paris," *Vogue* 91 (March 1, 1938), p. 107; "La vie des arts," *Marianne*, January 26, 1938, p. 11. Gaston Paris's photos are discussed in an im-

portant essay on the mannequins that appeared after this section was drafted: Elena Filipovic, "Abwesende Kunstobjekte: Mannequins und die 'Exposition Internationale du Surréalisme,' von 1938," in *Puppen, Körper, Automaten: Phantasmen der Moderne* (Düsseldorf: Kunstsammlung Nordrhein-Westfalen, 1999), pp. 200–218.

36. Man Ray's photos were commissioned for an article on the new Siegel mannequins published in *Vogue*, August 21, 1925. Willis Hartshorn and Merry Foresta, *Man Ray in Fashion* (New York: International Center of Photography, 1990), p. 17.

37. See, among others, Robert J. Belton, *The Beribboned Bomb: The Image of Woman in Male Surrealist Art* (Calgary: University of Calgary Press, 1995), for an extensive discussion of this issue.

38. Hugnet, "L'exposition surréaliste," p. 329. "Les artistes surréalistes . . . se sentaient tous l'âme de Pygmalion . . . On put voir les heureux possesseurs de mannequins . . . arriver, munis de mystérieux petits ou grands paquets, hommages à leurs bien-aimées, contenant les cadeaux les plus disparates."

39. A. M. Petitjean, "A propos de l'exposition surréaliste," *Nouvelle Revue Française* 26 (March 1, 1938), p. 515: "une espèce de putain."

40. Man Ray, "Resurrection des mannequins," typewritten statement, Man Ray archives, Centre Georges Pompidou.

41. Introduction to *Les mannequins* (Paris, 1966), English-language manuscript in the Man Ray archives, Centre Georges Pompidou.

42. The groundbreaking source here is Richard Martin's *Fashion and Surrealism* (New York: Rizzoli, 1987). The Surrealist mannequins are discussed on p. 50.

43. Dickran Tashjian, *A Boatload of Madmen: Surrealism and the American Avant-Garde, 1920–1950* (New York: Thames and Hudson, 1995), chapter 3, "Surrealism in the Service of Fashion," esp. pp. 68, 78–83. *Minotaure* 3, no. 10 (1937), illustrated in Hartshorn and Foresta, *Man Ray in Fashion*, p. 55. Domínguez exhibited the wheelbarrow as an object in the *Exposition Internationale du Surréalisme*.

44. Guetta, "L'expo du rêve," p. 13. Ironically, Dalí is not mentioned as the maker.

45. Wilson, "Surrealism in Paris," p. 144.

46. See my doctoral thesis "Themes in Picasso's Cubism, 1907–1918," Columbia University, 1988, pp. 21–24, where examples by Bonnard, Rodin, Lautrec, and Picasso are discussed. Several Man Ray photos continue this type in the Surrealist period, as in the *Nusch and Sonia* discussed below.

47. Nicole Parrot, *Mannequins* (New York: St. Martin's, 1982), p. 74. Some were cast in papier maché and colored with bright lacquers, including gold finishes. At the same time they became lighter, and more realistic skin tones also were developed.

48. Françoise Travelet, "Interview, Léo Malet," *La Rue*, no. 28 (1980), p. 52.

49. Petitjean, "A propos de l'exposition surréaliste," p. 515.

50. Man Ray, *Self-Portrait* (Boston: New York Graphic Society, 1988), p. 209.

51. Hérault, "Lettre de Paris: Surréalisme," clipping in Musée Picasso Archives.

52. Léo Malet, *Les confrères de Nestor Burma* (Paris: R. Laffont, 1988), p. 1243. Hugnet recalled that the mannequin was given over to Paalen ("L'exposition surréaliste," p. 334), but Malet's mannequin in fact appears, only minus its fishbowl, after Domínguez's.

53. Germaine Ferrari, *Matta, entretiens morphologiques, notebook no. 1 1936–1944* (London: Sistan, 1987), p. 217.

54. *Pérégrinations de Georges Hugnet* (Paris: Centre Georges Pompidou, 1978), no. 71. Hugnet opened his atelier "Livre-Objet" in 1934, and his sculptural bindings were discussed by Benjamin Péret in *Minotaure* in 1937.

55. "Ne plaisantons pas," *Paris-Midi*, January 20, 1938, clipping in Seligmann archives.

56. "Surrealism in Paris," *Vogue* 91 (March 1, 1938), p. 107. The photo is by Eggarter.

57. Wilson, "Surrealism in Paris," p. 144.

58. Illustrated in Emmanuelle de L'Ecotais and Alain Sayag, eds., *Man Ray, Photography and Its Double* (Paris: Centre Georges Pompidou, 1998), p. 123. According to Edouard Jaguer, Mossé was deported by the Nazis and died in a concentration camp (letter to the author, October 22, 1995).

59. Man Ray, *Self-Portrait*, p. 191.

60. Arturo Schwarz, *The Complete Works of Marcel Duchamp* (New York: Abrams, 1969), no. 303, p. 505.

61. Guetta, "L'expo du rêve," p. 13. (Guetta was normally a society columnist.) Jeffrey S. Weiss shows how standard this charge was in his discussion of "blague" in relation to Duchamp's readymades, in his exemplary *The Popular Culture of Modern Art: Picasso, Duchamp, and Avant-Gardism* (New Haven: Yale University Press, 1994), chapter 3, pp. 107–163.

62. Marcel Jean, *The History of Surrealist Painting* (New York: Grove, 1960), p. 281.

63. Laura Rosenstock, "André Masson: Origins and Development," in *André Masson* (New York: Museum of Modern Art, 1976), p. 146. Masson also painted a pansy in the mouth of the left-hand figure in *Métamorphose des amants* (1938).

64. Mary Ann Caws, "Ladies Shot and Painted," in *The Art of Interference* (Cambridge: Polity Press, 1989), p. 112. Although Masson specifies tiger eyes, her "peacock" reading is still plausible.

65. "Mad Dream Betrayal of New York Society," Sunday *Mirror* Magazine, February 24, 1935, p. 10. Clipping preserved in Surrealism scrapbook, Bibliothèque Littéraire Jacques Doucet, Paris, 8343.62, apparently compiled by Eluard.

66. Uwe M. Schneede, in *Die Kunst der Ausstellung* (Frankfurt: Insel, 1991), p. 96.

67. Michael Majer (Frankfurt, 1687), quoted in Kurt Seligmann, *The Mirror of Magic* (New York: Pantheon, 1948), p. 159 and plate 62. Plate 72 illustrates the frescoes of Nicolas Flamel, the alchemist who is named in the first street sign in the row of mannequins.

68. "Surrealism and Fashion," *London Bulletin*, no. 1 (April 1938), p. 20. For instance, the Lion of Belfort (lion head and human body) appears in *Une semaine de bonté*.

69. Reproduced in *XXe siècle*, no. 1 (March 1, 1938), p. 27. See also Herbert, *Paris 1937*, p. 128.

70. *Das interessante Blatt*, Vienna, February 24, 1938, p. 10.

71. "Veuve dont le sexe était remplacé par une ampoule électrique," Travelet, "Interview, Léo Malet," p. 52.

72. C. B. Morris, *Surrealism and Spain, 1920–1936* (Cambridge: Cambridge University Press, 1972), p. 20. Biographical details are found in Adam Biro and René Passeron, *Dictionnaire général du surréalisme* (Fribourg: Office du Livre, 1982), pp. 151–152. Espinoza died in Tenerife in 1939.

73. Raymond Lécuyer, "Une charge d'atelier," *Le Figaro*, January 22, 1938, p. 7.

74. Fraysse, "Un art d'insolite grandeur."

75. Wilson, "Surrealism in Paris," p. 144.

76. Maurice Henry, "Le surréalisme dans le décor," *Marianne*, no. 275 (January 26, 1938), p. 11.

77. *Man Ray*, Sotheby's sale catalogue LN5173, March 22–23, 1995, no. 182, p. 146. The object also recalls children's soap bubble sets, and as such was extensively used by Joseph Cornell.

78. Arnold Crane, conversation with Man Ray, June 12, 1968, transcript pp. 13–14, Oral History Collection, Archives of American Art.

79. In 1940 Ray made postcard-sized copy prints of an alternate view of his mannequin's head and sent them to friends such as Eluard. See Christie's, New York, *Photographs I*, October 5, 1995, lot 212.

80. Man Ray, "Resurrection des mannequins," typewritten statement, Man Ray archives, Centre Georges Pompidou.

81. The cooker is mentioned by B., "Ein Kunstsalon als Tollhaus," p. 2, confirming that Malet's mannequin was on view.

82. Léo Malet, *La vache enragée* (Paris: Hoebeke, 1988), p. 138.

83. Jean, *The History of Surrealist Painting*, p. 281.

84. "Where are the hares of Yesteryear? Happy Home Surrealism," *The Sketch*, London, January 26, 1938, p. 173.

85. Josef Breitenbach, "Internationale Ausstellung des Surrealismus in Paris," in T. O. Immisch, Ulrich Pohlmann, and Klaus E. Göltz, *Josef Breitenbach Photographien* (Halle: Staatliche Galerie Moritzburg, 1996), p. 86. Breitenbach was unsuccessful in getting his description of the exhibition and accompanying photos published in *Life* magazine (p. 80, note 17).

86. Rauschenberg's *Bed* (1955) is tied directly to the Surrealist tradition by its rather surprising inclusion in their 1959 Paris *Eros* exhibition. I refer to González-Torres's photographic posters of rumpled double beds. Conner's recent *Love Site* included a simulated double bed in the context of a history of postwar modes of seduction.

87. Jean, *The History of Surrealist Painting*, p. 281.

88. Amelia Jones, *Postmodernism and the En-gendering of Marcel Duchamp* (Cambridge: Cambridge University Press, 1994), p. 77.

89. Hérault, "Lettre de Paris: Surréalisme," clipping in the Musée Picasso Archives.

90. Wilson, "Surrealism in Paris," p. 144.

91. Hugnet, "L'exposition surréaliste," p. 326. He paints a picture of group discussion, in which balloons and irons were also proposed. Open umbrellas are associated with bad luck. Then Duchamp suggests coal sacks, used ones. These are borrowed from a "bois et charbons" warehouse (p. 327). Hugnet also recalls that the sacks were one of the first elements decided upon, and they subsequently had a liberating effect on the whole installation project. Henri-Pierre Roché recalled that it was difficult to find hundreds of umbrellas on short notice (in Robert Lebel, *Marcel Duchamp* [New York: Grove, 1959], p. 84), whereas Masson remembered the "superstitious" Georges Wildenstein opposing umbrellas (in Jean Paul Clébert, *Mythologie d'André Masson* [Geneva: Cailler, 1971], p. 60).

92. Translation by Carolyn Lanchner, in *André Masson* (New York: Museum of Modern Art, 1976), p. 145, of Clébert, *Mythologie d'André Masson*, p. 60.

93. Pierre Cabanne, *Dialogues with Marcel Duchamp* (New York: Viking, 1971), p. 81.

94. Brian O'Doherty, *Inside the White Cube: The Ideology of the Gallery Space* (Santa Monica: Lapis Press, 1986), pp. 67–69. I don't agree, however, that the sacks were "unobtrusive physically."

95. A. W., "Les surréalistes vont faire de nouveau parler d'eux," *Le Figaro*, January 17, 1938, p. 5, reprinted in Guiol-Benassaya, *La presse face au surréalisme*, p. 238. "Le surréalisme en liberté," *Le Journal* January 13, 1938, clipping in the Seligmann Archives.

96. Hérault, "Lettre de Paris: Surréalisme," clipping in Musée Picasso Archives.

97. *Harper's Bazaar* 73 (December 1939), pp. 58–60. These included some of Schiaparelli's newly "practical" collection: "warmth for coal-less Paris" (p. 58) and "straight skirts with a flap concealing pocket for passport and papers" (p. 126). Bellon's photograph is illustrated in Ian Dunlop, *The Shock of the New* (New York: McGraw-Hill, 1972), p. 209.

98. Cabanne, *Dialogues*, p. 81.

99. Gênet [Janet Flanner], "Letter from Paris," *New Yorker* 13 (February 5, 1938), p. 56. Marcel Jean, "The Relationship between Surrealist Artists and Writers," typescript of a talk of March 27, 1968, Museum of Modern Art Library, New York, p. 17.

100. Du Colombier, "Chez les surréalistes," clipping in Musée Picasso Archives. Jean, *The History of Surrealist Painting*, p. 281.

101. O'Doherty, *Inside the White Cube*, p. 69.

102. Man Ray, *Self-Portrait*, p. 233.

103. Grincheux Jovial [pseud.], "Surréalisme," *Beaux Arts* 75 (February 4, 1938), p. 2. He also mentions that the snails have "thinned."

104. Guetta, "L'expo du rêve," p. 13.

105. Hugnet, "L'exposition surréaliste," p. 330.

106. London *Times*, quoted in Dunlop, *The Shock of the New*, p. 209; A. W., *Le Figaro*, reprinted in Guiol-Benassaya, *La presse face au surréalisme*, p. 239, and Petitjean, "A propos de l'exposition surréaliste," p. 516. Often the popular, in the form of midway or sideshow, was not far from viewers' minds.

107. Wilson, "Surrealism in Paris," p. 144. "Surrealist Furniture Draws Paris Crowds," *Life* 4 (February 7, 1938), p. 57. Fraysse, "Un art d'insolite grandeur," p. 7.

108. See André Breton and Paul Eluard, *Dictionnaire abrégé du surréalisme* (1938; Paris: Corti, 1991), p. 6.

109. Daniel Abadie, "L'Exposition internationale du surréalisme, Paris, 1938," in *Paris-Paris, 1937–1957, créations en France*, exh. cat. (Paris: Centre Georges Pompidou, 1981), p. 74.

110. Flyer in Surrealism scrapbook, Bibliothèque Littéraire Jacques Doucet, 8343.28. Breton's lecture was probably similar to the one he gave in Prague in March, translated in *Manifestos of Surrealism* (Ann Arbor: University of Michigan, 1972), pp. 255–278. Hugnet's, changed to "L'objet utile," appears in his *Pleins et déliés*, pp. 125–127.

111. Ten interior and two exterior photos from the Ratton archives are illustrated in *Man Ray/Rare Works*, exh. cat. (Copenhagen: Fotografisk Center, 1996), pp. 19–36.

112. See *André Breton*, exh. cat. (Paris: Centre Georges Pompidou, 1991), p. 229.

113. De Beauvoir, *The Prime of Life*, p. 258.

114. Ibid.

115. Robert J. Belton, "Androgyny: Interview with Meret Oppenheim," in Mary Ann Caws et al., eds., *Surrealism and Women* (Cambridge: MIT Press, 1991), p. 68.

116. Tashjian, *A Boatload of Madmen*, pp. 43–45.

117. Whitney Chadwick, *Women Artists and the Surrealist Movement* (Boston: Little, Brown, 1985), p. 118.

118. Telephone interview, April 29, 1995. Alpert indicated that the size was modest, about 12 by 15 inches, and she likened her approach to Cornell's. The piece sounds comparable to that of another spouse, Jacqueline Lamba's *La femme blonde* (1936), illustrated in the *Dictionnaire abrégé*, p. 46.

119. Chadwick, *Women Artists and the Surrealist Movement*, p. 50. Alpert at the time "accepted as normal" Breton treating her "like a child."

120. "Le plus apparent [mécanisme surréaliste] consiste à détourner les objets de leur usage habituel. Puisque le parapluie sert à se protéger de l'eau, on fera un parapluie en éponges; puisque le fer à repasser doit glisser sur le linge, on fera

un fer à points. . . . Et l'on croira alors découvrir la singularité, le caractère magique de ces objets 'gratuits.'" Du Colombier, "Chez les surréalistes," clipping in Musée Picasso Archives.

121. "Surrealist Art: Strange Exhibits in Paris," London *Times*, January 21, 1938, p. 11.

122. Man Ray, *Self-Portrait*, p. 232. Péret was "one of several poets entrusted with the task of providing other attractions or distractions."

123. De Beauvoir, *The Prime of Life*, p. 258.

124. See photo in "Surrealist Furniture Draws Paris Crowds," p. 57.

125. Hugnet, *Pleins et déliés*, p. 342.

126. B., "Ein Kunstsalon als Tollhaus," p. 2.

127. Hérault, "Lettre de Paris: Surréalisme," clipping in Musée Picasso Archives.

128. André Breton, *Conversations: The Autobiography of Surrealism* (New York: Paragon, 1993), p. 142.

129. André Parinaud, "André Breton, entretien avec Marcel Duchamp," in *Omaggio a André Breton* (Milan: Centro Francese di Studi, 1967), p. 41. In this interview, Duchamp says that Breton's "essential quality was to be exacting," (p. 20), perhaps a shared trait.

130. Breton's essay is translated as "Lighthouse of the Bride," in *View*, March 1945. At that time Breton added a foreword in which he upped his estimate of the *Large Glass* to an epochal changing of the rules comparable in the field of art to Kant's *Critique of Pure Reason* in philosophy.

131. Interview with Robert Lebel, "Marcel Duchamp maintenant et ici," *L'Oeil*, no. 149 (May 1967), p. 19.

132. Duchamp to Breton, letter postmarked February 3, 1935, Bibliothèque Littéraire Jacques Doucet.

133. Duchamp to Breton, January 6, 1936, Bibliothèque Littéraire Jacques Doucet.

134. Cabanne, *Dialogues*, p. 81.

135. Benjamin Péret, letter to Marcel Jean, December 31, 1938, in Péret, *Oeuvres complètes*, vol. 7 (Paris: Corti, 1995), p. 349. Péret lists Hugnet, Eluard, Ernst, Arp, Man Ray, and Tzara in the group. Interestingly, Duchamp is not mentioned.

136. *The Writings of Marcel Duchamp*, ed. Michel Sanouillet and Elmer Peterson (New York: Da Capo, 1973), p. 192.

137. Breton, *Conversations*, p. 155.

138. Charles Duits, *André Breton, a-t-il dit passe* (Paris: Denoël, 1969), p. 108.

139. Tomkins, *The World of Marcel Duchamp*, p. 443. See also Robert Lebel, "Marcel Duchamp maintenant et ici," *L'Oeil*, no. 149 (May 1967), p. 19.

140. André Breton, *What Is Surrealism? Selected Writings*, ed. Franklin Rosemont (New York: Monad, 1978), pp. 273, 274.

141. Albert Flament, "Surréalisme," *Revue de Paris* 45 (February 1, 1938), p. 712.

142. Rouletabille, *Voilà* 8 (January 21, 1938), p. 2, clipping in Bibliothèque Littéraire Jacques Doucet, 8343.65.

143. Dunlop, *The Shock of the New*, p. 219.

144. Jacques Lassaigne, "Les adieux du surréalisme," *La Revue Hebdomadaire*, February 26, 1938, pp. 489–490, translated in Dunlop, *The Shock of the New*, p. 221.

145. André Lhote, "Du naïf au pervers," *Ce Soir*, January 22, 1938, p. 2.

146. Rouletabille, *Voilà* 8 (January 21, 1938), p. 2, clipping in Bibliothèque Littéraire Jacques Doucet, 8343.65.

147. Petitjean, "A propos de l'exposition surréaliste," p. 515.

148. Maurice Morel and Jean Bazaine, "Faillité du surréalisme," *Temps Présent* 2 (January 28, 1938), p. 4.

149. Marius Richard, "Surréalisme pas encore mort . . . ," *Toute l'Edition*, January 22, 1938, clipping in Seligmann archives.

150. "Surréalisme," *Beaux Arts* (February 25, 1938), clipping in the Seligmann archives. See also the Keystone press photo "Surrealism Inspires New American Fashions," May 2, 1938, in Christies, Geneva, *Livres Illustrés Modernes*, May 19, 1999, lot 5.

151. Serge, "Dans une odeur de café grillé . . . ," *Paris-Midi*, January 18, 1938, clipping in the Seligmann Archives. This brief account of the marvels of the opening is also accompanied by a sketch of Domínguez's *Jamais* and a generic Surrealist object among the vignettes.

152. Breton, *What Is Surrealism?*, p. 273.

153. Gênet, "Letter from Paris," p. 55.

154. Raymond Cogniat, "L'Exposition internationale du Surréalisme," *XXe Siècle* 1 (March 1, 1938), pp. 25–26.

155. Lassaigne, "Les adieux du surréalisme," p. 490.

156. Roger Lannes, "Le surréalisme en liberté," *Le Journal*, January 13, 1938; Richard, "Surréalisme pas encore mort . . . ," clipping in Seligmann archives.

157. Guy Crouzet, "Actualité du surréalisme," *La Grande Revue* (February 1938), p. 490, clipping in Seligmann archives.

158. Flament, "Surréalisme," p. 712.

159. Grincheux Jovial, "Le vernissage de l'exposition surréaliste," *Beaux Arts*, no. 264 (January 21, 1938), p. 2. Crouzet, "Actualité du surréalisme," p. 487, clipping in the Seligmann archives.

160. Jean Marechal, "Chez les surréalistes internationaux," *Le Petit Parisien*, February 3, 1938, clipping in the Seligmann archives.

161. Raymond Lecuyer, "Une charge d'atelier," *Le Figaro*, January 22, 1938, p. 7. Translated in Dunlop, *The Shock of the New*, p. 222.

162. See Kenneth E. Silver, *Esprit de Corps: The Art of the Parisian Avant-Garde and the First World War, 1914–1925* (Princeton: Princeton University Press, 1989), pp. 11–12. Silver notes that there were attacks against "the Judeo-German Cartel of Parisian Painting Dealers," which implicitly included Wildenstein, owner of the Galerie Beaux-Arts (pp. 8–9).

163. Louis Brunet, "Du surréalisme," *La Croix*, January 20, 1938, p. 1, reprinted in Guiol-Benassaya, *La presse face au surréalisme*, p. 225.
164. Du Colombier, "Chez les surréalistes," clipping in Musée Picasso Archives.
165. Petitjean, "A propos de l'exposition surréaliste," p. 515.
166. Simon Arbellot, "Les vieux enfants terribles," *Paris-Midi*, January 22, 1938, clipping in the Seligmann Archives.
167. As recounted by Dunlop, *The Shock of the New*, p. 202. Yet Penrose also reported surprising profits from the daily admission receipts.
168. Mark Polizzotti, *Revolution of the Mind: The Life of André Breton* (New York: Farrar, Straus and Giroux, 1995), p. 445.
169. Eluard, *Letters to Gala*, no. 210 (late July-August 1935), pp. 208–209.
170. Grincheux Jovial [pseud.], "Surréalisme," *Beaux Arts*, February 4, 1938, p. 2.
171. Levy, *Memoir of an Art Gallery*, p. 255. Levy closed his gallery, and entered the army in 1942.
172. Breton to Benjamin Péret, April 7, 1942, Bibliothèque Littéraire Jacques Doucet.
173. Baltimore Museum of Art archives. The bill is dated November 30, 1942, a little more than three weeks after *First Papers* closed.

3 Surrealism Goes to the Fair: Projects for an American Surrealist Display at the 1939 New York World's Fair

1. Illustrated in Gérard Durozoi, *Histoire du mouvement surréaliste* (Paris: Hazan, 1997), p. 344. Kristians Tonny, son of the gallery owner, was the only Dutch painter included (p. 345).
2. Julien Levy, "Application for Concession," January 27, 1938; Julien Levy and Woodner Silverman, "Surrealist House," undated typescript, stamped approved March 22, 1938. These and subsequent documents referred to are in D. W. F. Inc., file Pl. 630, New York World's Fair Archive, Rare Book and Manuscripts Division, New York Public Library. See also Julien Levy, *Memoir of an Art Gallery* (New York: Putnam's, 1977), pp. 206–207.
3. Proposal of March 22, 1938, as in note 2. See also Levy and Woodner Silverman, "Surrealist House," a bound volume that clearly accompanied the proposal. It exists in two versions. One from the Levy estate was exhibited at the Archives of American Art, in conjunction with the exhibition *Julien Levy: Portrait of an Art Gallery* at the Equitable Gallery, New York, 1998. It includes the review from *Vogue* with the Eggarter photos of the *Exposition Internationale*. In the midst of a gallery season, Levy probably did not travel to Paris to see the show himself but rather experienced it from reviews and accounts. I am grateful to Adam Boxer of Ubu Gallery for the opportunity to see a second, similar bound version of "Surrealist House" now in the collection of the Getty Research Institute.

4. Keith L. Eggener, "'An Amusing Lack of Logic': Surrealism and Popular Entertainment," *American Art* 7 (Fall 1993), p. 32.

5. Julien Levy, *Surrealism* (New York: Black Sun Press, 1936), pp. 15–17. On Duchamp as a guide, see also Levy, *Memoir of an Art Gallery*, pp. 19ff.

6. General Manager Maurice Mermey to Director of Exhibits and Concessions, carbon of memo of March 21, 1938.

7. I refer to Magritte's well-known painting *The False Mirror*, one of the hits in *Fantastic Art, Dada, Surrealism*, and the infamous eye-slicing scene of Buñuel and Dalí's film *Un chien andalou* (1928). One could also add the eye in Man Ray's *Object to Be Destroyed* (1932), or Georges Bataille's erotic novel *Story of the Eye*. Levy's idea to use the white area for projection of other images is closest to Magritte, however, which in turn looks back to Claude-Nicolas Ledoux.

8. Levy, *Memoir of an Art Gallery*, p. 207. He also proposed a "Feelie," with spectators grasping unseen concealed objects.

9. Levy, *Memoir of an Art Gallery*, pp. 210–212. The Bonwit's broken window was reported in the newspapers of March 17, 1939, so Levy's conversion was apparently after this date. Chronologies of Dalí indicate that he signed onto the project in May, rather late for a projected opening at the end of that month.

10. Dickran Tashjian, *A Boatload of Madmen: Surrealism and the American Avant-Garde, 1920–1950* (New York: Thames and Hudson, 1995), pp. 54–56.

11. March 17, 1939, quoted in Tashjian, *A Boatload of Madmen*, p. 87. A copy of the clipping is in the Dalí artist's scrapbook, Museum of Modern Art (microfiche 1.148).

12. *Art Digest*, April 1939, reprinted in Daniel Abadie, ed., *La vie publique de Salvador Dalí* (Paris: Centre Georges Pompidou, 1980), p. 7.

13. Interview with Peter Busa, quoted in Steven Naifeh and Gregory White Smith, *Jackson Pollock: An American Saga* (New York: Clarkson Potter, 1989), p. 410.

14. Levy, *Memoir of an Art Gallery*, p. 199. Levy did not believe the episode was calculated by Dalí. The window fracas was on March 16, the opening on the 21st.

15. "Listings," *New Yorker* 15 (June 17, 1939), p. 10.

16. Margaret Case Harriman, "Profiles: A Dream Walking," *New Yorker* 15 (July 1, 1939), p. 23, and Levy, *Memoir of an Art Gallery*, pp. 213–215. Harriman is also the source for the gallery sales results, and for identifying Levy's "rubber man" from Pittsburgh as W. M. Gardner, president of Gardner Displays, who took over the running of the pavilion in its second year (1940).

17. Meredith Etherington-Smith, *The Persistence of Memory: A Biography of Dalí* (New York: Random House, 1992), p. 243. According to James's biographer, he advanced 48 percent of the Fair funding: Philip Purser, *Poeted: The Final Quest of Edward James* (London: Quartet, 1991), p. 100.

18. The print purchased by the Metropolitan Museum in 1941 is titled and dated "April 1939" on the verso.

19. Nissan N. Perez, "Dali, Horst and the Dream of Venus," *Israel Museum Journal* 3 (Spring 1984), p. 56.

20. Ibid., p. 54.

21. In conversation Lisa Jacobs has identified this model as Laurie Douglas, a girlfriend of Lynes. He "discovered" her "exquisite beauty [and] full-figured body" in 1938, and she often appeared in his shoots through the 1940s, according to James Crump, *When We Were Three* (Santa Fe: Arena, 1998), p. 281. The print exhibited in the Guggenheim Museum's *Surrealism: Two Private Eyes*, vol. 2 (New York, 1999), p. 734, bears the label of photographer Murray Korman across the lower edge. There are no markings on the back. The catalogue attributes it to Lynes working in Korman's studio. The label is cropped in the unattributed version reproduced in Tashjian, *A Boatload of Madmen*, p. 59.

22. Korman (1901/2–1961) was primarily active as a theatrical photographer, and thus most likely was proposed by Rose. See Korman's obituary, *New York Times*, August 10, 1961.

23. Descharnes, vol. 1, fig. 719. He incorrectly attributes this photo to Lynes and identifies it as for a film, although I have not found a trace of one. For the attribution to Korman, see Barbara Lekatsas, *The Howard and Muriel Weingrow Collection of Avant-Garde Art and Literature at Hofstra University* (Westport, Conn.: Greenwood Press, 1985), no. 498, p. 61.

24. Elsa Schiaparelli, *Shocking Life* (New York: Dutton, 1954), p. 114. Shocking perfume was introduced in 1937 with a body-shaped bottle designed by Léonor Fini. The earliest ad for it is in *Harper's Bazaar*, December 1937, p. 132. See also Richard Martin, *Fashion and Surrealism* (New York: Rizzoli, 1987), p. 203. Dalí got James to give him the stuffed bear. See Etherington-Smith, *The Persistence of Memory*, p. 227.

25. Interestingly, the French pavilion featured a national art exhibition organized by the owner of Galerie Beaux-Arts, Georges Wildenstein. Completely ignoring the "future" theme of the Fair, he chose a historical display of French art before 1900. On the pavilion's upper floor was a rather "official" twentieth-century selection of about a hundred painters included Léger, Rouault, Derain, Braque, and Lhote, but no Surrealists. These Fauves and Cubists were only those of French nationality, thus excluding Picasso. See J. L., "L'art moderne," *Beaux Arts*, no. 339 (June 30, 1939), p. 4.

26. Fleur Cowles, *The Case of Salvador Dali* (Boston: Little, Brown, 1959), p. 104. See also *Art Digest* 13 (July 1, 1939), p. 12.

27. "*The Dream of Venus* by Salvador Dali," *Town and Country* 94 (June 1939), pp. 46–47.

28. Gerald Goode and James Proctor, telegram to Alfred Barr, May 30, 1939, in Dalí artist's scrapbook, Museum of Modern Art (microfiche 1.148). The same source also preserves the press release "Is Dali Insane?" cited below.

29. Lavinia, "Around the Fair," *New Yorker* 15 (June 17, 1939), p. 71.

30. *New Yorker* 15 (July 1, 1939), p. 8.

31. "Pay as You Enter," *Time* 33 (June 26, 1939), p. 10. Dalí had stirred up the issue of madness at least since his oft-quoted denial of "Conquest of the Irrational" (1935). See also "Not a Madman,—Dali," *Art Digest* 9 (January 11, 1935), p. 16.

32. Etherington-Smith, *The Persistence of Memory*, p. 245. While most of Dalí's biographers indicate that he left in September (e.g., Karin von Maur, *Salvador Dalí, 1904–1989* [Stuttgart: Staatsgalerie, 1989], p. 488), the *New Yorker* profile says that he sailed to France "two weeks ago" (p. 27), i.e., mid-June. He also claimed in *The Secret Life of Salvador Dalí* (1942; Figueres, Spain: Dasa Ediciones, 1986) never to have seen the completed pavilion (p. 377). He sailed on the *Champlain*.

33. James to Dalí, cable of June 21, 1939, quoted in Etherington-Smith, *The Persistence of Memory*, p. 245. Gala's reply, from the Pyrenees, came six weeks later (p. 246).

34. Levy, *Memoir of an Art Gallery*, pp. 217–218. This does have the hint of a cover story for Dalí's benefit.

35. Harriman, "Profiles: A Dream Walking," p. 27.

36. Excerpts appeared in "Dali Manifests," *Art Digest* 13 (August 1, 1939), p. 9. A reply by Chicago artist Dale Nichols allowed Dalí his madness, yet was not anxious to join him, as "common health measures should protect those who do not suffer from paranoia" (September 1, 1939, p. 26). Other art periodicals were silent on the "Declaration." Its entire text is reprinted in Levy, *Memoir of an Art Gallery*, pp. 219–222.

37. Levy to James, letter of July 15, 1939, quoted in Etherington-Smith, *The Persistence of Memory*, p. 246.

38. "Eleanor's Show," *Time* 34 (August 21, 1939), p. 31. See also "Tomorrow and 1940," *Time* 34 (October 23, 1939), p. 77, on the Fair's debts forcing it to reopen in 1940.

39. Manuscript quoted in Cowles, *The Case of Salvador Dali*, p. 103.

40. General Manager Maurice Mermey to Director of Exhibits and Concessions, carbon of memo of March 21, 1938.

41. George p. Smith, Co-Director of Amusements, to Gardner, carbon of letter of April 22, 1940.

42. Robert A. M. Stern, Gregory Gilmartin, and Thomas Mellins, *New York 1930* (New York: Rizzoli, 1987), p. 754.

43. "Vénus 39 rêve," *Marianne-Magasin*, p. 21, undated clipping in Surrealist scrapbook, Bibliothèque Littéraire Jacques Doucet, Paris, 8343.71. In part this recalls Matta's call in his "Architecture of Time" article (*Minotaure*, Spring

1938) for "walls like damp sheets which lose their shapes." Quoted in Lucy R. Lippard, ed., *Surrealists on Art* (Englewood Cliffs, N.J.: Prentice-Hall, 1970), p. 168.

44. "Dali's Surrealist Dream House at the World's Fair," *Vogue* 93 (June 1, 1939), p. 56. The exterior seems to have been slightly pink in the lower areas.

45. Levy, *Memoir of an Art Gallery*, p. 211. Levy recounted this to Dalí, who thought in terms of "a back-to-the-womb symbol" (pp. 213–214). Water would indeed prove successful for Rose, whose Aquacade revue was a big hit.

46. Schiaparelli, *Shocking Life*, p. 116. See also Palmer White, *Elsa Schiaparelli* (New York: Rizzoli, 1986), p. 170.

47. "Dali's Surrealist Dream House at the World's Fair," p. 56. The entry is best reproduced in *Life* 7 (July 3, 1939), p. 67.

48. Michele H. Bogart, *Public Sculpture and the Civic Ideal in New York City, 1890–1930* (Chicago: University of Chicago Press, 1989), p. 257. The bodily reentry into the womb also prefigures Nikki de Sainte-Phalle's 82-foot-long *Hon (Elle)*, which 100,000 visitors entered between her legs when exhibited in Stockholm during June-July 1966. Some of Dalí's bulbous female forms on the pavilion exterior, covered with patterned decoration, likewise foreshadow Sainte-Phalle's style.

49. Keith F. Davis, *The Passionate Observer: Photographs by Carl Van Vechten* (Kansas City: Hallmark, 1993), pl. 31, p. 116.

50. Carl Van Vechten, interview with William Ingersoll, March-May 1960, Oral History Collection, Columbia University, typescript p. 253.

51. Carl Van Vechten, letter to Fania Marinoff, Saturday, August 5, 1939, in Van Vechten papers, Rare Book and Manuscript Division, New York Public Library.

52. In the background of "Water-Bugs fun," *L'Illustration* suppl. 45 (July 1939), n.p.

53. Levy to James, letter of July 15, 1939, quoted in Etherington-Smith, *The Persistence of Memory*, p. 246.

54. Harriman, "Profiles: A Dream Walking," p. 22.

55. "Pay as You Enter," p. 10. *Time* also published two small topless photos of "puckish little Kelcey Carr," a veteran of "dives," and reported that one to four performed in five-hour shifts.

56. Mark Polizzotti, *Revolution of the Mind: The Life of André Breton* (New York: Farrar, Straus and Giroux, 1995), p. 403.

57. André Breton, *L'amour fou* (Paris: Gallimard, 1937), fig. 12, p. 92, entitled *L'air de nager.* See also *André Breton*, exh. cat. (Paris: Centre Georges Pompidou, 1991), cat. no. 215.

58. Levy, *Memoir of an Art Gallery*, p. 217. See also the unpaginated plates following p. 160.

59. Diana Cooper, *Trumpets from the Steep* (London: Hart-Davis, 1960), p. 16.

60. Robert W. Rydell, *Worlds of Fairs* (Chicago: University of Chicago Press, 1993), p. 137.

61. Edo McCullough, *World's Fair Midways* (New York: Exposition Press, 1966), p. 124.

62. David Gelernter, *1939, the Lost World of the Fair* (New York: Free Press, 1995), p. 126, reports on one source who recalled this display from adolescence. See also Rydell, *Worlds of Fairs*, p. 144.

63. Rem Koolhaas, *Delirious New York* (New York: Oxford University Press, 1978), p. 228.

64. Cowles, *The Case of Salvador Dali*, p. 104.

65. "Freud + Minsky = Dali," *Art Digest* 13 (July 1, 1939), p. 12. This is also the source for the quotations in the paragraph after next.

66. Now in the study collection of the Photography Department, Museum of Modern Art, New York. They are reproduced in Abadie, ed., *La vie publique de Salvador Dalí*, p. 76.

67. Dalí, *The Secret Life*, p. 371.

68. Eight are illustrated in *Dalí arquitectura* (Figueras: Fundació Gala-Salvador Dalí, 1996), cat. nos. 179–186. Some of the same images are also preserved in the Edward James Foundation. Since this study was finished, the Fundació has published 34 photographs by Schaal in its catalogue *Salvador Dalí Dream of Venus* (Figueras, 1999), with a detailed essay by Fèlix Fanés. Over 40 *Dream of Venus* photographs have emerged from the Schaal estate for exhibition at Jan Van der Donk, New York, January 2000.

69. "Dream of Venus" tape recording, Young-Mallin archive, New York.

70. "Vénus 39 rêve," p. 19, unidentified clipping as in note 5. The "admirable" Venus is said to be from a music hall troupe. See also *Life* 7 (July 3, 1939), p. 67.

71. Robert Descharnes and Gilles Néret, *Salvador Dalí, 1904–1989* (Cologne: Benedikt Taschen, 1997), no. 658, *Surrealist Dinner on a Bed* (1937). See also von Maur, *Salvador Dalí*, p. 487, on the Marx brothers collaboration in February 1937.

72. Oliver Jensen, "Fair Girlie," *Life* 9 (July 29, 1940), p. 55. She also termed the swimming "healthy." The extensive photos accompanying *Life*'s profile range from human interest to prurient.

73. Harriman, "Profiles: A Dream Walking," p. 23. See also Dalí, "Declaration of the Independence of the Imagination . . ."

74. Cowles, *The Case of Salvador Dali*, p. 104. See also Levy, *Memoir of an Art Gallery*, p. 205.

75. Dalí, "Declaration of the Independence of the Imagination . . . ," printed broadside, July 1939, quoted in Levy, *Memoir of an Art Gallery*, p. 222.

76. "Pay as You Enter," p. 10.

77. Which is not to overlook the usual reason given, Dalí's nonadhesion to Breton's group FIARI, as discussed by José Pierre in *Salvador Dalí retrospective 1920–1980* (Paris: Centre Georges Pompidou, 1979), p. 138. In his last preserved letter to Breton, Dalí regrets the Eluard "difficulties," which also could have come into play, given their continuing association. Yet Dalí closes with the expectation of seeing Breton and showing his new paintings. Letter of January 26, 1939, Bibliothèque Littéraire Jacques Doucet.

78. "Pay as You Enter," p. 10.

79. Levy, *Memoir of an Art Gallery*, p. 217.

80. "Pay as You Enter," p. 10.

81. Gelernter, *1939, the Lost World of the Fair*, p. 125.

82. Quoted in McCullough, *World's Fair Midways*, p. 123.

83. Ibid.

84. Ibid., pp. 124–125. Gelernter, *1939, the Lost World of the Fair*, p. 131, indicates that the promoters were fined.

85. Rydell, *Worlds of Fairs*, pp. 141, 143–144.

86. Herbert Drake, "Fun for All and It's All for Fun," *New York Herald Tribune*, April 3, 1939, section 11, p. 52.

87. Stanley Appelbaum, ed., *The New York World's Fair 1939/1940* (New York: Dover, 1977), p. 127.

88. Joseph Wood Krutch, "A Report of the Fair," *Nation* 148 (June 24, 1939), p. 723. He judged the show "rather ingenious" and found nothing to report to LaGuardia.

89. Drake, "Fun for All and It's All for Fun," p. 52. He reports that the real Sally Rand's proposal for a "Nude Ranch" was turned down by Fair officials.

90. Quoted in Tashjian, *A Boatload of Madmen*, p. 60.

91. "Hoopla and Honky Tonk," *New Yorker* 15 (July 8, 1939), p. 11.

92. Gelernter, *1939, the Lost World of the Fair*, p. 126. His 16-year-old respondent recalled audience members trying to make the topless models giggle. A similar story appears in E. L. Doctorow's *World's Fair* (New York: Random House, 1985), chap. 29.

93. Robert Rosenblum, "Remembrance of Fairs Past," in *Remembering the Future* (New York: Queens Museum and Rizzoli, 1989), p. 16. See also "Eleanor's Show," p. 31.

94. Clifford Orr, "Around the Fair, Foreigners and Natives," *New Yorker* 15 (July 15, 1939), p. 40.

95. Jimmy Ernst, *A Not-So-Still Life* (New York: St. Martin's, 1984), p. 151.

96. Stern, Gilmartin, and Mellins, *New York 1930*, p. 754.

97. Caption to Acme/UPI photo, datelined September 4, 1941, in Centre Georges Pompidou Archives. The caption also identifies the caged animal on the table as a porcupine. Etherington-Smith says there were 4,000 sacks (*The Persistence of Memory*, p. 270).

98. Herb Caen, a publicist who assisted Dalí, quoted in Etherington-Smith, *The Persistence of Memory*, p. 270.

99. André Breton, "Avida Dollars," *Arson* 1 (1942).

4 The New World: First Papers of Surrealism (1942)

1. William Shopsin, Mosette Broderick, et al., *The Villard Houses* (New York: Viking, 1980), p. 125. See this source for extensive illustrations of the original interior and its subsequent alterations.

2. Coordinating Council of French Relief Societies *Bulletin*, no. 5 (July 1942), p. 2. These bulletins are an important source for this section. At the old Council headquarters there had been an exhibit of Atget photographs from Berenice Abbott's collection, which raised $1,500.

3. The Coordinating Council was only in the Reid mansion for about a year; in early 1943 the mansion passed to the Women's Military Service Club rest center, and the Council moved across the circular drive to the north (Fahnestock) wing at 457 Madison. There Pagès's watercolors were reinstalled, and a French sailors' foyer and a cafe were opened.

4. Henry McBride, "Surrealism Gets Nearer," *New York Sun*, October 16, 1942, p. 27.

5. A more extensive portrait of the midtown art world has recently appeared. See Ann Temkin's essay "Habitat for a Dossier," in *Joseph Cornell/Marcel Duchamp . . . in Resonance*, exh. cat. (New York: Distributed Art Publishers, 1998), pp. 79–93.

6. Edward Alden Jewell, "Surrealists Open Display Tonight," *New York Times*, October 14, 1942, p. 26.

7. "Inheritors of Chaos," *Time* 40 (November 2, 1942), p. 47.

8. Spies no. 2725, illustrated in Sotheby's New York sale 7379, November 11, 1999, lot 129.

9. Coordinating Council of French Relief Societies *Bulletin*, no. 6 (December 1942), p. 7.

10. Coordinating Council of French Relief Societies, *Calendar 1943* (New York, 1942).

11. Elsa Schiaparelli, *Shocking Life* (New York: Dutton, 1954), p. 166.

12. Jimmy Ernst, *A Not-So-Still Life* (New York: St. Martin's, 1984), p. 222. "Miss" Peggy Guggenheim is listed in the catalogue as the first of eighteen "patrons" of *First Papers*.

13. Peggy Guggenheim, *Out of This Century: Confessions of an Art Addict* (1946; London: André Deutsch, 1983), p. 273.

14. On an official printed postcard dated "17 janv. 1941," which Breton had printed in *View* 1, no. 7–8 (October-November 1941), p. 5. On Duchamp's visa procrastinations, see Alice Goldfarb Marquis, *Marcel Duchamp = Eros, c'est la vie: A Biography* (Troy, N.Y.: Whitston Publishing Co., 1981), pp. 261–265.

15. Schiaparelli, *Shocking Life*, p. 168. She does not mention Surrealism, nor Breton, in particular.

16. Letter to Magda and Walter Pach, translated in Francis M. Naumann, "Amicalement, Marcel," *Archives of American Art Journal* 29 (1989), p. 47.

17. Harriet and Carroll Janis, interview with Marcel Duchamp, winter 1953, typescript, Philadelphia Museum of Art exhibition archives, p. 7-15.

18. "Artist at Ease," *New Yorker* 18 (October 24, 1942), p. 12. Could there be an irony intended in the use of "at ease," also a military term?

19. Matta to Gordon Onslow-Ford, letter of May or June 1942, quoted in Martica Sawin, *Surrealism in Exile and the Beginning of the New York School* (Cambridge: MIT Press, 1995), p. 214. For an extensive discussion of the reception of the first *VVV,* see pp. 214–220.

20. David Hare, interview with Dorothy Seckler, Archives of American Art, January 17, 1968, typescript p. 28.

21. Sawin, *Surrealism in Exile*, p. 213.

22. Breton to Benjamin Péret, letter of January 10, 1942, Bibliothèque Littéraire Jacques Doucet, Paris. In the same letter Breton says he is organizing a new issue of *Minotaure* (which ultimately never appeared, though to a large extent it was subsumed in *VVV*).

23. Robert Lebel, "Paris-New York et retour avec Marcel Duchamp, dada et le surréalisme," in Centre Georges Pompidou, *Paris-New York* (Paris: Musée National d'Art Moderne, 1977), p. 72.

24. André Masson, *Vagabond du surréalisme*, ed. Gilbert Brownstone (Paris: St.-Germain-des-Prés, 1975), p. 123.

25. The first number of Hugnet's *L'Usage de la Parole* (December 1939) includes poems of Eluard and Duchamp's "SURcenSURE," perhaps a punning spoof on Breton's censure of various Surrealists. The second has a cover by Ernst.

26. Ernst, *A Not-So-Still Life*, p. 206. This took place on July 17, 1941.

27. Breton to Gordon Onslow-Ford, letter of August 27, 1942, quoted in Sawin, *Surrealism in Exile*, p. 225.

28. Joseph Cornell papers, Archives of American Art, roll 1058: 883, note of Tuesday 28 [sic], 1942.

29. Breton to Benjamin Péret, letter of August 27, 1942, Bibliothèque Littéraire Jacques Doucet. In the same letter Breton indicates that he can borrow works of Esteban Frances from Gordon Onslow-Ford. His radio work obliged him to stay in New York, while Jacqueline and Aube vacationed on Cape Cod.

30. Breton to Benjamin Péret, letter of October 22, 1942, Bibliothèque Littéraire Jacques Doucet. He confirms the showing of two paintings by Remedios Varo, and decries the absence of Brauner and new works of Esteban Frances, never sent to New York.

31. Breton to Gordon Onslow-Ford, letter of August 27, 1942, quoted in Sawin, *Surrealism in Exile*, p. 225.

32. André Breton to William Baziotes, letter postmarked September 7, 1942, Baziotes papers, Archives of American Art, microfilm N70–21, 116. Calder also received an identical copy, now in the papers of his Foundation.

33. Ernst, *A Not-So-Still Life*, p. 234. Gerome Kamrowski was in fact included.

34. Sawin, *Surrealism in Exile*, p. 212. Goodwin had contributed a short poetic statement to the "Tanguy" issue of *View* (May 1942), and was included in a group show at Peggy Guggenheim's gallery in December 1946.

35. *New York Times*, January 11, 1955, clipping in artist's file, Museum of Modern Art. Nelson had a memorial show at the Riverside Museum that month. He had been included in an autumn salon at Peggy Guggenheim's gallery in October 1945.

36. Steven Naifeh and Gregory White Smith, *Jackson Pollock: An American Saga* (New York: Clarkson Potter, 1989), p. 861.

37. Peter Busa, quoted in Sawin, *Surrealism in Exile*, p. 230. From transcriptions of his notebooks, typescript p. 6, courtesy of Christopher Busa.

38. Christopher Busa, "Long Point Gallery," *Provincetown Arts* 7 (1991), p. 9.

39. Robert Coates, "Sixteen Miles of String," *New Yorker* 18 (October 31, 1942), p. 72.

40. Sidney Simon, "Concerning the Beginnings of the New York School: 1939–1943," *Art International* 11 (Summer 1967), pp. 17–18. Matta is speaking to Peter Busa but referring to the whole group, which also included Baziotes, Kamrowski, Pollock, and Motherwell.

41. Guggenheim, *Out of This Century*, p. 273

42. Schiaparelli, *Shocking Life*, p. 168.

43. Sawin, *Surrealism in Exile*, p. 226. The Janises' estimate is from the Duchamp special issue of *View*, and has been repeated since.

44. Duchamp to Man Ray, undated letter from 56 Seventh Avenue, New York. Man Ray papers, Getty Research Institute.

45. Harriet and Carroll Janis, interview with Marcel Duchamp, pp. 7-15, 7-17. Later he goes on to say that the cost was less than twenty dollars.

46. Ibid., p. 7-16.

47. Susanna Coggeshall, paraphrased in Sawin, *Surrealism in Exile*, p. 227.

48. Amelia Jones, *Postmodernism and the En-gendering of Marcel Duchamp* (Cambridge: Cambridge University Press, 1994), chap. 4. For the registering of *Mile of String*, see Arturo Schwarz, *The Complete Works of Marcel Duchamp*, 3d ed. (New York: Delano Greenidge, 1997), vol. 2, no. 488, p. 777.

49. Jewell, "Surrealists Open Display Tonight," p. 26. When Jewell previewed the show, Duchamp was still walking around, unwinding a ball of twine. It is probably Jewell's indefinite reference that has led subsequent writers to refer to paper birds, though Masson describes only squares of paper. No paper attachments are visible in the Schiff installation photos; presumably they were gone by the time of the opening.

50. McBride, "Surrealism Gets Nearer," p. 27.

51. I am grateful to Sandy Rohrer of the Calder Foundation for this suggestion.

52. Duchamp quoted in Rudi Blesh, *Modern Art USA* (New York: Knopf, 1956), p. 200. Duchamp later said that the string was guncotton and burned without a flame, "terrifying" but apparently without damage (Pierre Cabanne, *Dialogues with Marcel Duchamp* [New York: Viking, 1971], p. 86). Earlier he spoke of smoke and "smoldering but it didn't go any further" (Harriet and Carroll Janis, interview with Marcel Duchamp, p. 7-16).

53. Conversation with Ulf Linde, May 1995. I am grateful to Linde for pointing me toward some of the connections that follow, particularly "Recipe."

54. Dickran Tashjian, *A Boatload of Madmen: Surrealism and the American Avant-Garde, 1920–1950* (New York: Thames and Hudson, 1995), p. 219. He also evokes a connection to the "filaments and cracks" of *The Large Glass.*

55. Brian O'Doherty, *Inside the White Cube: The Ideology of the Gallery Space* (Santa Monica: Lapis Press, 1986), p. 72.

56. Coordinating Council of French Relief Societies *Bulletin*, no. 6 (December 1942), p. 5.

57. Duchamp quoted in Blesh, *Modern Art USA*, p. 200.

58. James T. Soby, "Matta Echaurren," *Magazine of Art* 40 (March 1947), p. 104.

59. "Inheritors of Chaos," p. 47.

60. "Agonized Humor," *Newsweek* 20 (October 26, 1942), p. 76. The reporter apparently spoke to Ernst, who is quoted as saying: "We like to paint as we dream, without control and with complete freedom."

61. Duchamp letter to Katherine Dreier, n.d. (c. September 1942), Dreier papers, Yale.

62. Ibid., letter of November 4, 1942. He also mentions that Dreier will receive a set of the photographs, which is preserved in her papers.

63. *Joseph Cornell/Marcel Duchamp . . . in Resonance*, plate 92, p. 112. To his right is a Mondrian-like abstraction, probably the same one visible in one of Schiff's photos (fig. 4.3). It is in fact an early painting by Robert Motherwell.

64. André Breton, "The Point of View: Testimony 45," *View*, ser. 5, no. 1 (March 1945), p. 5.

65. Harriet and Sidney Janis, "Marcel Duchamp, Anti-Artist," *View*, ser. 5, no. 1 (1945), p. 18.

66. "Agonized Humor," p. 76.

67. O'Doherty, *Inside the White Cube*, pp. 71–72.

68. Harriet and Carroll Janis, interview with Marcel Duchamp, p. 7-16.

69. Letter to Péret, October 22, 1942, Bibliothèque Littéraire Jacques Doucet.

70. "The Passing Shows," *Art News* 41 (November 1, 1942), p. 24.

71. McBride, "Surrealism Gets Nearer," p. 27. He probably refers to *Network of Stoppages* (1914) mentioned above.

72. Man Ray, *Self-Portrait* (Boston: New York Graphic Society, 1988), p. 191.

73. Peter Busa, notebooks, Peter Busa papers, courtesy Christopher Busa.

74. "Miles of String," *Art Digest* 17 (November 1, 1942), p. 7.

75. Coates, "Sixteen Miles of String," p. 72.

76. "Inheritors of Chaos," p. 47.

77. Catrina Neiman, *The Legend of Maya Deren* (New York: Anthology Film Archives, 1988), vol. 1, part 2, p. 152. The term also refers to what Deren called "a narrow sort of seat which apprentice witches were supposed to straddle for hours."

78. Telephone interview with Alexander Hammid, April 9, 1996.

79. Maya Deren, "'Witch's Cradle' Shooting Script," reprinted in Neiman, *The Legend of Maya Deren*, vol. 1, part 2, p. 163.

80. On August 15, 1943. Jennifer Gough-Cooper and Jacques Gaumont, "Kiesler, Duchamp, dada et le surréalisme," in Dieter Bogner, ed., *Friedrich Kiesler: Architekt, Maler, Bildhauer, 1890–1965* (Vienna: Locker, 1988), p. 291 and note 26.

81. William S. Rubin, *Dada, Surrealism, and Their Heritage* (New York: Museum of Modern Art, 1968), p. 160, a metaphor also used by Anaïs Nin, and underlining the mythic. See also John Bernard Myers, *Tracking the Marvelous: A Life in the New York Art World* (New York: Random House, 1983), who termed it a "dramatic labyrinth" (p. 35).

82. Cabanne, *Dialogues with Marcel Duchamp*, p. 86.

83. Masson, *Vagabond du surréalisme*, p. 123.

84. Royal Cortissoz, "George Bellows and Some Others," *New York Herald Tribune* (October 25, 1942), sec. VI, p. 5.

85. "The Passing Shows," p. 24.

86. Emily Genauer, "Surrealist Paintings Hung Surrealistically," *New York World-Telegram* (October 24, 1942), p. 7.

87. Dore Ashton, *The New York School, a Cultural Reckoning* (New York: Viking, 1973), p. 122.

88. Tashjian, *A Boatload of Madmen*, p. 379, note 34.

89. Blesh, *Modern Art USA*, p. 201.

90. Quoted in Sawin, *Surrealism in Exile*, p. 227.

91. Blesh, *Modern Art USA*, p. 201.

92. Duchamp to Dreier, letter of September 21 [sic], 1942, Beinecke Library, Yale University. Duchamp seems to have misdated this, for the day after the opening would have been October 15.

93. Schiaparelli, *Shocking Life*, p. 165.

94. Ernst, *A Not-So-Still Life*, p. 234.

95. Charles Henri Ford, letter to Henry Treece, October 31, 1942, Harry Ransom Humanities Research Center, University of Texas at Austin.

96. Jewell, "Surrealists Open Display Tonight," p. 26.

5 The Disembodiment of Surrealist Exhibition Space and Its Dissemination

1. Stefi Kiesler personal calendar, quoted in Dieter Bogner, ed., *Friedrich Kiesler: Architekt, Maler, Bildhauer, 1890–1965* (Vienna: Locker, 1988), p. 334, note 183. Other notations indicate Frederick Kiesler's contact with Breton and others earlier in 1942. See also Gough-Cooper and Gaumont's essay "Kiesler, Duchamp, dada et le surréalisme" in the same catalogue, p. 291.

2. Martica Sawin, *Surrealism in Exile and the Beginning of the New York School* (Cambridge: MIT Press, 1995), p. 235.

3. Interview cited in Virginia M. Dortch, ed., *Peggy Guggenheim and Her Friends* (Milan: Berenice, 1994), p. 10. Both Guggenheim and Duchamp left for London together before the Surrealist vernissage, where he hung the Cocteau drawings of the inaugural show of Guggenheim Jeune gallery.

4. "Inheritors of Chaos," *Time* 40 (November 2, 1942), p. 47; "Isms Rampant," *Newsweek* 20 (November 2, 1942), p. 66. Breton's object is illustrated in *VVV*, no. 2–3 (June 1943), p. 78.

5. Cynthia Goodman, "The Art of Revolutionary Display Techniques," in *Frederick Kiesler* (New York: Whitney Museum of American Art, 1989), pp. 68–75.

6. Ibid., p. 73.

7. Breton to Donati, letter of September 14, 1947, quoted in Sawin, *Surrealism in Exile*, p. 400. See also pp. 391–392, 395–399, for further details about the Maeght show.

8. Calvin Tomkins, "Not Seen and/or Less Seen," *New Yorker* 40 (February 6, 1965), p. 38. As biographer of both Rauschenberg and Duchamp, Tomkins's critical interests embody this link.

9. Dodie Kazanjian and Calvin Tomkins, *Alex: The Life of Alexander Liberman* (New York, 1993), p. 160. Duchamp produced a stain "portrait" of George Washington, which Liberman decided he could not use for *Vogue*. It was returned to the artist, along with fifty dollars for expenses.

10. "Ficelles de Marcel Duchamp," *VVV*, no. 2–3 (March 1943), p. 86.

11. Allan Kaprow, "The Legacy of Jackson Pollock," *Art News* 57 (October 1958), pp. 24–26.

12. For instance, in the Centre Georges Pompidou catalogue *Paris-Paris*, pp. 80–81, and Bruce Altschuler, *The Avant-Garde in Exhibition: New Art in the 20th Century* (New York: Abrams, 1994), pp. 126–127.

13. Grace Glueck, "A Rainy Taxi, a Tea Cup of Fur," *New York Times*, March 24, 1968, p. 28. The necklace seems related to the strand of hooks and shellfish worn by the nude model in two groups of Dream of Venus photographs.

14. Gerald D. Silk, "Ed Kienholz's *Back Seat Dodge, '38*," *Arts Magazine* 52 (January 1978), p. 116. Silk finds they "share related ideas," but that it was "unlikely" that Kienholz knew of Dalí's *Taxi* in 1964. Interestingly, the year of Kienholz's car matches that of the *Exposition* where the *Taxi* was first exhibited.

15. Robert Pincus-Witten, "Eva Hesse," in *Postminimalism* (New York: Out of London, 1977), p. 61. Hesse herself stressed the order of this work, saying, "Chaos can be as structured as non-chaos. That we know from Jackson Pollock" (ibid., p. 62). The photo of Hesse peeking through her ropes is published with this quote in *Life* magazine (February 27, 1970), p. 66.

16. Brian O'Doherty, *Inside the White Cube: The Ideology of the Gallery Space* (Santa Monica: Lapis Press, 1986), p. 72.

17. Rozsika Parker, *The Subversive Stitch: Embroidery and the Making of the Feminine* (New York: Routledge, 1989).

18. Catherine de Zegher, "Hatoum's *Recollection*: About Losing and Being Lost," in *Mona Hatoum* (London: Phaidon Press, 1997), pp. 90–105. De Zegher cites Pollock and Hesse as prior instances of the *informe*, but not Duchamp (p. 102). In this she repeats the curious omission of *Mile of String* in Yve-Alain Bois and Rosalind Krauss's study *Formless: A User's Guide* (Cambridge: MIT Press, 1997).

Conclusion

1. Interview with Hedda Sterne, March 31, 1995. Thus Breton's pointed anagram of Dalí's name, from c. 1941, boomerangs on the poet/exhibition organizer who thought of it.

2. "Surrealist Painting," *The Nation*, August 12 and 19, 1944, reprinted in *Clement Greenberg: The Collected Essays and Criticism*, ed. John O'Brian, vol. 1 (Chicago: University of Chicago Press, 1986), pp. 226, 230.

3. Michael Fried, "Art and Objecthood," *Artforum* (June 1967), reprinted in Gregory Battcock, ed., *Minimal Art: A Critical Anthology* (New York, 1968), pp. 116–147.

4. William S. Rubin, *Dada, Surrealism, and Their Heritage* (New York: Museum of Modern Art, 1968), p. 182. I can attest to the predominance of these views in art historical education in the mid-1970s.

5. Hal Foster, *Compulsive Beauty* (Cambridge: MIT Press, 1993), pp. xii–xiv.

6. Bettina Wilson, "Surrealism in Paris," *Vogue* 91 (March 1, 1938), p. 144.

7. Susanna Coggeshall, telephone interview, September 8, 1996.

Bibliography

Archival Sources

Archives of American Art: Alfred Barr papers; William Baziotes papers, microfilm N70-21; Joseph Cornell papers, microfilm roll 1058.

Archives of American Art, Oral History Collection: Man Ray, conversation with Arnold Crane, June 12, 1968; David Hare, interview with Dorothy Seckler, January 17, 1968.

Bibliothèque Historique de la Ville de Paris: Agence France Presse archives; Denise Bellon photo archives.

Bibliothèque Littéraire Jacques Doucet at Bibliothèque Sainte-Geneviève, Paris: André Breton correspondence to Salvador Dalí, Marcel Duchamp, Gordon Onslow-Ford, and Benjamin Péret.

Centre Georges Pompidou, Paris, Musée National d'Art Moderne archives: Man Ray archives.

Columbia University, Butler Library, Rare Books and Manuscripts Division: Varian Fry papers.

Getty Research Institute, Los Angeles: Man Ray papers; Josef Breitenbach photo archives.

Historic New Orleans Collection: Clarence John Laughlin papers.

Musée Picasso Archives, Paris: press clippings.

Museum of Modern Art, New York: Museum exhibition archives; photo archives; Alfred H. Barr, Jr. papers; James Thrall Soby papers.

New York Public Library, Rare Books and Manuscripts Division: New York World's Fair Archive, D.W.F. Inc., file Pl. 630; Carl Van Vechten papers.

Philadelphia Museum of Art, Department of 20th Century Art and Department of Prints and Drawings: Arensberg archives; Marcel Duchamp exhibition archives.

University of Texas at Austin, Harry Ransom Humanities Research Center: Charles Henri Ford papers.

Yale University, Beinecke Library: Katherine Dreier papers; Kurt Seligmann archives.

General Sources

Aragon, Louis. *Paris Peasant.* 1926; Boston: Exact Change, 1994.

Beauvoir, Simone de. *The Prime of Life.* New York: World, 1962.

Blesh, Rudi. *Modern Art USA.* New York: Knopf, 1956.

Centre Georges Pompidou. *Paris-New York.* Paris: Musée National d'Art Moderne, 1977.

Greenberg, Clement. *Clement Greenberg, the Collected Essays and Criticism.* Ed. John O'Brian. Vol. 1. Chicago: University of Chicago Press, 1986.

Holborn, Mark. *Josef Breitenbach, Photographer.* New York: Temple Rock, 1986.

Leiris, Michel. *Journal: 1922–1989.* Paris: Gaillimard, 1992.

Neiman, Catrina. *The Legend of Maya Deren.* Vol. 1, part 2. New York: Anthology Film Archives, 1988.

Parrot, Nicole. *Mannequins.* New York: St. Martin's, 1982.

Schiaparelli, Elsa. *Shocking Life.* New York: Dutton, 1954.

On Exhibitions and the New York World's Fair

Altschuler, Bruce. *The Avant-Garde in Exhibition: New Art in the 20th Century.* New York: Abrams, 1994.

Appelbaum, Stanley, ed. *The New York World's Fair 1939/1940.* New York: Dover, 1977.

Barr, Margaret Scolari. "'Our Campaigns': 1930–1944." *New Criterion,* special issue (1987).

Berlin Museum of Modern Art. *Stationen der Moderne.* Berlin: Berlinsche Galerie, 1988.

Drake, Herbert. "Fun for All and It's All for Fun." *New York Herald Tribune*, April 3, 1939, section 11, p. 52.

Dunlop, Ian. *The Shock of the New.* New York: McGraw-Hill, 1972.

Gelernter, David. *1939, the Lost World of the Fair.* New York: Free Press, 1995.

Goodman, Cynthia. "Frederick Kiesler: Designs for Peggy Guggenheim's Art of This Century Gallery." *Arts Magazine* 51 (June 1977), pp. 90–95.

Harrison, Helen A., ed. *Dawn of a New Day: The New York World's Fair 1939/40.* New York: Queens Museum and NYU Press, 1988.

Herbert, James D. *Paris 1937: Worlds on Exhibition.* Ithaca: Cornell University Press, 1998.

McCullough, Edo. *World's Fair Midways.* New York: Exposition Press, 1966.

O'Doherty, Brian. *Inside the White Cube: The Ideology of the Gallery Space.* 1976; Santa Monica: Lapis Press, 1986.

Platt, Susan Noyes. "Modernism, Formalism, and Politics: The *Cubism and Abstract Art* Exhibition of 1936." *Art Journal* 47 (Winter 1988), pp. 284–295.

Rosenblum, Robert. "Remembrance of Fairs Past." In *Remembering the Future.* New York: Queens Museum and Rizzoli, 1989.

Rydell, Robert W. *Worlds of Fairs.* Chicago: University of Chicago Press, 1993.

Schneede, Uwe M. "Exposition internationale du surréalisme, Paris 1938." In Bernd Kluser and Katherine Hegewisch, eds., *Die Kunst der Ausstellung.* Frankfurt: Insel, 1991.

Staniszewski, Mary Anne. *The Power of Display: A History of Exhibition Installation at the Museum of Modern Art.* Cambridge: MIT Press, 1998.

Troy, Nancy J. *The De Stijl Environment.* Cambridge: MIT Press, 1983.

On Surrealism

Ades, Dawn. *Dada and Surrealism Reviewed.* London: Arts Council, 1978.

Agar, Eileen. *A Look at My Life.* London: Methuen, 1988.

Balakian, Anna. *André Breton, Magus of Surrealism.* New York: Oxford University Press, 1971.

Barr, Alfred H., Jr. *Fantastic Art, Dada, Surrealism.* New York: Museum of Modern Art, 1936.

Belton, Robert J. *The Beribboned Bomb: The Image of Woman in Male Surrealist Art.* Calgary: University of Calgary Press, 1995.

Bibliography (side margin)

Biro, Adam, and René Passeron. *Dictionnaire général du surréalisme*. Fribourg: Office du Livre, 1982.

Breton, André. *Conversations: The Autobiography of Surrealism*. With André Parinaud and others. Trans. Mark Polizzotti. New York: Paragon, 1993.

Breton, André. *What Is Surrealism? Selected Writings*. Ed. Franklin Rosemont. New York: Monad, 1978.

Breton, André, and Marcel Duchamp. *First Papers of Surrealism*. Exh. cat. New York: Coordinating Council of French Relief Societies, 1942.

Breton, André, and Paul Eluard. *Dictionnaire abrégé du surréalisme*. 1938; Paris: Corti, 1991.

Caws, Mary Ann. "Ladies Shot and Painted." In Caws, *The Art of Interference*. Cambridge: Polity Press, 1989.

Caws, Mary Ann, Rudolf E. Kuenzli, and Gwen Raaberg, eds. *Surrealism and Women*. Cambridge: MIT Press, 1991.

Chadwick, Whitney. *Woman Artists and the Surrealist Movement*. Boston: Little, Brown, 1985.

Cone, Michèle C. *Artists under Vichy: A Case of Prejudice and Persecution*. Princeton: Princeton University Press, 1992.

De Salvo, Donna. *Staging Surrealism*. Columbus, Ohio: Wexner Center for the Arts, 1997.

Durozoi, Gérard. *Histoire du mouvement surréaliste*. Paris: Hazan, 1997.

Eggener, Keith L. "'An Amusing Lack of Logic': Surrealism and Popular Entertainment." *American Art* 7 (Fall 1993), pp. 30–45.

Eluard, Paul. *Letters to Gala*. New York: Paragon, 1989.

Ernst, Jimmy. *A Not-So-Still Life*. New York: St. Martin's, 1984.

Filipovic, Elena. "Abwesende Kunstobjekte: Mannequins und die 'Exposition Internationale du Surréalisme,' von 1938." In *Puppen, Körper, Automaten: Phantasmen der Moderne*, pp. 200–218. Düsseldorf: Kunstsammlung Nordrhein-Westfalen, 1999.

Foster, Hal. *Compulsive Beauty*. Cambridge: MIT Press, 1993.

Gough-Cooper, Jennifer, and Jacques Gaumont. "Kiesler, Duchamp, dada et le surréalisme." In Dieter Bogner, ed., *Friedrich Kiesler: Architekt, Maler, Bildhauer, 1890–1965*. Vienna: Locker, 1988.

Guggenheim, Peggy. *Out of This Century: Confessions of an Art Addict*. 1946; London: André Deutsch, 1983.

Guiol-Benassaya, Elyette. *La presse face au surréalisme de 1925 à 1938.* Paris: Centre National de la Recherche Scientifique, 1982.

Hartshorn, Willis, and Merry Foresta. *Man Ray in Fashion.* New York: International Center of Photography, 1990.

Hugnet, Georges. "L'exposition surréaliste internationale de 1938." *Preuves,* no. 91 (September 1958). Rpt. in Hugnet, *Pleines et déliés,* pp. 323–345. La Chapelle-sur-Loire: Guy Authier, 1972.

Jean, Marcel. *The History of Surrealist Painting.* New York: Grove, 1960.

Krauss, Rosalind, and Jane Livingston. *L'Amour Fou: Photography and Surrealism.* New York: Abbeville, 1985.

Lanchner, Carolyn. "André Masson: Origins and Development." In *André Masson.* New York: Museum of Modern Art, 1976.

L'Ecotais, Emmanuelle de, and Alain Sayag, eds. *Man Ray, Photography and Its Double.* Paris: Centre Georges Pompidou, 1998.

Levy, Julien. *Memoir of an Art Gallery.* New York: Putnam's, 1977.

Levy, Julien. *Surrealism.* New York: Black Sun Press, 1936.

Man Ray. *Les mannequins.* Paris: Petithory, 1966.

Man Ray. *Self-Portrait.* Boston: New York Graphic Society, 1988.

Martin, Richard. *Fashion and Surrealism.* New York: Rizzoli, 1987.

Masson, André. *Vagabond du surréalisme.* Ed. Gilbert Brownstone. Paris: St.-Germain-des-Prés, 1975.

Myers, John Bernard. *Tracking the Marvelous: A Life in the New York Art World.* New York: Random House, 1983.

Paris-Paris, 1937–1957, créations en France. Exh. cat. Paris: Centre Georges Pompidou, 1981.

Paul Eluard et ses amis peintres, 1895–1952. Exh. cat. Paris: Centre Georges Pompidou, 1982.

Penrose, Roland. *Scrap Book 1900–1981.* New York: Rizzoli, 1981.

La planète affolée: Surréalisme, dispersion et influences, 1938–1947. Exh. cat. Marseilles: Direction des Musées, 1986.

Polizzotti, Mark. *Revolution of the Mind: The Life of André Breton.* New York: Farrar, Straus and Giroux, 1995.

Purser, Philip. *Poeted: The Final Quest of Edward James.* London: Quartet, 1991.

Rioux, Gilles. "A propos les expositions internationales du surréalisme." *Gazette des Beaux-Arts* 120 (April 1978), pp. 163–171.

Rubin, William S. *Dada, Surrealism, and Their Heritage.* New York: Museum of Modern Art, 1968.

Sawin, Martica. "The Cycloptic Eye, Pataphysics, and the Possible: Transformations of Surrealism." In *The Interpretive Link,* exh. cat. Newport Beach, California, 1986.

Sawin, Martica. *Surrealism in Exile and the Beginning of the New York School.* Cambridge: MIT Press, 1995.

Schaffner, Ingrid, and Lisa Jacobs. *Julien Levy: Portrait of an Art Gallery.* Cambridge: MIT Press, 1998.

Simon, Sidney. "Concerning the Beginnings of the New York School: 1939–1943." *Art International* 11 (Summer 1967), pp. 17–18.

Surrealism: Two Private Eyes. 2 vols. Exh. cat. New York: Solomon R. Guggenhcim Museum, 1999.

A Surreal Life: Edward James, 1907–1984. Exh. cat. Brighton: Brighton Museum and Art Gallery, 1998.

Tashjian, Dickran. *A Boatload of Madmen: Surrealism and the American Avant-Garde, 1920–1950.* New York: Thames and Hudson, 1995.

Thirion, André. *Révolutionnaires sans révolution.* Paris: Laffont, 1972.

On Dalí

Abadie, Daniel, ed. *La vie publique de Salvador Dalí.* Paris: Centre Georges Pompidou, 1980.

Ades, Dawn. *Dali and Surrealism.* New York: Harper and Row, 1982.

Cowles, Fleur. *The Case of Salvador Dali.* Boston: Little, Brown, 1959.

Dalí, Salvador. *The Secret Life of Salvador Dalí.* 1942; Figueras: Dasa Ediciones, 1986.

Descharnes, Robert. *Salvador Dalí, 1904–1989: The Paintings.* Cologne: Taschen, 1994.

Etherington-Smith, Meredith. *The Persistence of Memory: A Biography of Dalí.* New York: Random House, 1992.

Fanés, Fèlix. *Salvador Dalí Dream of Venus.* Figueras: Fundació Gala-Salvador Dalí, 1999.

Harriman, Margaret Case. "Profiles: A Dream Walking." *New Yorker* 15 (July 1, 1939), pp. 22–27.

Maur, Karin von. *Salvador Dalí, 1904–1989.* Exh. cat. Staatsgalerie: Stuttgart, 1989.

Perez, Nissan N. "Dali, Horst and the Dream of Venus." *Israel Museum Journal* 3 (Spring 1984), pp. 53–57.

Salvador Dalí rétrospective 1920–1980. Exh. cat. Paris: Centre Georges Pompidou, 1979.

On Duchamp

Bonk, Ecke. *The Box-in-a-Valise.* New York: Rizzoli, 1989.

Cabanne, Pierre. *Dialogues with Marcel Duchamp.* New York: Viking, 1971.

Hultén, Pontus, ed. *Marcel Duchamp, Work and Life.* Cambridge: MIT Press, 1993.

Janis, Harriet and Sidney. "Marcel Duchamp, Anti-Artist." *View,* ser. 5, no. 1 (1945), p. 18.

Jones, Amelia. *Postmodernism and the En-gendering of Marcel Duchamp.* Cambridge: Cambridge University Press, 1994.

Joseph Cornell/Marcel Duchamp . . . in Resonance. Exh. cat., Philadelphia Museum and Menil Collection, Houston. New York: Distributed Art Publishers, 1998.

Lebel, Robert. *Marcel Duchamp.* New York: Grove, 1959.

Lebel, Robert. "Paris-New York et retour avec Marcel Duchamp, dada et le surréalisme." In Centre Georges Pompidou, *Paris-New York.* Paris: Musée National d'Art Moderne, 1977.

Naumann, Francis M. "Amicalement, Marcel: Fourteen Letters from Marcel Duchamp to Walter Pach." *Archives of American Art Journal* 29 (1989), pp. 36–50.

Naumann, Francis M. *Marcel Duchamp: The Art of Making Art in the Age of Mechanical Reproduction.* New York: Abrams, 1999.

Schwarz, Arturo. *The Complete Works of Marcel Duchamp.* 3d ed. 2 vols. New York: Delano Greenidge, 1997.

Tomkins, Calvin. *Duchamp, a Biography.* New York: Holt, 1996.

Index